HERITAGE AND HISTORIES

Of John Alexander Nelson and Vera Wilcox Nelson

HERITAGE AND HISTORIES

Of John Alexander Nelson and Vera Wilcox Nelson

Researched, Compiled,
Edited and Parts Written
By
Verda Nelson Jensen
And
Carol Jensen Lasson
1989

Reformatted and Republished
By
Bradley Nelson
2007

Wellness Unmasked Publishing
Mesquite, Nevada

First Edition, June 1989
Second Edition, August 2007

Wellness Unmasked Publishing
450 Hillside Drive
Mesquite, NV 89027

Published in the United States by Wellness Unmasked Publishing,
A division of Wellness Unmasked Incorporated, Mesquite, Nevada.

Library of Congress Control Number 2007935768
Heritage and Histories of John Alexander Nelson
and Vera Wilcox Nelson / Verda Jensen & Carol Lasson
p. cm.
Includes bibliographic references and index.
ISBN 978-0-9795537-1-4 (pbk.)

PURPOSE OF OUR BOOK

In commemoration of both John Alexander Nelson, Jr.'s, and his beloved wife, Vera Wilcox Nelson's one-hundredth birthdays, John's, September 13, 1888, and Vera's, March 25, 1889 it is our goal to have this history completed, published and available this year, 1989.

It has been said, "It's a wonderful thing to focus attention on a great life." This book focuses on the great lives of many loved ones, including John and Vera Nelson and their parents and grand-parents. I realize that none of these people were perfect and this book has not been written to portray any of these ancestors without faults or failings. They were certainly faced with many challenges and struggles, but they met their tests with hope and courage, with total commitment and with dedication to their families and to the church of Jesus Christ of Latter Day Saints.

Although there are stories and writings from each of these grand-parents and great-grand parents, we are focusing our main attention on the lives of John and Vera. They raised a family of seven children, four sons and three daughters, during difficult years which included the Big Depression years 1929-1935. They were grandparents to 37 grandchildren. According to our latest information, they had 116 great-grandchildren and four great-great-grandchildren so far. Their posterity will multiply considerably in subsequent genera-tions. John and Vera taught their children that they are children of a kind and eternal Heavenly Father who loves them and who hears and answers their prayers.

Their ancestors joined the Church of Jesus Christ of Latter Day Saints in the infancy of the Church, so both John and Vera were born into the Church and lived their entire lives as faithful members. They accepted every call issued to them in the Church and fulfilled their church callings with honor and success, often at their own or their family's great sacrifice.

Over the years, they traveled many, many miles, at their own expense, in all kinds of weather, to perform their church assignments. Often the roads were icy and snow-packed but they didn't let that stop them. Regardless of the weather, they would attend and preside at meetings in a district and stake which covered an area of over 200 miles square.

The more time I have spent working on the stories from the lives of John and Vera, as well as the stories from their ancestors, the more respect I have gained for each of them. I have a new love for them, for the trials of rearing large families and for the sacrifices they made for their Church. This is by no means a complete history of their lives, but it is my hope that John and Vera's descendants may find inspiration in these pages to enrich their own lives, to receive comfort and encouragement and to remember that we each have a heritage to be proud of.

John and Vera were both faithful in writing letters to their children who lived away from Great Falls, Montana. John typed his letters with the "hunt and peck" system and sent carbon copies to each one. His children, jokingly, kept track of who got the~ original and who received the carbon copy. They teased, "Daddy loved me the most," if they received the original. Upon the request of his daughters, John would send a few of his missionary experiences to them in letters. A wealth of information concerning family history was included in these letters.

John had a serious heart attack on July 9, 1960. He was not a person to just lie around, even for a recovery period after the heart attack, so he decided to spend a few hours each day talking into a Dictaphone and relating his life's experiences. His son, Robert, provided a Dictaphone for his use. (The Dictaphone was a device used during that time to record spoken words on a celluloid belt so they could be played back later for typed transcripts.) John began his Dictaphone tapes recalling events he had heard his parents tell concerning their move from Smithfield, Utah to Cardston, Alberta, Canada. He continued his tapes with stories about his childhood, his early youth, and his missionary days in Samoa and Tonga. While on his mission, he kept quite a complete Journal and it was from this journal that he was able to remember the details of the stories that he related. After his three year mission, he was called to remain in the Islands and to be the President to the Samoan and Tongan Island Mission for another three and one-half years.

Vera had been gifted with a keen memory and was able to offer help and support in helping John recall important details concerning events during the time they were married. Vera also was good to write in her journal and to keep accounts of interest concerning their life together.

Thanks are due to many people who have done preliminary work on this history. John and Vera's first grandson, John Nelson (Lovell's son), had the Dictaphone belts transcribed. The stories from these transcriptions have been of great help in preparing this book. Special thanks and gratitude to Margaret Carter Nelson (Lovell's wife) for typing John's journals. Margaret made the comment that she had never done anything more rewarding.

Thanks to Ruth Nelson Miller for all the effort she put into getting this book ready. Ruth and I had planned to work on this d book together when I retired from teaching school. However, shortly after my retirement, Ruth and her husband, Ivan Miller, d accepted a mission call to the London South Mission. Ruth felt it was important to get the book written, so she brought the records and tapes to me and with her good wishes said, "The book is up to you, Verda."

Thanks to each of the other members of John and Vera's family; Lovell, Bruce, Lee, Joyce Nelson McMaster and Robert Dale, for digging into their memory banks for some of these special stories. Thanks to them for searching through their old photo albums and sharing their treasured photographs. I have felt a great deal of love, support and encouragement from each one of them.

Thanks to my husband, Leon Jensen, who generously supported my quest. Because he, too, realized the need to complete this work, he continually offered me encouragement and inspiration. He also helped with editing the manuscript. He added great insight into the process of editing. Also, he didn't complain about my time-consuming task of assembling and organizing the information, nor the many hours I spent at the computer.

Special thanks are due to my dear daughter, Carol Lasson, who has worked by my side to edit, type, correct and encourage. She has given of her time and talents to get this work completed. She, too, has expressed a new love and concern for those we have written about.

Thanks to the other members of my family for their confidence in and support of me: to Lana, Julie, Jim, Joyce, and David. Jim helped me get started on the computer and helped by doing the Laser printing and to his dear wife Sandy for helping with the finishing touches.

I have written this book with the best factual materials available to me. Even though occasionally time may have dulled the memory of the storyteller, I have done the best I could. I found a little poem that tells my feelings about this special work. I will include it here:

CRUMBS OR COMFORT (OR)
THOUGHTS WHICH HAVE KEPT ME AWAKE NIGHTS

NO book's entirely perfect,
For errors will creep in.
Sometimes wrong information sent
Is what commits the sin.

And even printers make mistakes,
(For which they tear their hair.)
Sometimes two people disagree
On who, or when, or where.

It might have been the person
Who wrote the history
It might have been the typist,
Or blame can fall on me.

So, if you're dead before you're born,
Or married when you're three,
Or I've omitted anyone
Who sent themselves to me;

Or your last name is not your own,
Your picture not too good.
I ask you, please forgive the crime--
I did the best I could.

Harriet Jane Lamb Strandling

John and Vera both remained true to their convictions and testimonies, that God is our Eternal Father and His Son, Jesus Christ is our elder Brother and through His atoning sacrifice, we may be privileged to live again. They testified that by adhering to the commandments set out by Jesus Christ, eternal happiness will be the reward. It is my desire that each of us, as descendants or interested readers, will gain a love and respect for these Special people and that this love will help enrich our own lives and strengthen our own testimonies.

- Verda Nelson Jensen

A NOTE ON THIS NEW EDITION

In 1989 I scanned the original "Red Book," as this volume has come to be known in our family. My thought was to make it available to everyone in an electronic format, with no real thought of doing a reprint. The scanning technology that I had available provided me with digital images that left a lot to be desired, requiring a great deal of editing and correction. Over the next three years I tinkered with these scanned files on the occasional Sunday, but progress was slow. Finally, the Nelson Family Reunion that was planned for the Summer of 2007 provided the impetus that I needed to get it all done, and with only a few weeks to go I was able to get the help I needed in editing the entire book from a few of my brave cousins via email, and it all came together.

It was a wonderful experience and a great blessing to me to have the opportunity to do this republishing task. The Holy Spirit was there on many occasions as I worked from very early to very late during that final week to get this done, and I knew that the souls of our departed love ones were very much concerned that this special and sacred volume be completed. It was amazing how, during that final week of editing, the phone nearly stopped ringing, only to resume the moment the work was done. The photo of the old Mission Home that is shown on the back cover also mysteriously appeared at the top of a box in our den, just as Jean and I were doing the final touches to the cover. Neither of us recall ever seeing it before, but it strangely appeared 'just in time' to be on the cover. And so it went.

My special thanks go to my dear Aunt Verda Jensen and her daughter Carol Jensen Lasson for putting all of this together in the first place. I know that this work will yet touch many lives around the world. Above all, my appreciation goes to my Grandpa John and my Grandma Vera, to my father Bruce Nelson, Sr., and my mother Ruth, and to the rest of our ancestors that are up there pulling for us all to succeed down here, and to "overcome the world through faith in the Lord, Jesus Christ."

Bradley Brian Nelson, St. George, Utah - December 2007.

CONTENTS

PEDIGREE CHART

CHART NO. 1

DATE 30 June 1981

NAME OF PERSON SUBMITTING CHART
Ruth Nelson MILLER

STREET ADDRESS
280 North 2nd West

CITY Hyrum, Cache, Utah 84319 STATE

NO. 1 ON THIS CHART IS
THE SAME PERSON AS NO. _____
ON CHART NO. _____

SOURCES OF INFORMATION

NAME OF HUSBAND OR WIFE
Ivan Valaire MILLER

1 Ruth Maurine NELSON
BORN 4 Dec 1921
WHERE Cardston, Alta, Can
DIED
WHEN MARRIED 26 Dec 1940
WHERE

John Lovell NELSON
Bruce Allen NELSON
Ruth Maurine NELSON
Lee Carl NELSON
Verda Chloe NELSON
Joyce Ione NELSON
Robert Dale NELSON

2 John Alexander NELSON, Jr.
BORN 13 Sep 1889
WHERE Smithfield, Cache, Utah
WHEN MARRIED 1 Jan 1917
DIED 9 Dec 1963
WHERE Great Falls, Cascade, Mt.

3 Marth Vera WILCOX
BORN 25 Mar 1889
WHERE Lyman, Fremont, Idaho
DIED 29 Nov 1972
WHERE Ogden, Weber, Utah

4 John Alexander NELSON, Sr.
BORN 17 Oct 1854
WHERE Farmington, Dvs, Utah
WHEN MARRIED 9 Jan 1878
DIED 20 Sep 1942
WHERE Cardston, Albta, Can.

5 Ella Elizabeth THOMAS
BORN 9 Oct 1859
WHERE Lehi, Utah, Utah
DIED 30 Oct 1941
WHERE Cardston, Alberta, Can.

6 Samuel Allen WILCOX, Jr.
BORN 9 Mar 1850
WHERE Austin, Fremont, Iowa
WHEN MARRIED 28 Jan 1871
DIED 29 Oct 1908
WHERE Gridley, Butte, Calif.

7 Julia Ann LAUGHLIN
BORN 19 Sept 1853
WHERE Cottonwood, S.L., Utah
DIED 5 Nov 1913
WHERE 7 Nov 1913

8 Robert NELSON
BORN 4 Sep 1819
WHERE Muff, Donegal, Ireland,
WHEN MARRIED 12 Dec 1842
DIED 11 Feb 1902
WHERE Smithfield, Cache, Ut. [16]
CONT. ON CHART

9 Elizabeth JOSEPH
BORN 1 Nov 1819
WHERE Muff, Donegal, Ireland [19]
DIED 12 May 1902
WHERE Smithfield, Cache, Ut. [20]
CONT. ON CHART

10 Preston THOMAS
BORN 15 Feb 1814
WHERE Rockingham, North C. [21]
WHEN MARRIED 8 Oct 1856
DIED 10 Jul 1877
WHERE Franklin, Onieda, Ida. [22]
(1) Maria HADLOND
CONT. ON CHART

11 [blank]
BORN 27 Aug 1839
WHERE Cheltonham, Glous., Eng. [23]
DIED 29 May 1907
WHERE Franklin, Onieda, Ida. [24]
CONT. ON CHART

12 Samuel Allen WILCOX, Sr.
BORN 21 Mar 1819
WHERE Norfolk, St. Law, N.Y. [25]
WHEN MARRIED 17 Jan 1838
DIED 7 Apr 1898
WHERE Cedar Fort, Utah, Utah [26]
CONT. ON CHART

13 Martha Bolton PARKER
BORN 23 Jan 1820
WHERE Mountain, Dundas, Ont. [27]
DIED 23 Jan 1912
WHERE Wardboro, Bear Lake, Ida. [28]
CONT. ON CHART

14 David Saunders LAUGHLIN
BORN 26 Apr 1814
WHERE Dunbarton, New Hamp. [29]
WHEN MARRIED 11 Apr 1849
DIED 5 Dec 1856
WHERE Cedar Fort, Utah, Utah [30]
(2) Julia Ann ROCKER
CONT. ON CHART

15 [blank]
BORN 19 May 1828
WHERE Lower Canada
DIED 22 Jan 1891
WHERE Cedar Fort, Utah, Utah [31]
CONT. ON CHART

CONT. ON CHART (×16)

© 1977 The Genealogical Department of The Church of Jesus Christ of Latter-day Saints
Printed in United States of America

1

JOHN'S HERITAGE: ONE TO BE PROUD OF

In The Book of Mormon, Helaman told his sons, "Behold, I have given unto you the names of our first parents who came out of the land of Jerusalem; and this "I have done that when you remember your names ye may remember them; and when ye remember them ye may remember their works; and when ye remember their works ye may know how that it is said, and also written, that they were good."[1]

John and Vera were born of goodly parents and as ye remember "them and their works ye may know that they were good."[2] The following stories of these ancestors have been collected and edited from the Samuel Allen Wilcox, Sr. Family Bulletins and the John Alexander Nelson, Sr. Family Bulletins. In addition to these sources, information has been included from family letters, journals, family histories, and personal knowledge.

---

1   Book of Mormon, Helaman 5:6, p. 377
2   Ibid, p. 377.

HUSBAND	NEISON, Robert Sr.				Husband	Wife
Born	4 Sept 1818	Place	Muff, Donegal, Irlnd		Ward	
Chr.		Place			Examiners	
Marr.	12 Dec 1842	Place	Muff, Donegal, Irlnd		State or	
Died	10 Feb 1902	Place	Smithfield, Cache, Utah		Mission	
Bur.	12 Feb 1902	Place				

NEISON, Robert Sr 1818
(1) JOSEPH, Elizabeth

NAME & ADDRESS OF PERSON SUBMITTING RECORD
Mrs. Ruth Nelson Miller
290 No 2rd West
Hyrum, Utah

Husband's father: NELSON, Samuel 3rd
Husband's mother: (3) BURNS, Martha
Husband's other wives: (2) DIXON, Elizabeth

WIFE (1)	JOSEPH, Elizabeth	
Born	12 Sept 1818	Place Muff, Donegal, Irlnd
Chr.	1 Oct 1818	Place
Died	12 May 1902	Place Smithfield, Cache, Utah
Bur.	15 May 1902	Place

Wife's father: JOSEPH, John
Wife's mother: CARR, Martha or Mariah

FAMILY REPRESENTATIVE
Mrs. Ruth Nelson Miller
Relation to husband: gr dau

TEMPLE ORDINANCE DATA

	BAPTIZED (DATE)	ENDOWED (DATE)	SEALED
Husband	13 Dec 1849	15 Nov 1855	22 Jul 1855
Wife	BE 12 Dec 1863	EH	

	SEX	CHILDREN — GIVEN NAMES	WHEN BORN (DAY MONTH YEAR)	WHERE BORN (TOWN)	(COUNTY)	(STATE OR COUNTRY)	DATE OF FIRST MARRIAGE — TO WHOM	WHEN DIED (DAY MONTH YEAR)	BAPTIZED	ENDOWED
1	M	NELSON, Samuel	22 Jan 1845	Kilbrechan	Renfinshre	Sctlnd	3 Dec 1865 HERRIUS, Ann Jennette	18 Apr 1937	18 Dec 1849	15 Nov 1855
2	M	NELSON, Robert Jr.	4 Jun 1847	Greenock	"	"	4 Aug 1849		16 Jun 1855	27 Dec 1864
3	M	NELSON, Joseph	4 Jan 1850	"	"	"	UNID / 1 Jan 1877 COLLEN, Lydia Isabel	5 Nov 1934	CHILD	SD 12 Dec 1878
4	F	NELSON, Mary Elizabeth	4 May 1852	St Louis	St Louis	Mo.	7 Dec 1868 HATCH, Alveh Alexander	19 Apr 1924	16 Jun 1861	3 May 1870
5	M	NELSON, John Alexander, Sr	17 Oct 1854	Farmington	Davis	Utah	9 Jan 1879 THOMAS, Ella Elizabeth	29 Sep 1942	BE 11 Jun 1865	8 Dec 1868
6	M	NELSON, Robert James	17 Jun 1856	"	"		10 Apr 1882 SAXTON, Ellen	1 Jun 1906	1863	9 Jan 1879
7	M	NELSON, David William	2 Apr 1858	"	"		9 Dec 1860 ANDERSEN, Almira May	4 Mar 1891 / 4 Jun 1860	8 Jul 1866	10 Apr 1882
8	M	NELSON, Eliza Jane	1 Jan 1860	"	"		UNID		13 Oct 1866	9 Dec 1880
9	F	NELSON, Margaret Jane	12 Sep 1862	Smithfield	Cache	Utah	12 Dec 1878 TIDWELL, Royal Edwin	1 May 1956	11 Sep 1870	12 Dec 1878

OTHER MARRIAGES
#1 md (2) Abiah Ann SMITH
(3) Celia OTLIAN SKOG

SOURCES OF INFORMATION
Family records of George G. Nelson, Logan, Utah, & son of Robert Nelson, Sr.
Logan temple Patron files.

NECESSARY EXPLANATIONS
Wife left for Zion 1849, took 11 wks.
Left East for S.L. 1852, arrived Oct. 1852.

2

ROBERT NELSON AND ELIZABETH JOSEPH NELSON

Robert Nelson
Father of John's Father

Elizabeth Joseph
Mother of John's Father

John's paternal grandparents were Robert and Elizabeth Joseph Nelson. They were born in Donegal, Muff, Ireland. The following story has been handed-down from generation to generation. One summer morning a group of young people hired a local boatman to take them across the river for a picnic. It was not an ordinary river, but a wide open-end of a river where the tide came in every day. The group had a fine time and finally wandered back to the boat to cross the river to go home.

By that time, the wind had risen and the waves were running much too high for the little boat to cross. The boatman refused to attempt the crossing for fear that all would be lost, During the long night the boatman and the group of young people huddled in a lee of the bank and whiled away the time until daybreak when the winds stopped blowing and they were able to cross the river back to their homes.

Some days passed and to the consternation of Robert Nelson, towns-people were saying that the young men had kept the girls out all night for the wrong purpose and it wasn't long until the reputation of the girls was near ruin. A bad reputation could mean the girls could be cast from the church, ostracized from their society, or possibly even disinherited by their families. To save Elizabeth Joseph's good name, Robert Nelson married her.

3

In his own words, "I wanted a girl with some education, who could read and write and cipher, but I married her to save her a place in society."[3]

Seth Nelson wrote, "We can really be proud of such a man as our grandfather. Ambrose Woolford told me that Grandmother Nelson smoked a pipe, but was a good old soul. Grandfather and Grandmother Nelson lived until each was 84 years of age.[4]

After they married, Robert took his wife back to the old home at Greenook, Scotland located near Paisley. In the meantime, they heard the gospel of Jesus Christ preached by two Mormon Elders. They willingly accepted this message of truth and were baptized December, 1848 in Scotland. They worked there until they earned enough money to pay their passage to America, the "land of promise."

Three sons were born before they left Scotland: Samuel, Robert and Joseph. Robert died at the age of two on August 4, 1849. In 1849 they also left the "old country" and headed for Zion. They were on the sea eleven weeks. At times the sea was very rough; they thought the ship would sink and they would never make it to America. However, they arrived safely at New Orleans. From there they traveled up the Mississippi River to St. Louis, Missouri where they stayed long enough to earn money for their trip across the plains. It was here they joined the saints headed for Utah in the spring of 1852.

Elizabeth and her son, Samuel, walked all the way from the frontier to Salt Lake City, Utah arriving in 1852. Robert and another man had purchased one yoke of oxen and an old wagon in which they loaded the belongings of their two families. They took turns driving and walking to Salt Lake.[5]

Jane M. Tidwell, daughter of Robert and Elizabeth, recalls, "I have often heard mother relate stories of their first winter in Salt Lake City. They had no place to live but an old chicken coop which had

---

3   Letter from Seth Nelson to John Nelson.
4   Ibid.
5   "Tribute to our Pioneers, " by Jane M. Tidwell, January 3, 1930.

been cleaned and plastered with mud. Here they lived until the next spring when they moved out to Farmington, Utah."[6]

They lived in Farmington, Utah until about 1860 when they moved to Smithfield, Utah.

Jane M. Tidwell recorded, "We lived in a dugout and a wagon box until October then moved into our new one room log house with a dirt roof. The house was built on the lines of a fort. From the time we arrived until we raised our first crop and had it threshed, we lived most of the time on thickened milk and we did not have enough of that. When we threshed, we had to take our wheat with one team to Brigham City to have it made into flour. Mother's family was quite short of clothing but we had a few sheep and she prepared wool to make our clothes."[7]

Robert and Elizabeth were parents to nine children: three born in Scotland, one born in St. Lewis, Missouri, the next four born in Farmington, Utah and their ninth born in Smithfield, Utah.[8]

Jane recalled about her mother, "She also made soap and would give to those in need." Of her father she said, "Father was a hard working man in the early days. He was noted for his ability in cradling and stooking grain. He served as a school trustee in Smithfield for a number of years. He held the office of High Priest." Of both of them she eulogized, "They were true to the gospel for which they left their native land. They were firm believers in the law of tithing and taught it to all their children.[9]

---

6   Ibid.
7   Ibid.
8   Robert Nelson "family group sheet".
9   Tidwell, 1930.

HUSBAND Preston THOMAS

Born	15 Feb 1814	Place Rockingham, Richmond, North Carolina
Chr.		Place
Mar.	8 Oct 1856	Place Salt Lake City, Salt Lake, Utah
Died	11 Jul 1877	Place Franklin, Oneida, Idaho
Bur.	13 Jul 1877	Place Franklin, Oneida, Idaho

HUSBAND'S FATHER: Daniel THOMAS HUSBAND'S MOTHER: Nancy Ann MOREHEAD/Ann TURNER
HUSBAND'S OTHER WIVES: (1) 10 May 1838 Sarah Ann Jane MOREHEAD (2) Nov 1851 Maria FOSCUE

WIFE (3) Maria HADLOND

Born	27 Aug 1839	Place Cheltenham, Gloucester, England
Chr.		Place
Died	28 May 1907	Place Salt Lake City, Salt Lake, Utah
Bur.		Place Franklin, Oneida, Idaho

WIFE'S FATHER: Thomas HADLOND WIFE'S MOTHER: Rachel FRANKLIN

Husband Preston THOMAS Wife Maria HADLOND 1814
Ward/Examiner State or Mission Taylorsville Central

NAME & ADDRESS OF PERSON SUBMITTING SHEET
Sheila Nelson Zolman
2108 Champagne Circle
SLC, UT 84118

RELATION OF ABOVE TO HUSBAND: 2 gg dau   RELATION OF ABOVE TO WIFE: 2 gg dau
FOUR GENERATION SHEET FOR FILING ONLY YES [x] NO [ ]
DATE SUBMITTED TO GENEALOGICAL SOCIETY

LDS ORDINANCE DATA

	BAPTIZED	ENDOWED	SEALED TO PARENTS
HUSBAND	13 Jan 1844	6 Jan 1846	19 Feb 1857
WIFE	21 Jan 1846	19 Feb 1857	

SEX	CHILDREN (Given Names)	SURNAME	WHEN BORN	WHERE BORN (Town)	(County)	(State/Country)	DATE OF FIRST MARRIAGE / TO WHOM	WHEN DIED	BAPTIZED	ENDOWED	SEALED
F	Sarah Ann Jane	THOMAS	6 Oct 1857	Lehi		Utah	12 Jan 1882 Don Carlos HYDE	19 Jan 1946	6 Oct 1867	12 Jan 1882	BIC
X F	Ella Elizabeth	THOMAS	9 Oct 1859	"		Utah	9 Jan 1879 John Alexander NELSON	30 Oct 1941	9 Oct 1867	9 Jan 1879	BIC
M	Pinkney Preston	THOMAS	27 Jul 1861	Franklin		Oneida, Idaho	7 Nov 1889 Deborah WOODWARD	26 Oct 1925	12 Jun 1870	12 Jun 1889	BIC
M	Seth (Blair) Hadlond	THOMAS	9 Jan 1864	"		"	11 Sep 1901 Sarah ALSTON	5 Jul 1943	28 Jun 1874	24 Nov 1886	BIC
F	Mary Alice	THOMAS	28 Jun 1866	Fish Haven		Rich, Utah	5 Jan 1886 Jasper Jason HEAD	20 Dec 1926	28 Jun 1874	6 Jan 1886	BIC
F	Rachel	THOMAS	7 Dec 1869	Preston		Idaho	21 Dec 1887 St. Leon WOODWARD	29 Jan 1948	6 Oct 1877	21 Dec 1887	BIC
F	Rosabell	THOMAS	28 Sep 1871			B-Lake Idaho	2 Apr 1902 Samuel Heber KIMBLE	28 Nov 1946	28 Sep 1879	2 Apr 1902	BIC
M	Daniel Hadlond	THOMAS	24 Feb 1874	Franklin		Oneida	6 Jun 1900 Mary Ethel PRATT	6 Sep 1943	15 May 1882	19 Jun 1895	BIC
F	Letitia Dolila	THOMAS	24 Oct 1876	"		"	17 May 1900 George TEASDALE Sr.	Feb 1937	23 Oct 1884	17 May 1900	BIC

OTHER MARRIAGES
#3 md (2) 24 Jan 1900 Harriet Maria CARTER
#9 md (2) George TEASDALE Jr.

SOURCES OF INFORMATION
1. Family Bible in poss of Mary Ellen S. Thomas, Preston, ID
2. Franklin Ward Rec (GS 007,453) hush, wife, child #1,3-9

NECESSARY EXPLANATIONS
Wife aka Maria HADLAND

3/80

6

PRESTON THOMAS AND MARIA HADLOND THOMAS

Preston Thomas
Father of John's Mother

Maria Hadlond Thomas
Mother of John's Mother

John's maternal grandparents were Preston Thomas and Maria Had-lond. Preston was born in Rockingham, North Carolina on February 15, 1814. Maria was born in Cheltonham, Gloucestershire, England on August 27, 1839.[10] In February, 1844, Preston, his family, and a large number of their friends were baptized into the Church of Jesus Christ of Latter-Day Saints by Benjamin Clapp who was one of the First Council of the Seventy. Preston set out for Texas to find his brother Daniel Claybourne Thomas and to teach him the gospel. He found Daniel, taught him, and baptized him.

Later Preston Thomas sold his plantation and his black slaves to his Uncle Abner Thomas.

Around the time of Joseph Smith's death, Preston went to Nauvoo. He was there in 1846 when the city was burned by the mobs and the saints fled.

Brigham Young sent him back to Texas on a mission to get Lyman Wite to repent and come back to the church. After his mission he lived in Salt Lake City for a number of years and then established his home west of Lehi in Cedar Valley. In 1853 he was called on another mission back to Texas. He filled that mission and returned to Utah. Of some of his missionary work in Texas dated July 24, 1855, he wrote:

---

10   Preston Thomas "Family Group Sheet."

"'I have been preaching at Clinton, Dewitt Co., where I found several saints, whom I have re-baptized; they have all renewed their covenants by baptism, and are going to gather up in the Spring. I still continue to receive letters from various quarters, inviting me to go and preach, and asking me information about gathering, & c. Persecution rages more than usual in Texas. Whilst I was preaching at Clinton, during my last two sermons I was interrupted and insulted by a mob gathering round the court-house, and cursing, swearing and yelling like savages, and I thought it prudent to preach there no more. Everywhere the saints want to gather next spring, and I expect there will be a host of us going from Texas another season.[11]

In 1856 he was in St. Louis Missouri fulfilling another mission to help bring immigrant companies across the Plains to Utah. In this party of immigrants were Mormon converts from Cheltonham, England. Maria Hadlond was a member of this group. She had been baptized into the Mormon Church when she was a child of eight years old in Cheltonham. She had accompanied her parents out of England and had moved to Quebec, Canada where they lived for seven years. When Maria was fifteen years old, her family moved down to St. Louis, Missouri where her parents remained and are buried. She and her brother, Edward, and sister, Charlotte, joined with the immigrant company led by Preston Thomas. From St. Louis, they went down the river to New Orleans and from there to Galveston, Texas. Then they traveled overland to Salt Lake City.

Preston Thomas wrote the following:

> *Correspondence of Judge Thomas.*
> *En route for Utah*
> *Pannartic. No. Texas.*
> *Chocktaw Nation, Southside*
> *Canadian River, May 25, 1856.*
>
> *To the Editor of "The Mormon:"*

---

11   Nelson Family Bulletin, 1980.

Dear Sir:

I take up my pen to inform you and (through the columns of your paper) our numerous friends, of our whereabouts, progress, & c. We left our encampment on Matagardo, on the 7th of April, and since that time have every day continued our travels except Sundays and three other days. We are six hundred and seventy-five miles from our starting place. We crossed the Colorado River at La Grange, the Brazos at Waco, the Trinity at Dallas, and Red River at Preston. For three weeks we had very rainy weather, in the northern part of Texas, during which we were wallowing in the black prairie mud, which greatly retarded our progress.

We were hindered two days by high water, and one day in waiting for the saints to join us from Washington County. We were joined by one family of saints from the Guadaloupe Valley on the 12th of April, and by the saints from Washington Co. on the 21st. When we arrived near the place of rendezvous for the saints on the St. Gabriel's River we found they were gone; on our arrival in Ellis Co. we found Brother Clapp with his party were gone about three weeks previous, and the saints from the St. Gabriel had joined his party; when we crossed Red River we were informed they were just two weeks ahead, and when we arrived here, we were informed by the Indians they were about eight days ahead; so it seems we are gaining on them; what route they propose going I am not correctly informed. Sometimes I learn from travelers they design going up the Arkansas River, and then again that they are going up by Atchinson, and the Platt Routes.

We have at present thirty-four persons and eight wagons in camp. Br. John Ostler travelled with us from the southern coast as far as Dallas County, and then returned to join the elders in Ellis Co. He is a good and wise man, and rendered us very great service whilst with us. The saints became so attached to him that the whole camp deeply regretted his leaving us to go back, and he likewise desired to go home this year; but when he learned of his appointment by the Texas Conference to stay another year, he seemed reconciled to stay and labor another season in Texas.

Whilst we were passing through Ellis Co., Bro. Homer Duncan and Bro. Snedaker paid us a visit in camp, and spent a night with us; the hearts of the saints were cheered up by a discourse from each; they had been laboring with considerable success in that part of Texas; about fifteen persons had been baptized, and pretty fair prospect of others following their example. Bro. Duncan informed me that he had many calls for preaching. Bro. William Moody had gone to eastern Texas; these seem to be all the Elders now in that state.

Our camp moves along very harmoniously; we have not had a jar since we started; almost no sickness. The hearts of the saints rejoice from day to day, and the vast prairies and groves are made to reverberate with the songs of Zion as the saints journey along through the Indian lands. No serious accident has befallen us, and truly the hand of the Lord has been with us for good.

The Canadian River is the boundary between the Chocktaw and Creek Nations of Indians. This morning a notable Creek Indian came into camp, and I had a good deal of conversation with him; on his learning who we were, he invited me to preach to his people this afternoon. I consented, and he has gone away to assemble his friends.

It is Sunday to-day, and the whole camp, animals and all, seem to enjoy the rest, after a hard week's travel. I always rest on Sunday, and dedicate the day to rest and worship of Almighty God, but never rest on other days, except some unavoidable circumstances interfere. We feel that we have a long journey before us, and it will take a long time, with a great deal of exertion and industry to accomplish it; but I hardly think my old friends, with whom I have often crossed the plains, will charge me with not using sufficient diligence. We are now some 45 miles below Fort Gibson, and expect to pass that fort on the third day from this, where we *hope to receive letters and papers from many of our friends. For some time we have had no news from any quarter, only what we could gather from an occasional traveller whom we have met. The latest "The Mormon" that I have seen bears date 22nd March, and the latest dates from Utah, was some time in January. Judging from the clouds of grasshoppers we have seen for the last three hundred miles, our friends in Utah can have none this year, for they must have all emigrated to this country.*

I ask your indulgence for drawing so largely upon your columns, in publishing so long a letter, and also the privilege to publish another, with a list of all the names of the saints in camp when we leave the frontier.

May heaven's choicest blessings rest upon you, and crown your labors in New York with complete success; and may we be gathered to our mountain homes in safety, with all scattered saints, and stand at last in the celestial kingdom of our God, is the prayer of your devoted brother in the New and Everlasting Covenant.

Preston Thomas

("The Mormon"--June 21, 1856)[12]

Upon the company's arrival in Salt Lake City, Preston Thomas and Maria Hadlond were married in Brigham Young's office October 8, 1856 when Maria was seventeen and Preston was forty-two.

Maria Hadlond was Preston's third wife in polygamy. The other wives were Sarah Jane Morehead and Marie Foscue. He had twenty-two children with his three wives. Nine of these children were born to Preston and Maria Hadlond. John Alexander Nelson, Jr.'s mother, Ella Elizabeth Preston, was the second child born of this union.

Preston Thomas died July 15, 1877 in Franklin, Idaho. Maria died thirty years later on May 29, 1907 and was also buried in Franklin, Idaho.

---

12   "Nelson Family Bulletin," 1980

Husband	John Alexander NELSON		Wife	Ella Elizabeth THOMAS			1854
Ward Examiner	1.	2. L.TM	State or Mission	Taylorsville Central			

NAME & ADDRESS OF PERSON SUBMITTING SHEET
Sheila Nelson Zollman
2108 Champagne Cir
SLC, UT 84118

RELATION OF ABOVE TO HUSBAND: gg dau RELATION OF ABOVE TO WIFE: gg dau
FOUR GENERATION SHEET FOR FILING ONLY YES ☒ NO ☐
DATE SUBMITTED TO GENEALOGICAL SOCIETY

HUSBAND John Alexander NELSON (Stone Quarrier and Farmer) Sheet #1 con't on Sheet
Born: 17 Oct 1854 Place: Farmington, Davis, Utah
Chr.: Place:
Mar: 9 Jan 1879 Place: Salt Lake City, Salt Lake, Utah
Died: 29 Sep 1942/3 Place: Cardston, Alberta, Canada
Bur: 1 Oct 1942/3 Place: Cardston, Alberta, Canada
HUSBAND'S FATHER: Robert NELSON HUSBAND'S MOTHER: Elizabeth JOSEPH
HUSBAND'S OTHER WIVES: (2) 1892 Frances PURSER (Sealing Cancelled 20 Dec 1896)

WIFE (1) Ella Elizabeth THOMAS
Born: 9 Oct 1859 Place: Lehi, Utah, Utah
Chr.: Place:
Died: 30 Oct 1941 Place: Cardston, Alberta, Canada
Bur: 2 Nov 1941 Place: Cardston, Alberta, Canada
WIFE'S FATHER: Preston THOMAS WIFE'S MOTHER: Maria HADLOND
WIFE'S OTHER HUSBANDS:

SEX	CHILDREN Given Names	SURNAME	WHEN BORN (DAY MONTH YEAR)	WHERE BORN (TOWN)	COUNTY	STATE OR COUNTRY	DATE OF FIRST MARRIAGE / TO WHOM	WHEN DIED (DAY MONTH YEAR)
1 F	Maria Elizabeth	NELSON	7 Mar 1880	Smithfield	Cache	Utah	11 Sep 1901 Alonzo Bray LAMB	15 Jul 1947
2 F	Ella	NELSON	5 Jun 1882	"	"	"	23 Mar 1899 Joseph Franklin ALLEN	9 Jul 1962
3 F	Lileth	NELSON	9 Feb 1884	"	"	"	2 Sep 1902 Heber Chase SMITH	18 Jan 1975
4 M	John Preston	NELSON	3 Aug 1886	"	"	"		3 Aug 1886
5 F	Rachel	NELSON	28 Sep 1887	"	"	"	4 Oct 1912 William Adamson WOOLFORD	3 Apr 1971
6 M	John Alexander	NELSON	13 Sep 1889	"	"	"	1 Jan 1917 Martha Vera WILCOX	9 Dec 1963
7 M	Seth Henry	NELSON	15 Oct 1891	Cardston		Alberta, Canada	15 Dec 1916 Mabel Carrie HANSEN (1)	25 Jan 1975
8 M	Cleveland	NELSON	20 Mar 1893	"	"	"	1 Dec 1920 Hattie Luella BRONN	
9 M	Lorenzo Snow	NELSON	2 Jul 1896	"	"	"	1 Nov 1920 Mary Ireta TURNER	Deceased
10 F	Hazel (twin)	NELSON	15 Dec 1899	"	"	"	13 Apr 1919 Leo Milton BURGESS	29 Aug 1967
11 F	Irene (twin)	NELSON	15 Dec 1899	"	"	"		21 Jan 1900

LDS ORDINANCE DATA

	BAPTIZED (Date)	ENDOWED (Date)	SEALED (Date)
HUSBAND	1 Jun 1893	9 Jan 1879	9 Jan 187[9]
WIFE	9 Oct 1867	9 Jan 1879	
1	3 May 1888	15 Dec 1909	BIC
2	4 Sep 1890	5 Dec 1903	BIC
3	7 Jul 1892	12 Dec 1903	BIC
4	Child	Child	
5	1 Nov 1894	4 Oct 1911	BIC
6	1 May 1897	12 Jan 1910	BIC
7	5 Aug 1900	26 Aug 1923	BIC
8	7 Jul 1901	1 Dec 1920	BIC
9	13 Jul 1904	29 Jun 1933	BIC
10	14 Jul 1908	21 Nov 1924	BIC
11	Child	Child	BIC

NECESSARY EXPLANATIONS

OTHER MARRIAGES
#7 md (2) 15 Oct 1954 Elfrieda Bertha ELHERT

SOURCES OF INFORMATION:
1. Cardston and Wilford Ward Rec
2. Smithfield Ward Rec (GS 025,611) husb, wife, child #1,2,3,6

1854

FAMILY GROUP RECORD 1972 The Genealogical Department of The Church of Jesus Christ of Latter-day Saints

HUSBAND John Alexander NELSON (Stone Quarrier and Farmer) Sheet #2 cont from Sheet #1

Born	17 Oct 1854	Place Farmington, Davis, Utah
Chr.		Place
Mar.	9 Jan 1879	Place Salt Lake City, Salt Lake, Utah
Died	29 Sep 1942/3	Place Cardston, Alberta, Canada
Bur.	1 Oct 1942/3	Place Cardston, Alberta, Canada

HUSBAND'S FATHER Robert NELSON   HUSBAND'S MOTHER Elizabeth JOSEPH

HUSBAND'S OTHER WIVES (2) 1892 Frances PURSER (Sealing Cancelled 20 Dec 1896)

WIFE (1) Ella Elizabeth THOMAS

Born	9 Oct 1859	Place Lehi, Utah, Utah
Chr.		Place
Died	30 Oct 1941	Place Cardston, Alberta, Canada
Bur.	2 Nov 1941	Place Cardston, Alberta, Canada

WIFE'S FATHER Preston THOMAS   WIFE'S MOTHER Maria HADLOND

WIFE'S OTHER HUSBANDS

SEX	CHILDREN Last each child (whether living or dead) in order of birth. Given Names SURNAME	WHEN BORN DAY MONTH YEAR	WHERE BORN TOWN COUNTY STATE OR COUNTRY	DATE OF FIRST MARRIAGE TO WHOM	WHEN DIED DAY MONTH YEAR
12 M	Darrel Thomas NELSON	20 Dec 1901	Cardston Alberta Canada	7 Dec 1922 Mary CRITCHFIELD	4 Sep 1976
2					
3					
4					
5					
6					
7					
8					
9					
10					
11					

SOURCES OF INFORMATION   See Sheet #1

OTHER MARRIAGES   See Sheet #1

Husband John Alexander NELSON

Wife Ella Elizabeth THOMAS

Ward 1.

Examiners: 2. LJW

Stake or Mission Taylorsville Central

NAME & ADDRESS OF PERSON SUBMITTING SHEET
Sheila Nelson Zolman
2108 Champagne Cir.
SLC, UT 84118

RELATION OF ABOVE TO HUSBAND gg dau   RELATION OF ABOVE TO WIFE gg dau

FOUR GENERATION SHEET FOR FILING ONLY   YES [X]   NO [ ]

DATE SUBMITTED TO GENEALOGICAL SOCIETY

LDS ORDINANCE DATA

	BAPTIZED (Date)	ENDOWED (Date)	SEALED (Date) TO HUSBAND / TO PARENTS
HUSBAND	1 Jun 1893	9 Jan 1879	9 Jan 1879 Eli
WIFE	9 Oct 1867	9 Jan 1879	
	28 Jun 1910	14 Apr 1933	BIC

NECESSARY EXPLANATIONS   See Sheet #1

3/80

13

JOHN ALEXANDER NELSON, SR. & ELLA ELIZABETH THOMAS

John Alexander Nelson, Sr.
John's Father

Ella Elizabeth Thomas
John's Mother

John Alexander Nelson, Jr.'s father was John Alexander Nelson, Sr. He was born October 17, 1854 in Farmington, Utah, the fifth child of Robert and Elizabeth Joseph Nelson.[13] His family moved to Smithfield, Utah when John Sr. was a baby. It was here he learned to be industrious and earned his first dollar pulling weeds for his brother, Samuel.[14]

When John, Sr. was a young man, perhaps twenty years old, he and a boyhood friend of his, Tom Walker, spent summers cutting timber in the Wasatch Mountains. They were with a group of four other men, camping and enjoying the rugged outdoors. On this particular occasion, John was cutting off some of the limbs of the trees that had previously been chopped down. He was using a three and one-half pound axe. Tom came up unexpectedly just as John swung his axe. It caught Tom in the left shoulder and split his shoulder open.

The other men in the group were called. They put Tom in the wagon and bound his wound up tightly, so he wouldn't bleed to death. They got him down to Smithfield as quickly as they could and took him to the doctor, who took care of his wound. Tom was very fortunate and recovered completely, but he carried a scar all his life. He said,

---

13   John Alexander Nelson, Sr. "Family Group Sheet"
14   "History of John A. Nelson, Sr." written by Seth Nelson.

"I will never forget that morning that John Nelson, Sr. accidentally struck me with his axe."[15]

John Jr.'s mother, Ella Elizabeth Thomas, was born in Lehi, Utah on October 9, 1859. Her father was Preston Thomas and her mother was Maria Hadlond. John, Sr. and Ella were married in the Endowment House in Salt Lake City, Utah on January 9, 1879.[16]

Shortly after their marriage, in company with other young men, John Nelson, Sr. worked on the railroad for over a year in Oregon. It was here that he met one of the narrow escapes of his life.

With his companions he went out hunting for deer and shortly after leaving camp, the party divided, agreeing to meet on a certain night. John never reached the appointed ridge. Shortly after leaving the others, he found himself in very dense timber, the like of which he had never thought existed and he was soon completely lost. For 56 hours he wandered and only occasionally got a glimpse of the sun through the tall trees. He found no game and only shot one small rabbit.

John, Sr. became weakened and was beset by two spirits, who appeared to him as ordinary well-dressed men. They would continually stand across his path and turn him aside from the way he wished to go.

At night John, Sr. built a fire and the spirits would beat it out with clubs. When he would try to sleep, they would try to harm him, but on their every approach, another spirit (also dressed as a quiet gentleman) would drive the evil spirits away. When John, Sr. made his final effort to find his way out of the woods, the two men tried to stop him but were prevented from harming him by the other man.[17]

---

15   John A. Nelson, Jr.'s dictaphone tape.
16   John Alexander Nelson, Sr. "Family Group Sheet."
17   "History of John A. Nelson, Sr." by his son, Seth Nelson.

John and Ella lived in Smithfield from 1879 until the spring of 1890. Six children were born here: Marie Elizabeth, Ella, Lileth, John Preston (who died at birth), Rachel, and John Alexander Nelson, Jr.[18]

18   John Alexander Nelson, Sr. "Family Group Sheet."

2

JOHN'S EARLY YEARS

A SPECIAL NAME

When the Nelsons' sixth child, a baby boy, was to be blessed, his mother Ella asked the Stake Patriarch to perform the ordinance. As the Patriarch took the infant into his arms, he bent down and whispered to Ella, "What is this child's name to be?"

Ella responded, "His name will be Seth Thomas Nelson; the name that his father [John Alexander Nelson, Sr.] and I have chosen."

The Patriarch hesitated, "No, Sister Nelson, the Lord wants this child to be named 'John.'"

She looked at him in disbelief because her firstborn son, who had died in infancy, had been blessed with the name of John. She explained this fact to the Patriarch. However, the Patriarch could not be convinced.

"Sister Nelson, the Lord has instructed me that this child's name shall be 'John' and he shall be a missionary as John the Baptist of old. He shall proclaim the gospel of Jesus Christ throughout the world."

Consequently, the baby was blessed and given the name of "John Alexander Nelson, Jr.".[19]

John Alexander Nelson, Jr. has, indeed, lived up to the blessing given him as a baby. He has been a missionary, not only when he was called to be a missionary in the Samoan and the Tongan Islands, but wherever and whenever he could. He preached the gospel of Jesus Christ throughout his life.

John Alexander Nelson's Birth Certificate

The Church of Jesus Christ of Latter-day Saints

Salt Lake City, Utah,___19 May 1971___

I hereby certify that the following is a true and accurate extract from the records of The Church of Jesus Christ of Latter-day Saints, which records are in my custody:

Name ___– JOHN ALEXANDER NELSON JR. –___

Date of birth ___Thirteenth day of September, Eighteen Hundred and Eighty-Eight.___

Place of birth ___Smithfield, Cache County, Utah___

Father's name ___J. A. Nelson___

Mother's maiden name ___Ella E. Thomas___

Recorded in ___Alberta Stake, Cardston Ward, Record of Members, # 18300, Page 18.___

Entered on record ___1 May 1897.___

This is the earliest recorded entry in the Church records.

Historian of the Church and ex officio Custodian of its Records

---

19   Ruth Nelson Miller's family records.

BROTHERS AND SISTERS

John Alexander Nelson, Jr. was born in Smithfield, Utah on September 13, 1888. John was born into a family of four older sisters:
Marie Elizabeth, Ella, Lileth, and Rachel. Perhaps because these
sisters had experienced the death of a younger brother, they took
very good care of their new baby brother, "John." They pampered
and adored him. Fortunately for John, four more sons were later
born to his family: Seth, Cleveland, Lorenzo and Darrell and two
more sisters, Irene and Hazel, were also born to the Nelson family
or John could have been a pretty spoiled boy.

A CALL TO CANADA

In the spring of 1890 at a conference of the membership of the
Mormon Church in Logan, Utah, John Nelson, Sr. heard Charles
Ora Card call for volunteers to go to Canada to establish colonies
for the church there. Brother Card was a man one could follow with
safety. He had succeeded in carrying out many undertakings for
the church, including the over-seeing of the building of the Logan
LDS Temple.[20]

The September, 1988 issue of the "Ensign" says: "Fifty-five years after
the Prophet Joseph Smith's visit to eastern Canada, another man
in a place two thousand miles to the west penned his impressions
of Canada. From a tent on a cold, windswept grassy prairie called
Buffalo Plains near Lee's Creek in southern Alberta, he wrote in
May 1887, 'I am tired, and weary of traveling. I started to plow on
a new place in the wilderness one week ago yesterday and one week
ago today put in my first garden. It is a task to commence anew in
a new land far from home... but such are the trials of many of the
saints as present, but by the help of a kind Father in Heaven, we
will endure.' Such was the faith and determination of Charles Ora
Card (1839-1906) the man still referred to by many as Canada's
Brigham Young.'"

---

20   "History of John A. Nelson, Sr." by his son, Seth Nelson.

President Charles Card, who was president of the Cache Valley Stake in Logan, Utah, had earlier been commissioned by President John Taylor to find a place of refuge in Canada where members of the church could live their religion without harassment. In the wake of recent federal laws and court rulings prohibiting plural marriage, many husbands had chosen to leave the United States and support part of their multiple families from a distance rather than be thrown into jail and left unable to provide for them at all.[21]

John was the baby when his family left Smithfield, Utah for Canada in the spring of 1890. There were several of his mother's sisters and their husbands, Don and Sarah Hyde, Jasper Head and his wife Mary. They were all anxiously anticipating their move to Canada. It appeared to be a new country where they could get plenty of grazing for their stock and where there would be financial opportunities for growing families. However, polygamy may have been another reason for the move.[22]

On the genealogy family group sheet of John Alexander Nelson, Sr. it shows that John had taken another wife, Fanny Purser. There is no indication, however, that Fanny moved with the family to Canada. Perhaps his move to Canada was for the reason stated above, so that he could live with one family while supporting the one left behind rather than be thrown into jail for being a polygamist and be unable to support either family. Fanny and John's sealing was later cancelled December 20, 1896.[23]

John A. Sr. sold his land in Smithfield and obtained a good outfit. Then, he, his wife Ella, and their five children (the oldest of whom was ten-year-old Maria Elizabeth and the baby John, who was eight to nine months old) joined a company headed for Canada which was led by Johnny Woolf who had been over the route be-

---

21   "Edward J. Wood--Faith Personified," taken from the Sept. 1988 Ensign, The Church of Jesus Christ of Latter-Day Saints. Reprinted by permission.
22   John Nelson's dictaphone tape, no number.
23   John Alexander Nelson, Sr.'s, "Family Group Sheet."

fore. Mark Beazer, Ezra Hansen, and several others were also part of this party.[24]

A LONG, WEARISOME ROAD

From Smithfield to Cardston, Canada is approximately 700 miles. There were no freeways, bridges, gas stations or convenience food stores along that pioneer trail to make traveling easy. What a challenging trek for a group of pioneers with small children. This poem which was written by Lila Bennett Spencer describes another pioneer's journey, but since Ella Elizabeth had similar experiences, it is included here.

EMMA NEAT BENNETT, ALBERTA PIONEER

By Lila Bennett Spencer

She held the reins in blistered, sunburned hands,
And urged the weary team along through the tall prairie grass.
And the wagons lumped ahead like a giant, sluggish caterpillar
Seeking respite from the sun's hot breath.
The wind, the ever-present wind,
wrestled with the flapping canvas cover
And whipped her hair loose from its coil to sting her cheeks and smart her eyes.
Inside the wagon, in a sheltered corner, her fretful baby wailed in his nest of quilts
Until the wagon's sway stilled his cry.
The children walked beside on cracked and calloused feet,
heads bowed to the wind and sun, Prodding the cows with a crooked stick.
Her husband drove the wagon ahead, leading the way, setting the pace,
Shoulders square, eyes narrowed, seeing a vision lost to her.
A special call had brought them here, a call to irrigate this thirsty land,
To make a promised land. This, a promised land?
This land of blazing sun, and tall grass raked by wind,
moving like a restless sea around them, This treeless land?

"There's freedom there," they said, "And space to grow."

Space, yes, there was space. Limitless, barren space.
Her heart ached for the home she'd left and its remembered peace.
But her husband drove on, And she followed his lead

Through the wilderness.

---

24   John A. Nelson's dictaphone tape, no number.

LOSING THE ROAN DURHAM-SIRE BULL

John A., Sr. drove twenty head of two-year old heifers from Smithfield, Utah to Canada. Ella Elizabeth drove a wagon with a team of four horses. In John Sr.'s diary, he wrote of a prized roan, Durham-sire bull he had bought and taken along.

Ten to fifteen miles outside of Helena, Montana, the group had some trouble. Included in the group were two young men who had agreed to go along with the party to help drive the stock in exchange for board and lodging in their tent.

The two boys rode ahead of the group to find a good campground. Just a little ways from the campground, they saw some cattle. They decided they would like to have some fresh meat and consequently, they killed a little calf. They only took back to camp the portion of the meat they thought could be used, leaving the hide and the remains on the ground.

As they began distributing the meat, John Sr. was very angry that they had killed the calf and said that since it did not belong to them, they had no business killing it.

The next morning, just as they were about ready to round up their cattle and depart, a man rode into their camp. He said, "Gentlemen... don't leave. One of my cows came down to the ranch. She cried all night for her calf. I followed her to the remains of her slaughtered calf. I noticed horse prints in the dirt around where the killing had taken place. One of the horses of the riders wore horseshoes. That is not something that is common in these parts. I followed those footprints of the shod-horse and they led me to your camp. I am sure that one of your party has killed my calf. Just wait here until I go into Helena to get the sheriff. You will not be able to get away from us as I can see you are not traveling very fast."

About this time, the rancher noticed the two-year-old Durham bull that belonged to John, Sr. He said, "If you will give me this animal,

I will forget the incident and I will not call the sheriff and you can be on your way."

There was no alternative. John, Sr. realized that should the sheriff come out, there would be greater troubles, so he said, "All right, you take the bull." He never quite forgave the boys for their foolish stunt that cost him his prize bull, but he gave up his bull so they could continue on their journey.[25]

FORDING THE SUN RIVER

It became necessary to ford the Sun River at the area now known as Fort Shaw, Montana. It was in the spring of the year and the water was at a high stage. Ella was driving her own team that weighed about 1600 pounds. They were harnessed to pull. In order to cross the river, John put Ella's team on his wagon as lead team and took his wagon over first, leaving one of his team to pick up later when he went back for Ella's wagon.

John got over successfully with his wagon and then his trail wagon. He was going back to get Ella. He was riding Old Barney and leading Old Frank. Barney got down a little too low in his fiord and went in a deep hole.

He went under the water with water covering his head. As he came up, naturally John had slipped from his horse's back, but he grabbed for Old Barney's harness.

He climbed up on the horse and hung on tight and Old Barney took him out of the water.

The other horse, Old Frank, came up on the opposite side of the stream. With that experience behind them, they were able to get the other wagons across safely. They felt that the Lord had been protecting them all along their journey.[26]

---

25 John A. Nelson's Dictaphone tape, no number.
26 Ibid.

CANADA, OH CANADA

PEOPLE OF SUPERIOR MOLD

On arrival in Cardston, Alberta, Canada, the family found a log cabin which they used until they could build a home of their own. It was in this cabin that John, Sr. and his second daughter, Ella, were stricken with a mountain fever and were only saved by the administration of the Elders. John Sr.'s son, Seth, said, "That experience taught father that men and women who seem ordinary neighbors, suddenly become angels of mercy who carry to the sick ones all available luxuries, provide food, wood, water and the best that could be found. Those who assisted him and his family at that time have always remained to him, men and women of superior mold."[27]

This cabin was very near where the great Alberta Temple now stands.

HOMESTEADING

Shortly after John Sr.'s family arrived in Canada, they were able to take up a homestead, which gave them land, if they would put buildings on it and improve the property. The government offered this to encourage people to come and settle the land and become citizens of Canada.[28]

THE ROCK QUARRY

On this homestead, there was a wonderful rock quarry; it had beautiful sandstone that was in the hill in layers. Dirt had to be moved off the top of it, and then holes were drilled into the rock with giant blasting powder to make the rock available for use. Blasting was common for many years after the quarry was opened.

John Jr. wrote: "Rock didn't cost very much in those days, however, but my father used to haul the rock into Cardston, which was about

---

27   History of John A. Nelson, Sr. by Seth Nelson.
28   John Nelson's Dictaphone tape, no number.

three miles away. The rock sold by the perch, which was so many hundred pound weight of rock. It was hauled with heavy planks in the bottom of the wagon, and heavy post-like logs around the edge of the bed of the box of the wagon. They would pile the rock on top of that."

John continued, "It didn't take many rocks to be piled on the wagon to weigh two tons. Father always hauled with two teams. I was his oldest son and as a boy of 6 or 7, I would haul a load of rock behind Father's team with the trusty old team, Sam and Dan. I remember playing around the quarry until my father got the two wagons loaded up. Generally we would take two loads every day, one in the morning, and then have lunch at home, and return for a second load in the afternoon. All I had to do was sit on a sack of straw on the load of rock, and then drive old Sam and Dan along behind my father's wagon. Sometimes I'd fall asleep before we'd get into Cardston."

"This rock was used for the foundation of many homes in the Cardston area. Also many houses were built from the rock from the quarry. The foundation for the tabernacle on Temple Hill in Cardston has rock donated by my father. Father started a rock house for his family, but like the shoemaker's kids who had no shoes, this home was never completed. Mother thought it best that he build a frame house, so that is the way it was."

"There was no mechanical means of lifting the rock in those days. Father could lift several hundred pounds of rock onto a wagon by getting it up onto his knees, over onto his breast, and then up on the wagon. It was a hard way to make a living."

CARDSTON'S STONE AGE

A book entitled Cardston and District--Chief Mountain Country Volume II contains an article written by Albert E. Schindler, "Cardston's Stone Age Period," which records that stone was a very popular building material in the Cardston area, as early as 1888. He wrote:

> On November 9, 1888, a petition was presented to the Honorable E. Downey, Minister of the interior in Ottawa, by C. O. Card, Francis Lyman and John W. Taylor, requesting the privilege for the Cardston colonists to use the local stone for building and other purposes. Permission, of course, was granted and the colonists didn't even have to pay the standard five per cent tax on the stone because, according to the government files, the Cardston quarries weren't even considered as established quarries.
>
> Many of Cardston's early buildings used the stone for the foundations. The first complete structure to be built of stone was the Tithing Office, built about 1890. These grand old structures stand as ready witnesses to the fact that, dropped into an environment of conflict, hardship and struggle, as our forefathers were, the human soul seems often stimulated to produce finest mark.
>
> Sad, yes, even a pity that the stone building boom in Cardston flowered with such promise, then all too quickly faded into history. Barely twenty years and it was all over. After 1912, when the Canadian Pacific Railway took over the A. R. and I. Railway to Cardston and Medicine Hat, brick became very cheap resulting in Cardston's brick yard and stone quarry being phased out as uneconomical.
>
> Although Cardston's stone-age period was short-lived, it was colorful, imaginative and impressive. To be sure, in the course of time, other great estates and mansions will come and go, as things must, but will anything ever be able to equal the noble dreams of Cardston's stone builders?

A GROWING FAMILY

Seth was born October 15, 1896, a year after the family arrived in Canada. Other children born to the family were: Cleveland born March 20, 1893, Lorenzo (Ren) born July 2, 1896, the twin daughters, Hazel and Irene, born December 15,.1899. Irene died January 21, 1900, when she was just about six weeks old. Darrel Thomas Nelson was the last child born to the union of John Alexander, Sr., and Ella Elizabeth Thomas Nelson. He was born December 20, 1901.

About the year 1907, John, Sr. sold his homestead and went to Woolford, about 8 miles east of Cardston, which was a better farming district. Here he lived until about 1909, when he went to Nampa, Idaho, and remained there until the dedication of the temple in 1923, when he returned to Cardston.

During his early years in Cardston, he worked as a carpenter leaving the imprint of his saw and hammer on many of the frame buildings that still stand there. The Woolf hotel which stood on the east side of main street was erected by him and Joseph Wight.

Whenever the Cardston boys of the "nineties," told stories of strength and prowess, they never failed to tell of the great strength of John Nelson, Sr. and his brother-in-law, Jasper Head. At pulling sticks and side-holts, they found no rival.

3

YOUTHFUL DAYS IN CANADA

ELLA CALLED TO BE A MIDWIFE

Ella's son, John Alexander Nelson, Jr., recalled the following about his mother, Ella Elizabeth Nelson:

"Two years after my parents moved to Cardston, Alberta, Canada, from Smithfield, Utah, my mother was chosen by the First Presidency of the Church to go to Salt Lake City and take a special training in obstetrics. Mother yielded obedience to the call. Father was willing that she should go. I was between three and four years of age and Mother took me along. We had to go to Lethbridge, a distance of fifty miles, to take the closest train."

"We were to be gone for three or four months while Mother was in nurses' training school. I remember going to the school with her. I couldn't write, but she gave me a pencil and a paper."

"Mother graduated with honors and was given many of the things pertaining to this type of work. Plastic bones and things showing the human body and the mechanism of it, so that she would know just what to do in the delivering of a baby.

"On her return to Canada, Mother was soon in demand as a mid-wife. There was another woman there by the name of Hammer. Her health was not always good, however, and she couldn't go as much as my mother could. Although my mother had a family of ten living children (five boys and five girls), she made necessary arrangements to take care of the women who needed her. Some of Mother's children were born during the time she performed her duties as the mid-wife. My older sisters remained home and took care of the smaller children."

"My sister Mimie, (Maria Elizabeth) was a second mother to me and some of the younger children. She stayed home and looked after the home while mother was out among the sick. Mother built up a great reputation and she was always willing to go and never refused. There were no phones in those days, no means of communication, only by letter or word of mouth. But Mother seemed to know when there was some woman in trouble who needed her help and assistance. There was an inspiration that seemed to hover over her and tell her when she was needed."

"I remember Mother and Father both telling how Mother would get out of bed at midnight, or somewhere during the night, get dressed as quickly as she could, even put on her hat and coat, and take a chair close to the door with her little satchel, waiting for a rap to come. A man would come for her and he would be amazed to see Mother sitting at the door, waiting for him. He would say, 'How did you know I was coming?'"

"She would reply, 'Well, I just felt impressed. I woke up with a start, jumped out of bed and felt that shortly somebody would rap on the door for me, so here I am, ready to go.'"

"Mother always had a lot of faith, and I am sure, as I have heard her tell it many times, before attempting to deliver a child, she always had a prayer with the family. She was very successful because of her prayerfulness, her faithfulness and her willingness to yield to the call of the First Presidency of the Church. Heavenly Father must have loved my mother a great deal because he gave her such a special gift."

"Mother didn't only help the women who gave birth to babies, but she had learned how to cope with the various diseases: smallpox, typhoid fever, and the diseases common to that time. Her tools were a pair of scissors, a ball of cord string and some sort of antiseptic."[29]

NO DISCOUNT FOR CASH

Seth Nelson, son of Ella Elizabeth, recalled that his mother charged five dollars for delivering a baby. Included in this fee was a week's care for the mother and family. One time he was sent to collect after such a delivery and the woman gave him four dollars and fifty cents, saying she was taking a fifty cent discount for cash. As he put the money on their kitchen table and told his mother the proposal, Ella became irate and insisted he return for the full amount saying, "I don't give discounts!" It was a small sum, but good for the times and bought the family many of the things they could not have otherwise afforded.[30]

JOHN'S LOVE FOR HORSES

John loved horses. One of his favorite stories that he loved telling to his children and grand children was about a childhood memory with a horse. It happened when he was seven or eight years old. His father, John Sr., had taken a trip and his children were all anxiously awaiting his return. On the day he was scheduled to arrive, they sat out by the house and watched with eager anticipation. At last the wagon came into sight with Father Nelson sitting in the driver seat. From a distance, there appeared to be another person in the front

---

29   John Nelson's Dictaphone tape, number 2.
30   "Ella Elizabeth Thomas History," by Seth Nelson.

seat of the wagon. As the wagon got closer and closer, the children were all sure that their father was bringing home a visitor.

When the wagon pulled into the yard, the children could see that the visitor had especially long ears. In fact, yes, it wasn't a human visitor at all, but a little PONY!

Much to the delight of his eager family, Father John unloaded the pony from the wagon. The pony, however, was not too friendly and ran up on a side hill. But his struggle to keep from having a rope put around his neck was in vain, and he soon became a favorite pet of the family. What a thrill.

THE KIDNAPPING

In Cardston in about the year 1899, there was a man called Dr. Brandt, who had purchased the drug store. He had a reputation for being a scoundrel and a cheat because of a story that he had allegedly swindled one of the local citizens, Jim Layton, out of a great deal of money.

The story claimed that Jim had sold his ranch and that he had been enticed to invest the money he received for the ranch in Dr. Brandt's drug store. After a period of time, because Jim wasn't getting any dividends back on his investment, he contacted the Canadian Drug Inspector to come and investigate the drug store operations. The inspector found that the shelves were apparently lined with bottles of medicine which contained nothing but colored water. A lawsuit followed, but during this time Dr. Brandt was still in business.

John said, "Dr. Brandt appeared to be a heavy drinker. One day my sister Lileth and her friend, Miss Umay, both about twelve-years old, went into the drug store. Dr. Brandt and one of his drinking buddies forced these two young girls into the back room of the store. The men left to continue drinking their liquor. They had evil desires and ambitions toward these two young ladies."

"After the girls had been locked in for several hours, the men returned, both 'dead drunk.' As they opened the door, the girls bolted and ran and got away from the men. Lileth came running home, frightened to death and all out of breath. She told Mother about their being kidnapped."

"Father and I had just returned with a load of hay from up on the ranch. I was about nine or ten years old at the time. Mother ran immediately and held the gate for us as we drove into the yard. Father was still sitting on the hay when Mother excitedly repeated the disturbing events. Father got down off the wagon, taking my hand with him. He was so angry, I wondered if he even realized I was with him! I wondered what was going through his mind as we raced the three or four blocks to the drug store."

"At that time, in Cardston, there was a wooden sidewalk on Main Street. Just as we got almost in front of the drug store, the doctor appeared."

"Father said, 'Stop where you are! Don't move or I'll tromp you right through this sidewalk. If you aren't out of Cardston by tomorrow night, you won't be able to get out. Now, I warn you, leave our town or I'll come after you. Don't ever show your face in Cardston again!'"

"I was standing on the sidewalk, watching all of this, trembling for fear of what father would do to Dr. Brandt. But after this warning, father turned and we both went back home. Lileth was there when we returned and she asked, "What did you do, Pa?""

"Father replied, 'After tomorrow night we won't have to worry about Dr. Brandt being in Cardston any more.'"

"Dr. Brandt left Cardston; where he went no one seemed to know. His wife stayed on and sold the business and their lovely big home and probably met Dr. Brandt at an appointed location."-

LON LAMB'S WILD RIDE

"The spring I was fourteen years old, I was living with my oldest sister, Mimie, and her husband Lon Lamb. Lon was the foreman on Simm Wolfe's ranch. This was located about seven miles from Cardston on the east side of the St. Mary's River. My brother-in-law, Lon, had the job of breaking some wild horses. I was helping him, as much as I could at that age."

"In order to break the horses, we first had to separate them from the pack by putting them into a small corral. One day as we were trying to separate a big black gelding from the pack, he ran into the little corral followed by an old work mare. I yelled to Lon, 'You'd better get the old mare out before you catch the gelding.'"

"He responded, 'I'll catch the gelding and you open the gate and let out the mare.' As Lon threw the lariat over the black gelding's neck, he had made the loop so big that the rope caught one front foot and the shoulder of the gelding."

"The corral was so small, Lon was not able to let out all the loops in the rope and as he ran past the old work mare, she kicked at him and the loop in his hand was hit by her hind heels making the loop fly up over Lon's head. At this instant, the wild gelding made a leap for liberty trying to jump the eight-foot-high fence. The black gelding balanced on top of the corral for a few seconds before going over the fence. All this time, the rope was around Lon's head and body."

"I shouted to Lon, 'For goodness sake climb the fence. He responded and climbed up the fence just as the wild horse was at the end of the rope--starting down through the trees on the outside of the corral. By this time the rope was also tangled around both of Lon's feet and as the horse raced on, Lon was dragged in the dust. The horse dragged him around the gravel yard and around the rocks and stumps of the St. Mary's River. Instead of crossing the river, the horse ran up over the prairie and passed the buildings of the ranch."

"By this time, his wife, Mimie, had been alerted and came running to observe her dear husband being dragged by the wild horse. I jumped on a pony that we had been breaking, and followed as fast as I could, adding a prayer that I have never forgotten. 'Oh, Lord, please stop this horse long enough for Lon to be released from the rope.' My prayer was answered. The horse stopped momentarily and Lon was able to reach up and take hold of the rope and the knot released. The black gelding ran on."

Lon lapsed into unconsciousness. He was badly torn and bruised by the wild ride over the rocks and stumps. When I saw his condition, I raced back to the ranch to get the buckboard. The buckboard was a little four-wheeled buggy with an iron railing around the body of the box. Mimie ran out with some blankets and quilts and we got into the buckboard.

When we reached Lon, he was conscious. The blood and lacerations on his body were terrible to behold. We got him into the buckboard and back to the ranch.

"It was necessary to ride to Cardston for the doctor. I knew that I could reach Cardston faster by swimming the river with my pony than by going around to the bridge. It was about three miles into Cardston by swimming the river, and seven miles by going across the bridge. I swam the river with my pony. I never forgot how very cold the water was. I kept my feet in the stirrups so that I would not be swept off the horse. The horse ran as fast as he could go."

"I went first to the livery stable and I hired a team and buggy so that I could take the doctor out to take care of Lon. I tied my pony to the side of the buggy. It was fortunate to find the doctor in his office."

"We had a hurried ride back the seven mile road to the ranch. The doctor was very skillful and he took care of Lon's wounds. He told Lon, 'It will be two or three months that you will have to remain on your stomach as you lie in bed. These sores will have to heal, but you are lucky to be alive.'"

"Mimie was expecting her first child in about one month. I will always remember the strength and character she displayed in caring for her husband. Lon never fully recovered from this accident. He had trouble with one of his legs the rest of his life. But after being dragged by a wild horse, Lon was indeed lucky to be alive!

HIT OVER THE HEAD WITH A QUIRT

"When I was a young man, about 17 years of age, my father sent me out to look for a few stray cattle that had his brand on. These cattle had strayed down the reservation near the town of Magrath, Alberta, Canada. I rode down that way looking in fields and pastures or wherever I would see a herd of cattle. I figured on staying that night at my Uncle Jasper Head's place while I looked around that vicinity."

"I had been riding part of the day and it was the middle of the afternoon when I reached the outskirts of Magrath, (which at that time was a growing town.) I noticed some cattle over in a pasture, and going down along side of the fence, I came to an opening that had pole bars across it. The bars had been dropped down at one end, so I stepped my horse over the end of them and rode out into the field where the cattle were. I was just going slowly looking at the brands, when a large man rode up on a big grey horse. He briskly rode up to me and without saying a word, he hit me across the face with a quirt loaded with shot. [A quirt is a riding whip with a braided leather lash and a short handle.] The riders in those days nearly always had that type of weapon attached to the saddle, either snapped on the side or with a hand hold around the horn."

"As he hit me across the face with this quirt he said, 'I'll teach you to leave my bars down!'"

"I told him as soon as I could get my breath, being terribly surprised at the wicked blow he gave me, which left a mark on my face, 'I did not leave them down.' He didn't believe this but he kept striking at me. The only thing that saved me was that I was on a little quicker horse than he was. I was a younger man, just a boy so to speak, but I could have hit him over the head many times with my quirt. I detached it from my saddle and struck him across the back a time or two because it looked to me that it was either fight or die. I was talking all the while of my innocence, telling him that I did not leave the bars down."

"We were traveling south, and as we were fighting, we rode upon a little hill which was only a few blocks from where he first struck me. There I saw a horse with a saddle on it tied up to the running gears of a wagon. [Running gears of a wagon are just the gear without the box on it.] I said to my pursuer, 'Perhaps the man that owns that horse is the one who left your bars down.'"

"He looked over at the horse with the saddle on and then we both rode over to the little shack on the property. We saw a big overgrown boy, perhaps 14 or 15 years of age, asleep on a bed with only a mattress on it. It was in the month of August and very warm. This man shouted out to the boy and said, 'Did you leave my bars down?'

"The boy, as he rose from his sleep, said, 'Well, yes I did, I expected to go right back out of the field but I came here and I was tired and I laid down on this mattress and must have gone to sleep.'"

"The thing that I noticed more than anything else, even perhaps more that the terrible mark across my face, was the thought that this man did not apologize to me, even after the boy on the bed had confessed that he was the one who left the bars down.

I'd like to suggest a lesson, 'Always be man enough or woman enough to confess to a wrong. If you are wrong, do not be afraid to apologize.'[31]

---

31   John Nelson's dictaphone tape #15.

HORSE SENSE

"We were living in Canada, when my Grandmother Thomas (mother of Ella Elizabeth) died in Salt Lake City. My mother's brother, Seth, lived adjoining us through the field. I was a young man about seventeen years of age. My Uncle Seth came down and wanted to know if I would do his chores so he could attend his mother's funeral. I told him I would be happy to. He had a lot of fine horses, so he told me to hook up a team of four of them and do some plowing. He thought he would be gone about a week. So Uncle Seth, my mother Ella, and several other relatives, left by train from Lethbridge headed for Salt Lake."

"The first morning I planned to do a little plowing. I noticed that one of the horses acted a little skittish and awkward. I did not realize that this horse was a big three-year-old colt who had never had a bridle or harness on him before. I was determined to carry out my uncle's instructions. So I bridled this horse up, tying him, as luck would have it, next to his mother. He went in the barn, he ate the oats, and he never moved. I harnessed him up, but when I started out, he didn't seem like he wanted to go. I got him going. His mother the mare bit at him. He acted a little ornery for the first half of the day, but I worked him all day and the rest of the time Uncle Seth was gone."

"I've never forgotten Uncle Seth's reaction when he arrived home. 'John, that horse has never been broken. I had intended to break him this spring, but just never got around to doing it.'"

"I felt rather foolish, but also very fortunate that I had not experienced more trouble than I had by not knowing that this horse had never been hooked up before.'"

QUICKSAND

The following is a short story about John's brother-in-law, Chase Smith, husband of Lileth, from John's dictaphone stories.

"We were living in Cardston at the time of the event. Chase had come up to Cardston from Salt Lake City, Utah to visit with his uncle, Sam Kimball. Perhaps his main reason for staying in Canada so long was his attraction to my beautiful sister, Lileth. Chase had grown up as a city boy and was just learning to ride horses. I had invited him to come ride with me one day. I was several years younger than he."

"We were looking for some cattle that had been lost. We came to a spot we called a big soap hole or a mud hole. It was quick-sand, very spongy and if an animal got out in the middle of it, many times the animal would sink and never get out. As we came near the quick-sand hole, we saw a cow struggling in the middle. She had a young calf lying out on the bank. She had gone in to get a drink and had become bogged down in the quick-sand."

"I said to Chase, 'The only way we can help her is for both of us to put a rope around her horns and pull. When she struggles, we can pull and help her and maybe get her out.'"

"We threw a lariat around her big horns, and as she struggled, we pulled back with the strength of our two saddle horses. Finally, after working with her for some time, we succeeded in landing her high and dry, out of the quick-sand. She was completely exhausted. We took the rope from her horns while she was lying there on the ground."

"With great compassion, Chase walked up to her, speaking to her gently. Quickly, she jumped to her feet and if it hadn't been that my saddle horse was standing close by, he may have gotten one of her big horns through him.

Chase made a comment that has stayed with me these many years when he said, 'That animal doesn't seem to have any appreciation in her soul. Here we helped her out of the quick-sand and then she took after me and would have gored me with those terrible, wicked horns she has, if it had not been for your saddle horse.'"

"I have thought about that many times in my lifetime. It is a lot like people. Sometimes we help people and they don't appreciate it. There might come a time when they could help us, but they decline. They may go the other way. Thanks to a kind Father in Heaven this negative kind of person is few and far between."[32]

ICE JAM ON ST. MARY'S RIVER

"For a year or so before I went on my mission, I was keeping company with a young lady named Margaret Hansen. She and her family lived in Aetna, Alberta, Canada. I was living with my parents in Woolford, about fifteen miles away. I had to cross the St. Mary's River to get to Margaret's house. When the river was low, I would usually ride my horse and cross at a shallow part of the river. It was another fifteen mile ride if I went around by the Kimball Bridge when the river was too high to cross."

"I went over to visit Margaret on a Sunday afternoon in the spring of the year. The river had been frozen all winter with the exception of a few spots where the fords were. After spending a nice afternoon with Margaret and family and since it was such a long ride back to Woolford, Margaret's brother, Oliver, asked me to stay all night. He said that I could get up early on Monday morning and head for home. I decided that my parents wouldn't worry about me, so accepted his invitation."

"As I got to the river the next morning, I could see large cakes of ice floating down the river, but I had a good safe horse and didn't think much about the ice cakes. After I got out into the river part way, suddenly, here came a great wall of ice and water. I could see that I could neither go ahead or back and all I could do was to dodge the big blocks of ice that were coming right towards me. I hadn't realized it, but the day before there had been an ice jam up the river and now that the ice jam was breaking up, it was causing the flash flooding."

---

32   John Nelson's dictaphone tape, #42.

"My horse and I were both extremely frightened. The water was getting deeper, so that the water came way up above the skirts of the saddle. I kept my feet down in the stirrups.

I had always been taught the value of prayer by a spiritual mother. I prayed that the Lord might protect me and that my horse and I would not be hit by one of the ice blocks.

I struggled for a long time before I was able to get out of that icy cold water. I was soaking wet."

"When I returned home, I found that my father had been walking the floor, worrying about me all the while that I had been in the river. Father was not an outwardly spiritual man, but he had a premonition that something was the matter with me. We had been very close as father and son and he sensed that I was in trouble. He, likewise, had prayed to the Lord what whatever trouble I was in, I might have the Lord's help to save me."

"I appreciate the training from a good mother who instilled within me the value of prayer, and also the love and concern of my own dear father whose prayers, together with my own, were answered by a kind and Heavenly Father."[33]

REN AND JACK CROSS BUTTE LAKE

"Early in the spring, perhaps March or April, the year I was about nineteen years old, I was out plowing in the field west of my father's home. Out in the distance, there appeared to be two individuals out in the middle of Butte Lake. The lake was about a mile and one-half long and three-fourths of a mile wide in some places. The lake was a favorite spot for recreation, as we would skate there in the winter when it froze over, or swim or boat on it in the summer. In the winter, the young people would get their horses with sharp shoes on and hitch them to a sleigh and have great fun sliding over the slick ice."

---

33   John Nelson's dictaphone tape #42.

"I kept my eyes on the two figures, but they were too far away for me to tell what they were doing. After I had plowed for several hours, I got on my saddle horse, and rode down around the lake to see what was going on. To my surprise, I discovered two young men: my younger brother Ren and his friend Jack Purnell. The boys were about twelve- years old at this time."

"They had built a raft from logs and poles and rowed out on the south side of the lake. They got some long poles to push themselves out onto the lake. The warm days of spring had caused the ice to begin breaking up and the ice had honey-combed around the shore. Through an opening in the ice, the boys had worked their raft out into the middle of the lake. The wind had become very strong and the boys were not able to get back to the shore."

"They had decided the best thing to do was to use their long poles and push themselves across to the other side of the lake. This way, they could take advantage of the wind to help blow them across. As they got to about a block from the north shore of the river, they found the water was too deep for their poles to touch the bottom of the lake. The ice had broken up all around them and had closed the opening for them to get through. They found themselves stranded!"

"When I first saw them, they were both standing on a corner of the raft in icy-cold water up to their knees. They appeared to be nearly frozen. They had been out on the lake all afternoon, but had been unable to yell loud enough to attract my attention."

"I could see there was nothing that I could do by myself, so I rushed back and notified the neighbors. They brought lariats and lines from the harnesses and all of the rope that could be located. We all went onto the north side of the lake and quickly improvised a raft. We tied all of the ropes together and I took the rope out with me on the raft to go to the rescue."

"I worked very hard with an ax and club to break up the ice in an attempt to reach the boys. I shouted to them to keep working and to try to come directly towards me. If I could get a hold of their raft and tie the ropes onto it, the men on shore could pull us all in to safety."

"When I finally reached the boys, they climbed onto my raft.

Ren spoke, 'Can you see that little white bird sitting on the corner of the raft? It's such a beautiful little bird and whenever he came to the raft, we were warm. We haven't been cold while he was with us, but when he left, we got cold again.'"

"Both boys told me that they had been praying very hard to Heavenly Father, to help them. I told them to keep praying so that the little bird might come again and keep them warm until we could get to shore. With great effort, the men on shore were able to pull us to safety."

"The boys were overjoyed to be rescued. Their prayers had been answered. They had been protected by a kind Heavenly Father when He sent the little white bird as a messenger of hope and love to them. The bird had given them courage and warmth and made them feel that all would be well with them. Through their great faith and prayers, they were saved from an icy grave."[34]

---

34   John Nelson's dictaphone tape #46.

.

4

JOHN, THE MISSIONARY

JOHN'S MISSION CALL

"When I was nineteen years of age living in Woolford, Alberta, Canada, with my parents, I received a call to go on a mission. (Dec. 14, 1910) This call came from Salt Lake City, Utah 'Box B.' 'Box B' was known the church around as the Office of the First Presidency Of the Church. Whenever a young man or woman received a letter from 'Box B,' it meant missionary work. My Bishop had asked me previously if I would be willing to accept a mission call. I had agreed, with the consent of my parents.   I had been preparing all summer and fall to get ready for this mission.[29]

---

29   John Nelson's dictaphone tape #46.

Three handsome young brothers:
Cleve and John--front; Seth--rear.

PRESIDENT EDWARD J. WOOD

"My Stake President, Edward J. Wood, had talked to me and asked me if I would like to go to the Samoan Islands. I had heard him speak so many times of his mission there. He had been called to serve twice in his young life to these islands. President Wood had

President Edward J. Wood and his Counselors

given much service and sacrifice to missionary work. When he was a young man, twenty-one years of age, he was engaged to be married. He went to his Stake President to get a temple recommend, so he could take his bride-to-be to the temple to be married, but instead he learned of his mission call to the Samoan Islands.[30]

"A little over a month later, in September 1888, he was en route to three and a half years in Samoa, and was one of three missionaries to join a missionary couple sent six months earlier to open up the mission. He returned in 1892 and married his high-school sweetheart, Mary Ann Solomon. They had two children and then in 1896, four years after his return from Samoa, at the age of twenty-nine, he

30   Ensign Magazine,"Faith Personified", Edward J. Wood, Sept. 1988--page 50-56. Used by permission..

was called again to Samoa, this time as Mission President. This call separated him from his wife and family for two more years.[31]

Jay Todd, Managing Editor of the "Ensign" magazine wrote some of President Wood's feelings as he departed for the Samoan Mission:

"Today was the greatest trial of my life. Never before did I realize what leaving home was. Poor Mary Ann fainted away and little Glen almost broke his heart and I felt as I never felt before. For no other reason on earth could I ever be induced to leave my dear little family than the Gospel.[32]"

READY AND WILLING

John recorded on his dictaphone tape: "Because of the good reports that President Wood had given me, I was pretty well sold on the Island Mission. When my letter from 'Box B' arrived on December 19, 1909, asking me to accept a mission call to the Samoan Islands, I was ready and willing to go. I was to go to Salt Lake City for Missionary Training, and then to Vancouver, British Columbia preparatory to sailing for Samoa."

"A farewell meeting was held for me at my home ward. I had prepared a little speech, and others spoke, giving me advice and counsel. I also received some seventy-five or eighty dollars as a contribution to help me on my way.[33]"

ENTRIES FROM JOHN'S DIARY

"I now begin to keep a record of all my doings both spiritual and temporal, praying for the Lord to inspire me to write only those things that will be beneficial and interesting to those who may read it in the future."

---

31   Ibid.
32   Ibid 1.
33   John Nelson's dictaphone tape #26.

"On December 19th in the middle of the afternoon I bid my Mother, Lorenzo, Hazel and Darrel 'goodbye.' The rest of the family were planning to go to the train depot the next day. The night of the 19th, I went to Aetna and stayed at the home of Miss Margaret Hanson, the girl with whom I had been keeping company.

John and his sister, Rae. Likely taken about the time John left for Samoa.

"The next morning I bid her and her folks 'goodbye' and in company with her brother, Oliver, I left for Cardston where I met my father and two brothers, Seth and Cleveland. At two o'clock that afternoon I bid Father and Seth 'goodbye.' Cleve was going as far as Lethbridge with me and returning the next day. In Lethbridge, Cleve and I attended a fine theatre. The next morning we both took the same train for a distance of sixteen miles. He then left me and I took the 11 AM train going south."

"I had a very pleasant journey, reaching Emmett, Idaho on December 24, and in the afternoon of the same day I rode out to my sister's place at Bramwell. The next day was Christmas and with her and her family, I spent the day very interestingly. At night attended a dance."

"During the holiday week, my time was taken up mostly talking to Ella and Joseph of things at home. For the latter part of the week, my sister Mimie arrived from Salt Lake where she had been visiting."

MY TRAINING TIME IN SALT LAKE CITY

"On January 8th I left for Salt Lake arriving there on the 10th. I stayed with my sister Lileth Smith and her husband, Chase. Chase was one of the sons of the late President Joseph F. Smith. He had been in Canada a lot and I knew him. He was a very fine man. I stayed with them while I went through the church missionary training school. This I enjoyed immensely.

"Lileth and Chase were so kind to me and I loved being with them. Lileth and Chase were a little surprised one day, when I went through their home and raised all of the windows, and as loudly as I could, I sang, 'Come, Come, Ye Saints.' When they asked me why I wanted the windows raised, I told them I wanted all of their neighbors to hear and to join the ranks of the Mormons.

John's diary continues, "I loved the missionary training period. There were classes held with talks by the members of the First Presidency. These wonderful men gave such good instructions to us and I enjoyed this time immensely. These training sessions took about three weeks. They helped me to know what to expect on my mission and helped me to prepare for my work that was ahead. I was very anxious to get to Samoa to begin teaching the gospel of Jesus Christ to the people in that faraway land."[34]

CAN'T BE PERSUADED

"One morning, while I was staying at Lileth's home, my Uncle Dan, one of my mother's brothers who was a prominent attorney in Salt Lake City, called me on the phone. He said, 'Johnny, I understand that you've received a call to go to the Samoan Islands on a mission. Now, that's a far away country and you won't learn much while you're there because you will speak in a foreign, unknown tongue. What you should do is have your mission changed and go to an English speaking mission so when you return home, you will be more fluent, have a greater knowledge of the Gospel and of the

Lileth Nelson Smith and Heber Chase Smith Family from left, Heber Jr., Ella and Alice. Circa 1910.

world and of everything in common. So why don't you let me intercede for you and have your mission changed to some English speaking country?'"

"It didn't take me long to tell him 'no,' because I was filled up with going to the islands. I said, 'Thanks a lot, Uncle Dan, I appreciate your concern and interest in me, but my mind is made up. I am accepting the missionary call to wherever I have been called. Since my call is to the Samoan Islands, that is where I'll go. So, I don't think it would do you any good to intercede for me."'[35]

GUIDE ON TEMPLE SQUARE

"Daily at the Bureau of Information on Temple Square, volunteers told groups of tourists the wonderful stories about the tabernacle, the temple, and the migration of the Mormons from Nauvoo into the Great Salt Valley. We young men, who were preparing to go on missions, were very much interested in these stories and the things that these men were telling. We availed ourselves of the opportunity of going along with various groups as they went through the Bureau of Information, through the Assembly Hall and the Tabernacle and had stories told to them of the hardships of the Latter-Day Saints when they first arrived in the Great Salt Lake Valley."

"This was all very inspiring and many people from various parts of the United States and Europe Joined the groups. After I had been listening to the volunteers for a little while, I was asked if I would like to help take some groups through, for many times they were short of help. The volunteers who worked there were from many professions who, when they had two or three hours of time, would go over to the Bureau of Information and take tourists through the center. Groups left every hour. Many times, there would be thirty-five to forty people in a group, especially during the tourist season."[36]

WE MISSED OUR TRAIN

"I was set apart on January 21, 1910, to serve as a missionary to the Samoan Islands. On the night of January 22, 1910, at 11 P.M., in company with ten other elders, I left Salt Lake City, en route to Vancouver, British Columbia. I visited my Aunt and Uncle in Portland. "

---

35   Ibid.
36   John Nelson's dictaphone tape #26.

"From there we went to Seattle where we could go up the coast to Vancouver and take the boat for our field of labor. Melvin J. Ballard, who was then President of the Northwestern States Mission, had arranged for tickets for all of the missionaries who were going across the ocean. He gave us all instructions for the coming journey."

John and his missionary companions... John is in front at right. This picture was likely taken in Seattle just before the group left for the islands -- 1910.
Notice the stacks of lumber behind the elders.

"There was an older, married man among the group who was going to New Zealand. President Ballard had given all of our tickets to this man, with instructions that he was to be the 'Presiding Elder.' President Ballard then gave us all instructions. He said that we could go take in the sights of the city. He said to be sure and be back in time to catch the train that was bound for Seattle."

"Ten of us were there at the station on time for the train. We went in and found our places on the train. President Ballard was standing on the platform but the Elder who had our tickets had not yet returned from visiting some friends that he knew in Portland, Oregon. Just as the train was about to leave, President Ballard, very much chagrined and very much put out with our 'Presiding Elder,' came into the car in which we were waiting and said, 'You men had better get off, because the Elder who holds your tickets has not yet arrived.'"

"All ten of us got off the train, luggage and all. We all stood on the platform with President Melvin J. Ballard as the train pulled out without us. Just as the train was rounding the corner out of sight, here came our missing Elder on the run.

President Ballard gave that Elder a good scolding and added, 'You might be the means of all these Elders missing their steamship.'"

"President Ballard was kind and quickly forgave the delinquent Elder. There was another train to Seattle in three hours. President Ballard said that he thought we would be able to get there in time to make our connections so we could catch our steamship in Vancouver."[37]

---

37   John Nelson's dictaphone tape #24

MY FIRST STREET MEETING

"Everything went all right and we arrived in Vancouver, British Columbia in plenty of time. In fact, some of the missionaries who were laboring in Vancouver met us and invited us to come and see one of their street meetings. Since we had several hours to wait, we joined them. They told us what to do. We were to stand out as if we were part of the crowd in the street."

"They had a song and a prayer and then one missionary stepped out and started speaking. A large crowd had gathered by that time. It wasn't long before the Elder in charge was getting a lot of argument from a man who was standing in the crowd. Pretty soon, the arguments got very heated. And then, of course, even more people stopped. It wasn't long until two policemen came along and broke up the meeting and the crowd was dispersed in all directions. We had seen one way that the Elders teach the gospel in North America. It was a little disturbing. I wondered what my experiences would be in Samoa. We missionaries got back together, however, and were glad that we had that little experience of seeing how missionaries worked in America."[38]

HANDS UP

"We took the steamship and traveled on down to Victoria, B.C., January 28, 1910. The purser came in to the various state rooms and said, 'This is the last chance you'll have to post a letter before sailing out to sea. So we're going to stop here for two hours. You can write your letters and walk up town, since it is only a few blocks to the Post Office and post your letters there.'"

"We all got busy and we wrote to our families. Another Elder and I were a little slow in getting our letters written. It was about nine or ten o'clock in the evening and darkness had set in. Along the path to the Post Office from the wharf, there was a wire fence on one side and a very heavy hedge on the other. We had to walk through the

---

38   Ibid.

dark for perhaps three or four blocks. We could see big street lights on the other end right at the exit to this path. As we were going to the Post Office, there were two of the other Elders from our group, coming towards us as they were returning from the Post Office. We could see them under the big street light just as they entered the dark part of the path.

In the darkness, as they came close to us, I stuck out my hands as if holding a gun and said, 'Hands up!'"

"It wasn't a premeditated act of mischief, but just one of those boyish tricks. Immediately, all four hands went up. We quickly apologized and told them who we were, but one of the Elders was so frightened, we couldn't get him to put his hands down. He became hysterical. I learned my lesson! I have thought about this often and my boyish trick. I felt sorry to have frightened him so badly."[39]

JOHN'S DIARY CONTINUES

"On the morning of the 29th of January, 1910, at 3 a.m., I was suddenly awakened with a terrible feeling not seeming to know just where I was or what I was doing. I tried to dress, but all in vain. I rolled from my bunk onto the floor and there I laid until Elder Miller helped me to dress. This is my main recollection of the first few days of my trip on the big steamship."

"Elder Miller took me out on deck. Here I found several of the other Elders feeding fish in grand style (meaning they were vomiting). This seasickness stayed with me for two days and then I was alright, William Orr said, 'If I ever have my way, none of my relatives will ever cross the ocean.' Elder Jones said, 'If I ever hit land, there I'll stay.' Elder Hatch said, 'I would rather follow a thresher for a month than ride a boat for one day.' What did I say? Let me see, I said, 'Take life as it comes, up hill or down.'"

---

39   Ibid.

"February 1st--Storm not very bad.. Miller and I talked most of the day of our past lives. A girl lay in an adjoining room singing. 1000 miles from land, 1337 miles from Honolulu, made 280 miles the last 24 hours. A pretty sick bunch on board."

"February 2nd--1054 miles from Honolulu, 1288 miles from Victoria, rough sea, feeling pretty good."

"February 3rd--Feeling fine. 729 miles to Honolulu. Made 325 miles last 24 hours. Wrote a letter home. Sailors practice fire drill, sat up till late."

"February 4th--Very warm, made 345 miles today. Wrote letters to Margaret and folks. A concert at night."

"February 5th--Arrived at Honolulu at 3:30 p.m. Took in all the sights of the city. Ate my fill of bananas. Left at 11 p.m. Sweat quarts while walking around the city. Went to a theatre in a roof-less building."

"February 6th--Sunday. All of Elders gathered in our room and took turns reading the Bible and singing songs. At night a meeting was held in the dining room. A sectarian minister did the preaching. We helped him sing. He preached on the dashing waves and then prayed for our safety. He announced a meeting for the next Sunday."

"February 7th--Raining but very warm. The other Elders with myself were leaning over the side of the boat when a large wave came and nearly drowned us. Saw great flocks of flying fish about the size of small trout. Have been pulling sticks." [Apparently a game.]

"February 8th--Held a celebration, games of all sorts, boxing, wrestling. I was running a wheel barrel race and a big awkward Englishman fell down on top of me and nearly broke my leg. The third class was competing against the second and the former took all the prizes. The seconds were supposed to be gentlemen and were not rough enough, so lost out."

ARRIVING AT FANNING ISLANDS

"February 9th--At 8 a.m. arrived at the Fanning Islands, left at 12. Did not pull clear up to shore as the water was too shallow. Natives freighted cargo to shore in small boats. None of passengers were allowed to get off, only two who remained on the island.

A number of fish were caught by passengers, until several large shark came and took the hooks and bait from the lines.

One fellow took a large meat hook and fashioned it to a rope and put meat on it and let it down into the water. The sharks were too smart and kept clear of it. The island was certainly a picturesque little spot. Large coconut trees stood high. Two native boys came to the ship trying to sell post cards. After all the cargo was unloaded, the two passengers were next and as they were lowered into the row boat, the passengers on board sang the song 'Goodbye Friends, We're Going on to Suva.' We were not long in leaving the island from view."

"I read all afternoon. At night the third class passengers gave a concert and dance on deck. Such a time as we never had before! Irish songs, Scottish songs and English songs galore and a waltz in between. After the show, two Elders and myself took some chairs on deck and prepared for a sleep. We are close to the equator."

"February 10th--Today crossed the equator at 10:30 a.m. A very mild day, read and talked most of the day, not much doing."

CROSSING THE EQUATOR

"There is an old custom that the day the ship crossed the equator, the whales, polliwogs and the fish of the sea will sanction anything that might happen on the ship. On board was a man named Jack Johnson who was, at one time, the champion boxer of the world. Jack was being banished from America for white slavery practice and was planning to go to Australia for refuge. The day we crossed the equator, the captain of the ship appointed Jack as the Sheriff and distributed little circular letters around the ship telling of this old custom."

"If any one was asked to do any kind of stunt and they refused to do it, they were taken before Jack Johnson, the world fugitive. He would pronounce the penalty. There was one young man who had spilled his dinner plate. Jack had sentenced him to jump into the swimming pool on the ship. It so happened that the young man could not swim, He jumped into the deep end of the pool. It was quite exciting for a few minutes as the young man came up two or three times and then disappeared into the pool. It was Jack Johnson, himself, who jumped in to save the man's life. He was all right, but the penalty backfired on Sheriff Jack Johnson."

"Another man's penalty was to be shaved by an attendant who had a big wooden razor and a bucket of flour mixed up with water as the lather. It didn't matter what kind of clothes he had on. They just slopped this lather all over the poor man. It was a lot of fun, and made the crossing exciting."[40]

JOHN'S DIARY CONTINUES

"February 11th--Very warm. Physical exercises 6:45 by Dr. Newman. I had a wrestle with George Pack. Sweat for an hour after. At night we attended a dance, no ladies in attendance. A young Chinaman has found a friend in the Elders and hangs around quite close."

"February 12th--828 miles from Suva, made 350 miles, passed some small islands which were very beautiful. It is so warm we cannot read, write or talk. Good Night!"

"Missed the 13th as we crossed the equator."

"February 14th--Very warm. Passed the day in fun." "February 15th—Physical exercises. At night, came in sight of Suva, but did not pull into harbor until next morning."

---

40   John Nelson's dictaphone tape # 24.

"February 16th--Landed at Suva and took in the sights with other boys. We were mighty glad to walk on solid ground once more. The Moana left at 7 p.m. Elders Pack, Miller, and myself who were to stay in Suva. Went to the wharf to bid 'goodbye' to the rest of the party. At night, slept fine in a bed that did not rock."

"February 17--We walked to Flag Staff Hill where we were permitted to look through a glass and view different parts of the Island."

"February 18--Walked to the prison, hospital and other places of interest which are located just outside the city. At night we took our shoes off and ran races on the sand in the moon light."

"February 19 and 20th--not much doing."

"February 21st--The New Zealand boat arrived bearing Elder Bowles, who was on his homeward journey."

"February 22nd--Too lazy to write or eat, very hot. Went to wharf to bid farewell to Elder Bowles."

"February 23rd--Went to an election and band practice. Not feeling very well."

"February 24th to 26th--Elder Pack sick. At night we visited the Church of England."

"February 18th--Elder Miller and I took sick and such a sickness I will never forget! We could neither sleep, eat or lie down. A tropical fever which most white people get on landing here. We did not do much sightseeing after getting the fever."

OUR WET ARRIVAL

"March 9th--Our welcome ship came at last to bear us to Samoa and we were a happy lot. Left Suva at midnight. I was a little sea sick the first day out. We reached Samoa at 5 o'clock in the evening on March 12th, 1910. The ship anchored some distance from the shore and we were compelled to go ashore in a little row boat. On landing we met nobody we knew as the Elders were not expecting the boat so soon. However, a gentleman came up and asked if we were not 'Mormons.' We told him 'yes' and he sent a boy to lead us to the mission house two miles away. It was raining in torrents and we were wet to the skin before we arrived. Oh, what a long two miles, but we looked for a brighter day!"[41]

41   John Nelson's diary, 1910.

5

JOHN'S MISSION

FIRST RECOLLECTIONS OF SAMOA

Following a soggy beginning in Samoa, John recorded, "We were received very kindly by Elder Burton K. Farnsworth and shortly after Mission President William A. Moody came in. Dry clothes were furnished us as our trunks were left downtown. We had supper, then went to singing practice."

"Sunday school was held at 8 a.m. We then had breakfast at 10. I read until meeting time at 3 p.m. The three of us were called up to speak.

It was a rather peculiar sensation to stand up before a congregation who could not understand a word you spoke to them and who stared at you as though you were a being from a new planet.

The three of us occupied three minutes and ten seconds and that was plenty before such a lot of starers."

"Elders Miller and Pack were appointed to labor in Tonga and I in Samoa. They left for Tonga Sunday night on the same boat we had arrived on the night before."

"March 14th--My work as a Missionary now begins. I arose at 6 a.m. o'clock and helped to mow the lawn before breakfast, then studied for awhile, until I helped to clean house and then went visiting. Worked again on the lawn at sunset."

"March 15th--Studied for awhile and then went up town and delivered some tracts. A lady gave me a pie. Visited several families."

JOHN'S FIRST COMPANION

President Moody assigned Elder George Brown to serve as John's first missionary companion. Their first assignment was to go on a proselyting trip, beginning in the village of Maasina, where John had contracted the itch. John wrote, "I have a severe case of itch and Elder Brown put a clear carbolic salve on it. I say! It took the skin off!"

While crossing a stream, Elder Brown slipped and fell in and got soaked. This is just one of the many times such a thing happened to these two young missionaries. Their experiences were just beginning. They met a family who were members of the church in Maasina and they treated them with kindness and gave them a place to stay, a place to bathe, and food to eat.

John wrote of his first meal:

"I will never forget my first devil fish.

For supper, we had a bird and the whole thing was cooked; eyes, bill, toes; but amazingly, it sure tasted good!

Samoa is a great place to work up an appetite."

SAMOAN ANTS

John's diary continued: "Lying down at night, around the lamp, watching little ants kill and carry off larger ants, gave me more courage than I had felt for a long time.

I made up my mind that this mission was going to be a choice experience and that I was determined to enjoy it as much as I possibly could."

Another experience with these Samoan ants came soon after.

John remembered, "It was the first Sunday after my arrival in the Islands. I was called on to give a talk at Sacrament Meeting. As I stood before the audience, I looked down to see all brown-faced natives, resembling the American Indians I had left on the prairies of Alberta, Canada. I realized that there would only be a very few members who would be able to understand me, as my thoughts and words had to be spoken in English."

"As I began my talk, a peculiar sensation penetrated my body. It seemed that my entire body was literally being eaten alive. I have never experienced such a feeling before in my life.

I could actually feel something crawling up my sleeves, up my pants legs, down my back and even in my hair. As I looked down at the missionaries in the congregation, I noticed that they were all smiling, almost an 'evil' smile. I learned later that they were likely recalling their first experience with the same sensation, 'being eaten alive by SAMOAN ANTS.' I later learned that SAMOAN ANTS loved the new blood from America. It was a peculiar situation, for sure, but the ants never seemed to bother the natives, or those who had been in the Islands for some time, but they seemed to know the newcomers."[1]

A SPECIAL WITNESS

John told this story: "Soniatu is a little village built on the Church plantation on the Island of Samoa, located about three miles in-land from the ocean. It was a very fertile area and crops of bananas, taro, coconut, and other produce were grown there. At this period of time, the only way to get these crops down the mountain to the ocean to get ready for shipment and sale was for the natives to carry two baskets, perhaps 100 pounds in each basket, with a stick put through the basket and lifted across their shoulders. They could trot the three miles without even setting the baskets down to rest.

---

1   Ibid.

When questioned, "Don't you get tired?" they would reply, 'When I get tired, I just bounce the load to the other shoulder.'"

"There were usually a lot of Americans, Australians, or New Zealanders who had come to the Islands and set up their business there on the coast. Some of them were jewelers or pottery salesmen. I had just been in the islands for two weeks, when a special missionary conference was held at Soniatu. All of the missionaries, from all over the mission, had been together for several days for a spiritual feast. We had shared each other's testimonies and received instructions from our beloved Mission President, William A. Moody."

"President Moody and six or seven of the elders, myself included, were waiting for the natives to get their loads on to the little row boats to take their produce out to the waiting big ships. Then we would get the natives to row us out to the waiting boats for our trips back to our field of labor."

"The big boats could not come all the way into the land at this port, but had to dock about 30 or 40 feet out. This was a span of water about arm-pit deep that we had to cross to get out to our ship."

"It wasn't a very busy port. As we looked down the road, several of us noticed a man, dressed in a brown suit, coming towards us. As we glanced at him, we thought perhaps he was one of the merchants or traders. No one paid much attention to him. He arrived almost to where he had to go around in the bush to pass the baskets of taro that were obstructing the path.

Instead of him going around the baskets, he just began walking on the water. He went out around the boat, which was immediately in front of us. We were all astonished!

We stood there, almost with our mouths open, as we saw this fine, symmetrically-built man, walk on top of the water. He just kept walking as though he were walking on land. The natives did not appear to notice him, but all of the elders and President Moody saw him. He walked around the boat and came back onto the land and down the path."

"As we stood there in amazement, President Moody, who was a very spiritual-minded man, said, 'This man may be John, the Revelator, who was banished to the Isle of Patmos. He was given the promise that he should never see death, but that he should remain upon the earth until the second coming of the Savior. Or it could be one of the three Nephites spoken of in the Book of Mormon, who were also given the same promise - that they should live upon the earth until the Savior comes in all His glory and that nothing could molest them, neither cold, heat or anything of that sort. The only thing that would bother them were the sins of the people on the earth.

"We were all shocked. We stood there pondering what we had seen. We were not mistaken. Our eyes had beheld this person. Each one of us had seen him. We all felt as though it must be John, the Revelator who had been left upon the earth to preach the gospel of Christ. It was a spiritual experience for each of us and it is my testimony that he was real... whoever he was. We witnessed that he walked upon the water, just as the Lord, Jesus Christ had done when he lived.2

JOHN BECOMES A TEACHER

"I had obtained a fair school education, and it didn't take me long to take a normal training. This is what I did. Just before I left for my mission, and immediately after, I found there was a normal training going on in the islands. Many of the missionaries who had done a little college work could quality for the art of teaching. I prepared to do this.3

2   John Nelson's dictaphone tape #4.
3   John Nelson's dictaphone tape #26.

MY FIRST ROW BOAT RIDE

"One of my first assignments on arriving in Samoa was to Pago Pago, on the island of Upolu, where the mission headquarters were located. This is the largest island of the Samoan chain. I had stayed there at the mission home for about ten days and was then assigned by President Moody to go with my companion, Elder George Brown, on a proselyting trip around the islands. Elder Brown was from Draper, Utah. He had been on his mission for three years and was on his last leg of his mission. I'm sure he was getting anxious to go home. We had planned the trip to take about thirty days of good missionary walking to get around the island. We expected to hold meetings and teach the gospel as we traveled. I didn't know the language at all, but I knew this would be a good learning time for me, and would help me become acquainted with the customs of the people and perhaps have some experience with the language. Elder Brown was to be my teacher."

"One afternoon we came to a place where the water from the ocean backed up into a bay for about eight miles. It was just about one-half mile across the channel by water to get to the little village on the opposite shore. Elder Brown knew if he could get someone to row him across the bay, it would save us about sixteen miles of walking. He went into a house and asked several old women if they would row us across."

"One of the women consented. The Samoan people are very helpful and kind. Elder Brown planned to have them row him across first and then come back for me. He got into the canoe, pulled his hat down over his ears, and the woman rowed him across without any trouble. He had traveled that way many times before and seemed very unconcerned about it. The woman then rowed back to get me. I had never been in a row boat before! I had my books and some extra clothing wrapped up in some oilcloth. I, too, pulled my hat down tight over my ears.

I was frightened to death. The waves were gigantic. It was like a roller-coaster ride. You would ride high onto a swell and then drop way down, taking our breath away each time.

The woman seemed nervous as she sensed that I was so frightened. I'm sure she felt that I would capsize the little row boat. I couldn't speak to her, as I didn't know her language."

"As we got about half way across, the wind died down. The waves were not so high.

Then suddenly a giant swell came and we just went from the bottom of the swell, right up to the top and then we tipped over! Head first!

My clothing and books were lost. The old woman was an experienced seaman and she quickly recovered my possessions and we both swam to the up-side-down row boat. I looked up and could see Elder Brown on the opposite shore, laughing at me."

"Elder Brown sent the other woman out in another canoe. She came right up along side of me and said, 'Oso.' I had learned a new word; it meant 'jump!' I was to jump from the up-side-down row boat, on which I was sitting, on to her canoe. I made a valiant attempt, but, lo and behold, I was too heavy and tipped her, canoe and all, right into the bay. There we were. Two canoes, two women and a mighty green new missionary, all floating in the bay." "The women were used to the water and in a few moments they had one of the canoes righted and they held it tightly so I could climb into it. They handed me a paddle. With one woman on one side and one swimming on the other, and me in the canoe with the paddle, we made it to the shore. Elder Brown was getting such a 'kick' out of all of this. I was provoked at him that he was laughing so hard.

I thought 'What am I doing here? I would rather be at home. I don't think this is any fun.'

Here I was; my feet were tired from hours of walking around the island. I was dumped into the bay by two Samoan women whom I couldn't even understand. My watch had stopped in the salty water and to top that all off, there stood my missionary companion, laughing his sides off!"

"Elder Brown turned out to be a good helper. He thanked the women for their help. We were too embarrassed to accept any more help from them. We got another family to let us come in. They saw the situation and gave me a sheet to put on while Elder Brown washed the sea water from my clothing. Then he hung them on a bush to dry. In just a few hours in the tropical climate my clothing was dried again.

Can you imagine how my white suit looked? But it didn't matter. We were out doing the work of the Lord and an unpressed suit of clothing didn't matter very much. I later learned that any time you started out on a trip; you start with nice, clean clothing and in a very short distance, if you aren't wet with perspiration, you're wet with the rain.""4

BATTLE OF FORGIVENESS

"This little story is one of the first experiences I had after arriving in the Samoan Islands on my mission sometime in May of 1910. I was still working with Elder George Brown."

"We were out proselyting one afternoon and as we went from one village to another one close by, the path took us up over a ridge that was very rocky and dry. As we were tired, we sat down on a large rock to rest. After a few moments of resting and visiting with each other I looked over the rocks and down a little valley below us and saw two men about a city block apart. One man was walking and the other one seemed to be crawling on the ground toward the other. I drew Elder Brown's attention to the men. After watching them for a little while, Elder Brown said, 'This is going to be interesting, as

---

4   John Nelson's dictaphone tape #13

no doubt these men have had a fight earlier in the day. A place has been suggested for them to meet and forgive each other before the sun goes down.'"

"There was an old Israelite law that the sun shall not descend on the wrath of two friends. They must meet at an appointed place and ask each other's forgiveness; rub noses as a sign of friendship and be friends thereafter."

"We watched them for about an hour. The one man seemed to have been beaten so badly that he could not walk. They seemed to be in no hurry to come together. They were looking at the sun and as the bitterness had not all left their souls--because of the terrible blows they had given each other--they took all the time they could before the sun sank beneath the horizon. They appeared to be converted to the law. They likely knew what the people of their village would say if they did not repent and forgive each other. These two men submitted themselves to this law.

Just as the sun was nearly out of sight, they met. The one helped the other to his feet, and embracing each other, they wept as only those who truly forgive can weep."

"By this time, Elder Brown and I had become so interested in the event that we had left our seat on the rock and wound our way down the hillside so as to view the happenings at closer range. We finally met the men and saw their emotions, their true repentance, and their willingness to again be friends. The stronger of the two almost carried his friend and brother back to the village where they were met with songs of thankfulness that a real battle had been won by both of them - the battle of forgiveness."

"To carry the story a little further, I soon found that a native holding the Priesthood of God, who became angry at his brother, would often let the sun go down on his wrath. I always thought it was because Satan worked harder to overthrow a man who held the priesthood of God."5

ELDER WILFORD M. THORNOCK

"As a new missionary to the Islands, Elder Wilford M. Thornock, who was just a young man, scarcely nineteen years old from Paris, Idaho, became very homesick. It seemed as though even with the help of the District President and all of the other missionaries, nothing could get him out of this terrible feeling he had of being homesick."

"One day our Mission President, Don C. McBride, was holding a missionary conference on the Island of Tutuila. There were 25 or 30 of us in the meeting house at Mapasono, all sitting in a circle. Each elder was to report his progress and bear his testimony as to the work in the Island during the last month or so."

"When it came to Elder Thornock's turn to make his report, he was sitting by a window. He got up and made mention of the fact that he had been very homesick and that he had not accomplished as much as he would like to have done. Then he said, 'However, I know . . .' and just then he stopped and looked as though he was speaking with a person at the window. Then he said, 'Well, I do.'"

"Then he turned again to the missionaries and tried to talk again, 'I know that...' and he was stopped again. He was trying to say, 'I know that God lives.' The third time as he tried to speak, he was still unable to complete the sentence; he once again said just, 'I know that. . .'

Suddenly the adversary, who had been outside the window challenging his words, came to the window in great power, grabbed him, threw him down on the seat, and struggled with him until he went black in the face."

"This may sound like a fairy-tale, but it's true. It was a testimony to all of us present of the power of the adversary. President McBride

5   John Nelson's letters to his daughters

jumped up immediately and asked us all to stand. As we stood, he raised Elder Thornock up from the seat, on which he had become prostrate and asked one of the Elders to hold him up as President McBride laid his hands upon Elder Thornock's head. We exercised our faith, while President McBride said, "In the name of Jesus Christ, I command the adversary to immediately depart and leave Elder Thornock."

"Elder Thornock slumped over again on the seat, as weak and as limp as a dishrag. The first words that Elder Thornock spoke as he sat up again were these, 'I know that God lives.' This was the beginning of a great missionary career for Elder Thornock."

"A few days after this occurrence, Elder Thornock was assigned to be my missionary companion. We were staying the night in the Mission Home, sleeping in separate rooms. In the middle of the night, Elder Thornock arose and came into my room and touched me on the arm. We were sleeping with mosquito netting hung from all four corners of the ceiling, perhaps three of four feet high and tucked around under the mat so the mosquitoes could not get to us.

As Elder Thornock touched me on the arm, I was quickly awakened and jumped up immediately. I felt the same power and evil feeling that had been in the meeting a few days before."

"Elder Thornock said to me, 'That same spirit is bothering me again.' I sat him down on the edge of the bed and laid my hands upon his head and said, 'In the name of Jesus Christ, I rebuke the adversary from bothering Elder Thornock any more.'

I did this in great humility and fearing, very fearful, because of the power that had been given me as a missionary and as a servant of God. The evil spirit left the room and did not bother Elder Thornock, anymore.'

"The next day I was teaching school in the lower part of the mission home, when this same evil spirit tried to get a hold of me. After dismissing the children from school, I laid down on the cement floor. Elder Thornock came down in a little while to see where I was.

I became angry with him and told him to leave me alone. The spirit of the adversary was in my body."

"A little while later, I got up and went upstairs and attempted to write a letter to my family in Canada. While I was writing, President Don McBride and President Butler, the conference president, stopped by the mission home on their way around the island. They stayed only a short time and resumed their trip. They had traveled about three miles away, when all of a sudden, President McBride said, 'There is something the matter with Elder Nelson. We must return to the mission home at once.'

"They came into my room and realized that I was not myself. I was still sitting in the same chair where I had been when they had visited me previously. Both came and laid their hands upon my head and without me ever asking or saying a word, they said, 'In the name of the Lord, Jesus Christ, we rebuke the adversary from Elder Nelson and it was done. I never felt that evil presence again.'6

ELDER THORNOCK'S HEALING

"After my arrival in the Samoan Islands, in the year 1910, my first few months were spent learning the language. A great deal of our time was spent in reading the Book of Mormon and the Bible and other literature printed in the Samoan language."

"One Saturday, a few months after my arrival, I was studying at home with my missionary companion when Elder wilford Thornock came to visit. He had been my companion for a short time and we had developed a genuine concern for each other. Elder Thornock was presently living with a family of saints, about three miles around the bay from us."

6   John Nelson Dictaphone Tape #11

"Elder Thornock was not well. He had been in failing health for several months. The doctors had diagnosed the problem as tuberculosis. The doctor, who was treating him, recommended that he return to America for better treatment. The tuberculosis was getting well-seated in his lungs. The doctor told him to drink as much milk as possible while he was still in Samoa. There were very few cows on the islands, and milk was very scarce. The natives obtained their milk from the coconuts. The Governor's secretary heard of his plight and arranged for him to get some milk."

"At this time, Elder Thornock had been assigned a native Samoan as his missionary companion. They had not been able to communicate with each other and although Elder Thornock had studied the language, he just couldn't speak or understand the Samoan language. Elder Thornock said, 'I've got to get out of this terrible, loathsome and damp country. I am so homesick. I want to go home, but before I do, I have come to get you to give me a blessing. I want you to administer to me with this holy oil, consecrated for the healing of the sick.'"

"I had not had much experience in administering to the sick or using the consecrated oil and I told Elder Thornock as much. However, I told him that we should take the oil and walk out into the bush. I suggested that we go down the path towards the village he had just come from and take the path that led into the thick forest. There we could be alone."

"We followed a trail until we came to a big log that had been blown over and was obstructing our path. I told him that this seemed to be a good place, as it was quiet there and no one would disturb us. I told him that we could give our thanks and gratitude to our Heavenly Father and tell Him of Elder Thornock's troubles."

"I anointed Elder Thornock with the holy oil. As I did, it seemed as though the beautiful spirit of the Lord came to us in such abundance.

I have never forgotten that marvelous feeling of love that we had in our hearts for each other and for the work of the Lord. In the prayer I uttered, even though I could hear my voice, the words did not come from me.

I promised Elder Thornock that he should remain in the Islands, and that he would be healed immediately and remain to fulfill a long, useful and successful mission. As I said, 'Amen,' the spirit of the Lord was powerful in both of us. As I removed my hands from his head, we took each other by the hand and ran down the path like two little boys. We each returned to our own village."

"Elder Thornock was healed. He didn't need any more medication. His body returned to full strength and he did stay and become an outstanding missionary in the Samoan Islands. We both acknowledged the power of the priesthood and the goodness of our Heavenly Father in answering the prayers of His servants, even young, inexperienced missionaries."7

ELDER THORNOCK RECEIVES THE GIFT OF TONGUES

"A short time after this experience, Elder Thornock was staying with a group of missionaries at the Mission Home in Pago Pago. After we had all retired for the night, I could hear Elder Thornock pacing back and forth on the veranda. I got up and asked if he was having a problem. He said, 'The Samoan language is running through my mind so fast that I cannot sleep.' He was given the gift of the Samoan language by a kind Father in Heaven. "

"Elder Thornock was one of the best scriptorians I have ever known. He could memorize the scriptures easily and he had a gift of explaining them. Elder Thornock was a powerful missionary and he stayed in the Islands for nearly four years to complete a long and successful mission."8

7   Story written by John A. Nelson
8   John Nelson's Dictaphone tape #4

CENTIPEDE IN MY POCKET

"I wish to relate a story that was a shock to me and an experience that I do not wish to have happen again. One morning when I had been out tracting with my companion, we stopped at the home of a family who were members of the Church. They always allowed the missionaries to stay in one big room where they had prepared mosquito netting hung from each corner of the room and from the ceiling. There were mats for us to sleep on and the nets were tucked under the mats so that the mosquitoes couldn't get in to us."

"We had a very nice evening with this lovely family and then a good night's rest. The next morning as I was putting on my trousers,

I put my hand in my pockets to straighten them out, and in my right hand pocket, I felt something rough. It was like a chain and as I pulled my hand out from my pocket, there it was - a large centipede on the back of my hand!"

"Centipedes in the islands are as poisonous as rattlesnakes. Everyone feared them. If the natives ever saw one going under their sleeping mats, they would not go to bed until the centipede was found. If the centipede was not found, the natives would not sleep in that house. If anyone should be bitten by one, it would mean certain death."

"I shook my hand and the centipede flipped to the floor.

The man of the house saw it and immediately shouted, 'Centipede!!' The children and the man's wife came running to look for it. Centipedes always try to hide under a mat or anywhere they can. There was a great commotion and confusion. The children then ran outside. My companion and I also ran outside of the building because we also knew the hazard of the centipede. The man of the house was able to find it and quickly kill it."

"I have never forgotten that little incident because I related it to Apostle Paul's experience. One time in his life he was shipwrecked.

When he went ashore with his companions, they decided to build a fire. As Apostle Paul picked up a stick of wood, a centipede came out of the wood and onto the back of his hand. He flipped it into the fire and it burned."9

ELDER CHRISTENSEN PERFORMS A MIRACLE

"I had only been a missionary for a short time when I was assigned to labor with Elder Christensen. He had been in the Island about two or three years and was assigned as my Senior Companion at this time. We were traveling from the mission headquarters to Soniatu, a distance of about thirty miles. We were traveling on foot."

"Elder Christensen was walking in front of me. We were nearly through the village of Aua when we stopped. Just as we looked up the path, we noticed an elderly native with a cane, feeling his way along the path.

He was blind. Elder Christensen raised his hand to the old gentleman's eyes and in the native Samoan language, he said, 'In the name of Jesus Christ, our Savior, I command you to receive your eyesight.'"

"The old gentleman looked around for a moment and opened his eyes and of course, he could see! I had no idea how long he had been blind, but he ran down the path, apparently so astonished he could scarcely believe what had happened to him. He shouted, 'I can see! I can see!'"

"I testify that Elder Christensen performed that miracle in my presence, using the power of the Lord and the Holy Melchizedek priesthood that he bore."

9   John Nelson's Dictaphone tape #4

ALL AROUND TUTUILA, SAMOA

"In the spring of 1910, I was teaching school as my missionary assignment in Tutuila, Samoa. My mission president had planned for my companion and I to make a trip around the Island when school closed for the summer. My companion contracted an illness and rather than no one going on the proselyting mission around the Island, the President decided that it would be a good experience for me to go alone."

"I had been teaching English, but did not have the Samoan language learned to any great extent. I took my Samoan Bible, my English Bible, my English Book of Mormon and my Samoan Book of Mormon with me. I also took a hymn book that was published in English. It would take about a month to make a complete trip around the Island. I planned to walk between the villages and just follow the ocean all the way around."

"There was never any problem with food or lodging, as the natives would welcome you into their home, no matter where you stopped. They would prepare a nice mat in a corner and place a mosquito net that hung from the four corners of the ceiling to protect you from the insects. They would tuck the net under your mat and you would be protected. I found that the native custom was to all gather for the evening meal just as the sun was sinking beneath the horizon. Also, their custom, thanks to the Catholic missionaries that preceded me, was to read a few verses from the Bible, sing a song and then have a prayer. I found that it fell to my lot to lead the family in this custom."

"The first night of my trip I stopped at the home of a family with a lot of children. They handed me their Bible and wanted me to carry out their tradition. I'm sure I didn't read their Bible very well, as I was not yet very familiar with their language. When it came time for the song (I must admit that I was never very good at music), I told them I would sing in English. I opened my song book to the beautiful hymn, 'We Thank Thee Oh God for a Prophet.' This was

79

always one of my favorite hymns and I sang it with a great deal of feeling."

"After the song, I prayed in English. When I had finished, the father asked me to sing again. I repeated the same song, singing all of the verses. It touched my heart as I thought about what was happening to me. Here I was, a young elder in a foreign country 7,000 miles from home, not understanding the language of the people, yet the message of love from that song, 'We Thank Thee Oh God for a Prophet,' filled that home. There was a spirit of missionary work and the spirit of the gospel seemed to be in attendance and it had filled the hearts of those humble natives."

"I have never enjoyed an evening any more than that night, alone in the faraway Island among people not of my faith, talking to these natives in broken English and broken Samoan.

There was an understanding for each other. They gave me a good bed and I thanked them for their hospitality and kindness. Especially deep in my heart was my gratitude of my experiencing the beautiful spirit of the missionary program."

"As I completed my travels, I felt as though I was walking hand-in-hand with the spirit of the Lord. The people were so kind to me and eager to help me with the language or to give me food or a bed for the night. What a glorious month I had, building my testimony, getting acquainted with the Samoan people and depending on the Lord for direction and help. I knew that my Heavenly Father was with me to sustain me. He gave me courage to bear my testimony, albeit a weak one, to these marvelous people."

"I think this was the only trip that I ever made alone. I know that if I did not have a white companion to go with me, I'd have a native companion to go along. The native companions were a great help in teaching me the language and helping me to adjust to the customs and traditions of these people.

6

JOHN'S MISSION CONTINUES

ENTRIES FROM JOHN'S DIARY

For the first few years that John was out on his mission, his diary was quite complete. It was from this diary that he was able to recall so many of the stories and details concerning his mission. It would not be practical to include John's entire diary in this book, but we have chosen some entries to be included just the way he entered them in his diary.

March 16, 1910 -- Arose at six, attending to breakfast, went to the English Consul to register, but could neither register at the British or the American Consul. So my protection is poor in Samoa. Visited two families.

March 20, 1910 -- Attended Sunday School and meeting at night, but oh, what a jabbering lot. Not one word did I catch. After meeting at night, a Seventh Day Adventist and his wife came in to debate with President Moody. Oh, what weak arguments they put up. The wife seemed to be the best preacher. I could not stay awake until the debate was finished, although it was interesting.

April 1st, 1910 -- Studied, visited a few families and thought of what I must learn before I make a successful faifeau (missionary).

April 26th, 1910 -- Stayed home all day and tried to learn a few words. I have been able to use a few words and things look a little brighter than when I first started. God certainly helps those who try. But, may He help me to try a little harder.

April 28, 1910 -- Elder Farnsworth cut my hair close to the head and in turn, I clipped his likewise.

May 6th, 1910 -- For supper had a bird and the whole thing was cooked, eyes, bill and toes, but it sure tasted good! Samoa is a great place to work up a good appetite. Lying down at night around the lamp, watching little ants kill and carry off larger ones, gave me more courage than I have had for some time. Just to see how little things could accomplish so much renewed my spirits.

May 7th, 1910 -- I had my first ride in a Samoan canoe. Found it rather hard to steer and after I had gone out in the bay for a considerable distance, a boy had to swim out and help me back.

May 13th, 1910 -- Sunday the drum was sounded at 7 A.M. and Sunday School took up. The mats were arranged in rows and the men sat on one side of the house and the women on the other. About 15 people attended. At ii A.M. a class was held for the purpose of learning to read and study the Book of Mormon. Afternoon meeting was held at 3 P.M. The elder in charge desired that I should speak a few minutes, even though it was in English and no one could understand me. Elder Brown did most of the speaking. I dismissed. At night, Elder Brown went to see if some people were ready to be baptized and I went to hold prayers in another family. I asked an old woman to help me sing "Hope of Israel." After praying, chatted with the people as best I could and kept them laughing at my "flowery language" and we all seemed to enjoy the evening.

May 16th, 1910 -- Studied until 2 P.M. We baptized two girls, Elder Brown officiating. ~Held a meeting and confirmed the girls. Ate two dinners today within one-half hour of each other, Samoa is a fine place to eat often.

May 24th, 1910 -- Studied for awhile, took a swim (five of us), and then Elder Brown and I left for our proselyting trip. Elders Brown and Bennett had a wrestle. We reached a large village; went to the Mayor's house and watched four chiefs play a game called "Lafa-le-tupe." Had supper, after which we had some nice gospel talks.

May 25th, 1910 -- Arose early and left, going as far as Falefa; wading a stream on the trail. We were a little wet, but the hot tropical sun soon dried us out. Some style to traveling in Samoa! We were met at Falefa by Pres. Jensen and John Butler. We changed missionary companions here, Pres. Jensen and I going together. We visited the Pulenuie's home and had a good time.

May 28th, 1910 -- I visited. I try to use all the words I know. I know that I shall enjoy this work as soon as I can talk good. But, oh, did you ever try to pull a hen's tooth out with your specks?

May 31st, 1910 -- Came to a family of Saints where we stopped and visited. A woman gave her two-year old son a whipping that would have killed a good-sized dog. Many good talks along the trail. Saw the mail boat pass going to Apia. I doubt there is any mail for me. A ship is the only thing that looks natural to me in Samoa, and that has a sickly feeling when I look at it.

June 2nd, 1910 -- Today it has been raining most of the time. A meeting was held in this house at 7 A.M. We had a loaf of bread and a can of salmon for breakfast. A treat from home! Pres. Jensen stopped here for dinner on his way to Pesega.

Our clothes are on the line and the color of them would frighten a white woman to death, let alone a native.

My shirts are stained with cocoa-nut juice and it won't come out in the wash.

June 3rd, 1910 -- Today has been fine. Our clothes dried fine. A native carried our mail from Pesega. I received four letters and two post cards: Mother, Cleve, Margaret, Earl Talbot and Seth. Visited a sick man.

June 7th, 1910 -- Today 9:30 A.M. Priesthood meeting commenced with Pres. Jensen in charge. The first two hours of the meeting was taken up in the discussion of temporal matters, such as: the building of the Soniatu Road, how to raise money to pay for the moving-picture outfit and whether to continue it or not. Other little matters were attended to and then we had a recess for ~5 minutes, eating oranges brought from Tonga. Pres. Moody spoke for an hour and a half and his instructions were GRAND! I only hope that I can obey some of them. He spoke on getting the language and gave us some good pointers. All of the Elders spoke in turn and the Spirit of God was with us. The Saints brought us in a fine dinner. I went to Apia with Pres. Moody, came back and wrote letters.

June 9th, 1910 -- Finished my letters and made ready to journey with Elder Brown. We left Pesega at 3:30 P.M. visiting with three families. Stayed all night at the home of a minister. Left and visited with several families today. Stayed with a man who is very much interested in the Gospel. He treated us fine, killing chickens for our dinner and then fixed us a fine bed. I think his heart is touched. We left him a book to read. I am beginning to understand and enjoy listening to the natives talk.

June 12th, 1910 -- We went on to the next village and stopped at a large house, where we were treated well. Elder Brown took sick and we stayed here for the night. A nice bed was soon fixed for him and the net placed over it. I sat up trying to talk for awhile with the men of the house, but I soon put them to sleep with my jabber. Now comes the trying part.

Two beautiful young ladies stepped in. I dare say they were beautiful in features, if not in thoughts. They were very willing to help me with the language and I was soon taking down words by the score.

One of them left me and went to cheer Brother Brown. She asked him if she could get in his bed with him, Of course, she was told to "Go away!" By this time, I was startled with the same question. I immediately told her to leave and then I retired.

We thanked God for the strength He gave us in resisting tempta-tion, as we know that the evil one is ever trying to ensnare the Elders of Israel. Oh, God, ever be with us and keep Us pure.

June 24, 1910 -- Today we had two canoe rides. Leaving the village where we had spent the night, we soon came to a long bay. A man showed us the way to a bridge, which we crossed. We found that it did us no good, as we came in contact with more water. We then returned, but "Oh" that bridge!   A person must have a pretty level

Samoan Relief Society Sisters

head to walk it. A round cocoa-nut pole, three or four span of trees long and water below about 20 feet deep. We came back to the same place but the old man did not seem willing to help us this time. An old lady, who happened along, took pity on us and took us across in a canoe. We had not gone far, until we had struck another bad place. We were lucky enough to find a fellow with a canoe at the crossing who helped us over. We stopped at the first place we came to and a man asked us to spend the night at his house. We took him at his bargain and washed our dirty clothes.

July 2, 1910 -- Walked to Soniatu where I found ten letters, which, of course, made me feel happy. I never appreciated a good letter so well in my life as I do now.

August 1, 1910 -- Meeting held and Elders separated. I was appointed to labor at Soniatu. My first experience on the plantation was to take thirty men and keep them busy at work. I found I had my hands full, but never-the-less, I jabbered away and finally, as the days went by, they obeyed me. I had no trouble in keeping them at work. First we went over the ground and cut the bush and then came along and planted the nuts. I enjoyed this work as I did lots of talking and thus mastered the language. President Moody decided that it was well to start school, as we had thirty-five children in the village. I was appointed to corral them on Monday morning.

The bell was rung and they circled. A wilder bunch I have never beheld!

But, I did my best to tame them. The first two weeks were the worst. I was forced to whip many, but after that they realized that I was the ruler and they cooled down and I ruled them by kindness. I shall never forget those days.[42]

VARIETY OF RESPONSIBILITIES

John added a note in his diary that the records he had kept during a certain period of time, were lost while going to Pesega. Without dates of entry in his diary, he wrote the following:

"Many were the good meetings I attended in Soniatu. I was appointed to visit all of the Relief Society meetings and help the sisters

42   John Nelson's diary, 1910.

with the lessons. This I found to be a great pleasure. I also visited the different organizations, as this branch is thoroughly organized."

"Elder Bennett and I took turns going to Apia, it took about a week, with the natives to buy provisions and sell their taro. I was in charge of the store, which we kept at Soniatu for the benefit of the Saints. We would to sell to non-Mormons. This and the school kept me busy. I had certain hours in which I was working at the store. All my spare time I was visiting among the Saints and working on the Plantation. My testimony was made strong while laboring here."

"One night Elder Bennett and I were aroused from our beds to go and administer to a sick man.

When we entered the house, five people were holding the man down, as he was out of his head and in terrible pain. I administered the oil and the moment my hand touched his head, he was quiet.

We then sealed the anointing and he was sound asleep before we took our hands from his head. He did not move again the remainder of the night and in the morning, he was well."

"The Saints in this village depend entirely on the Lord in case of sickness and their faith in administrations is almost complete. The Lord is bound to keep his promises when we obey.[43]

SURPRISE PARTY FOR JOHN

"The first of March, 1911, it was almost a year to the day since I was called to be a missionary to the Samoan Islands. I had served that first year on the Island of Soniatu. Now I was called to leave Soniatu and go to Tutuila, the American Island. When the saints of Soniatu learned that I had been called to leave them, tears came in their eyes whenever I met them. A surprise party was given by the village and the school. They tried hard not to let me know what they were going to do, but I heard too many whispers. About seven

43   John Nelson's diary, p. 6, 1910.

o'clock at night I was sent for and told to go to the largest house in the village. When I arrived, a lot of people were there. I must admit I was a little surprised to see so many people out."

"The first thing on the program was a fine supper and about seventy-five of us sat down to eat at once. Supper over, we had games of all kinds, songs, and dancing. Speeches were made and I made the last speech. I thanked the people for their kindness to me.

I admonished them to treat all Elders as they had treated me and the Lord would bless them.

The students from my school then sang some songs and it was then that I felt I was going to leave them, for each song told how badly they felt. (Samoan songs always suit the occasion.) All arose and bid me goodbye, as I was going to leave early the next morning. I did not realize that I had become so attached to these native people. Tears were shed by many as we embraced and said, 'good-bye.'"[44]

TUTUILA, JOHN'S NEW FIELD OF LABOR

From John's diary: "Early the next morning left for Apia and there prepared for my journey. In company with President McBride, we set sail on the Dawn at 5 o'clock in the evening, headed for Tutuila. The water was smooth and we did not get sick. (John had recorded earlier that he would become sea-sick whenever he had to sail.)"

"We arrived at Tutuila in the morning, and oh, how beautiful that Island looked as we pulled into the large bay. I have not the words to do justice to a good description of the beautiful sights which were before me. I was sorry when the Captain told us to go ashore as my eyes wanted to feast on the beautiful scenery. The Bay is about two and one-half miles long and one-half mile wide. The mountains rise high all around, but at the opening of the sea. The Government

---

44   Diary, p. 12, 1911.

buildings are on the west side. Stores are dotted here and there and villages are clear around, with just a short space in between."[45]

John recorded little until two months later, when he wrote about the conference held with all of the missionaries:

"Conference was held at Mapusaga. I was called to speak in the first meeting. A good spirit prevailed throughout the Conference and several people were baptized. I was appointed to preside over the Pago Pago branch with Elder Wilford Thornock as my companion."

"I shall never forget the first meeting I held in that branch. Elder Thornock was a sick with sore eyes, so I went to church alone. There was not a very large congregation, only about thirty present. I gave out the song, expecting some of the natives to lead and sing, but all was quiet. I struck a note and sang the song clear through, without anyone to help me. I prayed. Then I ask some of the members to join in singing, which they did. I then preached for about a half-hour and then dismissed. I shook hands with all the people and told them I wanted to get acquainted. They seemed a very friendly lot."

"President McBride gave me instructions to hold more meetings, as there was only two meetings held during the whole week and these were Sunday School and an afternoon meeting on Sunday. The Saints turned out well for awhile. We finally had to give up the extra meeting on Sunday, but continued to hold one when the moon was bright. A Samoan does not like to get out at night, especially to a meeting. We also started a singing practice on Friday nights, which proved quite a help to our meetings."

"School was started with about thirty-five children and held four days a week. I taught the advanced class and Elder Thornock the small children. My daily routine of work was school, visiting and studying."[46]

---

45   Diary, p 13, 1911.
46   Ibid.

BRINGING THE SAINTS BACK TO THE FOLD

"After I had been in the Samoan Mission for about a year, the mission president, William A. Moody from Arizona, wrote to the First Presidency of the Church concerning a special problem in the mission. Some years before, a mission president had taken the priesthood authority away from branches of the Church when they refused to move three miles inland, at his request. The Church had purchased eight hundred acres of land on the island of Upolu. It was the mission president's plan to establish a permanent Mormon Village and let the people work on the coconut plantation, giving each family a plat of land."

"As near as I could make out, the mission president did not have the sanction of the authorities of the Church in Salt Lake City when he took the priesthood authority away from these members.

When the mission president made the call to these saints, most of them refused to move. They had lived on the seashore all their lives

---

. These natives loved the ocean, they loved to fish and hunt turtles. To insist they move three miles inland and keep them there with nothing but a fresh water stream running through the eight hundred acres was too much to ask. Consequently about 2,500 of the Saints in this area of the Church apostatized."

"It is not my place to condemn or judge this mission president. He did establish a village in the beautiful valley of Soniatu where those who followed him were taught the principles of the gospel. This valley was the shape of a horse shoe and the opening of the horse shoe led out towards the ocean. The mountains rose high all around in the other parts of the valley. The mountains were high and covered with beautiful trees of all kinds: the wild banana tree, the banyan tree, and various types of vegetation that grow so perfectly in the South Pacific Islands."

"After my mission president, President Moody, had written to the First Presidency of the Church concerning these people who had apostatized, he received instructions to choose an Elder from the field to work with these people and see if some of them could be brought back into the 'fold'. I was the Elder chosen and along with a native Elder by the name of Philipo, we were set apart to do this work. We began immediately. Philipo was a wonderful, powerful man, both in stature and in the knowledge of the Gospel of Jesus Christ.. He had been converted when he was just a young man and now he was approximately 45 years of age. He was not married."

"He was my tutor to a great extent. As we visited with these fine people, Philipo would asked me questions and I would try to answer them. Because of this good practice, I was blessed with a good knowledge of the Samoan language and it wasn't long before I could carry a good conversation and could explain the principles of the gospel as Philipo had taught me. I give Philipo the credit for being a wonderful teacher, and he taught me the principles of the gospel in a simple way that I could teach the natives in return."

"We were successful in bringing many of these saints back into the Church. As we visited their homes, the natives seemed to enjoy listening to me preach, even though the language was not always correctly spoken. They seemed to think that I knew more than the native Elder, Philipo."

"Philipo was a little radical in some of his teachings and I often had to chastise him and tell him to adhere to the principles of the gospel.

He would tell the people, if they didn't believe a certain principle of the gospel, to tear it out of their Bibles or Book of Mormons.

I could not go along with this practice and told him that was not an acceptable thing to do. However, he was a very impressive missionary and he was loved by the native people. He had a talent of exciting and enthusing the saints."

"We worked with these people for some time. Many Of the men were Elders, or Priests, or Deacons. Their names had never been taken off of the records of the Church. They had never been excommunicated, even though they had apostatized. We didn't bring them all back into the fold, but there was over 1,000 who did come back into activity in the Church. All we had to do was rekindle the spark that was in their hearts and they rebuilt themselves up again to become a strong body of the Church."

"This was a very enjoyable assignment and I learned to love and appreciate Philipo. He was somewhat of a prophet. One time we were climbing a mountain. I became very thirsty before we got to the top. Philipo said he had been to the top of this mountain on a previous occasion and he knew there was a big log at the top that was pulled over for the natives to sit on and rest after they reached the top. Philipo suggested that he would hold back his speed and I could go on ahead.

He said, 'When you get to the top, sit on the log and look over to the side and you will see a big orange. I can see it in my mind right now. I don't know who put it there, but I'm telling you that you'll find one.'"

"So that's exactly what I did. I went ahead of him. I got to the top of the mountain, perhaps five minutes before he got up there and I sat down on the log and looked across. There was a big orange, just as Philipo had predicted. I know that he didn't put it there and I know that we hadn't met any natives along the way who could have left it. Philipo hadn't been over this trail for several months. I got up and with my pocket-knife, I cut it in two pieces. I left part of it for Philipo when he arrived at the top of the mountain. However, he would not eat it. He said, 'That orange is a sacred orange and it's for you. That orange was put there by someone, I know not who, but I prophesied to you that it would be there. It was! That orange is for you, and I'll not touch it!'"

"The natives of Samoa were superstitious in many ways and in this case, Philipo was exactly that! He and I sat down and thanked the Lord that we had traveled thus far in safety. For six months, we visited with people who had once been active members of the Mormon Church. It was a real pleasure, as well as a difficult task, to induce them back into the Church. Many of them were so bitter they wouldn't even talk to us. But if we could get into their homes, get their attention, and get them to listen to us, we were able to bring them back into the Church."[47]

WHO MADE TUTUILA?

"I had been set apart, by the laying on of hands by the Mission President, to go to Tutuila and preach the gospel of Jesus Christ to the natives there. As the war vessels went to this little island of Manua, the people were loaded aboard ships to take them to Tutuila where they could be taken care of, fed and given housing. They were an entirely different type of people than those on the island of Tutuila. They appeared wild, uncouth, untamed and practically .uncivilized."

"Several hundred of these people from Manua arrived at the little town of Pago Pago, Tutuila where the headquarters of the Church was located. They were dispersed to homes among the villagers. The missionaries were very much a part of the local scene and the natives were used to seeing us around town. However, we became quite a novelty to these misplaced persons and for some unknown reason, they paid particular attention to me. I say this in all humility, not that I was anything special, but these people seemed to take particular notice of me. The only special thing I could think of, was that I had been set apart to teach these people the gospel."

"As I walked down to get my mail at the post office one afternoon, one of these wild Samoans made the remark in the Samoan language, to one of his friends, 'That fellow thinks he made Tutuila.'" I interrupted him abruptly and said, 'Brother, you are mistaken. I didn't

47   John Nelson's Dictaphone tape #14.

make Tutuila, but the Lord, God in Heaven made this island. After He got through making this Island, there was just a little fragment left and He threw it over there and made Manua, the island where you came from.'"

"Then he grinned to think that I understood the language and then he listened to me as I told him, right there along the highway, the story of the restoration of the gospel.

I told him how I had come out as a missionary, left my home 7,000 miles away, to teach him and his people the true plan of Jesus Christ. I told him to pay heed to my words and invited him to come out to our Church."

"It wasn't long before we were holding special meetings every evening at 7:00 P.M. in the chapel for these people of Manua. They were interested and filled the chapel. Many conversions were made by teaching them the gospel. They became humble saints. So I had the opportunity of teaching the natives from the Island of Manua, although I never traveled to their island."[48]

MORE DIARY ENTRIES

John's diary was sporadic after this. He wrote several experiences, but not daily entries. There appears to be a span of time when nothing was recorded. John apparently served in Tutuila until February, 1913, when he wrote the following excerpt in his diary:

February 26, 1913. Wednesday, bid Elders and Saints "Goodbye" and set sail for Upolu in a row boat. A good wind was blowing and the sails were hoisted and we were only three hours until we reached Upolu. We sailed down along the coast after resting at Fastootai and spent the night at Mulimui, landing at Pesega the next morning. I was busy for several days, visiting and attending to business in general.

---

48   John Nelson's Dictaphone tape #28.

Sunday morning, President Allred of the Savaii Conference spoke. He rebuked the women for their fine dress and told them that they were getting proud. His sermon caused feelings among the Samoan sisters, but I hope it will do good in the end. More white and Samoan missionaries spoke at this meeting.

On Monday, General Priesthood meeting convened at 6:30 A.M. Much power was manifest when the native brethren spoke. I spoke for some time on the duties of the priesthood and what is expected of them. President Rhead spoke a short time.

Immediately after this meeting, the General Relief Society meeting convened. Several of the sisters spoke very interestingly. President Allred of the Savaii Conference was called up to speak. He stood before a very cool audience because of his critical remarks about the sister's clothing in his talk on Sunday.

Some of the sisters arose and left the meeting. Others held their ears and a bad spirit went through all the meeting.

Brother Allred sat down, because he could not talk. I told him to get up and finish what he had to say, even if they all left. He arose and talked for a few more minutes and then Sister Wilcox called on me. I arose and tried to make the sisters feel good, but found them quite angry. I told them a story about my watch only having one hand on it, but only a few would laugh. They gradually felt better, as more sisters spoke. After the meeting, Brother Allred had a good talk with some of the leading sisters and they felt all right or at least seemed to be feeling better.[49]

---

49   John Nelson's diary, 1913.

MISSIONARY INSPIRATION

"This is a story I remember about President Willard Smith and his wife while they were laboring in the Samoan Islands, before he became the President of the Mission. He was taking a trip with his~wife and one or two of his children. We had an old horse on the Island of Tutuila that was a fixture around the mission farm. The Elders had nicknamed him 'Old Hand Organ' because he was so lazy and slow.' It took a pretty good switch to persuade him to move along as fast as the rider wanted him to go."

"Brother and Sister Smith were using him on this trip. They were going around the Island one day and many of the Elders were going on ahead of them, back towards the mission home. Brother and Sister Smith were perhaps several blocks behind. Sister Smith was riding 'Old Hand Organ.' There was a very bad, steep spot on the trail."

"Elder Ransom, who had been one of my companions, was with the Elders in the advance group. When they came to this hazardous place along the trail, he stopped. The other Elders went on ahead, but Elder Ransom sat down on a rock beside the trail. He was in a position to be of service if any problem occurred as the rest of the party came along on the horse. As Brother Smith came to this spot leading 'Old Hand Organ,' for some unknown reason, the horse slipped and fell.

Elder Ransom was sitting in just the right spot to grab Sister Smith and pulled her from the horse's back as the horse rolled over the cliff and way down to the bottom, where there was a wild stream of water rushing by."

"Where the horse fell was jagged shale rock and had Sister Smith fallen with the horse, she would have been badly hurt or even killed. The horse wasn't hurt very badly, however, and the Elders were able to walk down and around to another place and bring 'Old Hand Organ' the mile or so down the coast. Everyone thanked a kind Father in Heaven for giving Elder Ransom the inspiration that he might be needed at that particular dangerous crossing."[50]

---

50   John Nelson's Dictaphone tape # 28.

7

PRESIDENT JOHN A. NELSON

A NEW CALLING

I had been laboring as a missionary in the Samoan Islands for three years. Much of this time was spent teaching school. I would do missionary work during vacation times and after school in the evenings and Saturdays and Sundays. I was teaching in a large cement building and had 35 to 40 students."

"One day after school, I noticed in the distance, two men coming down the beach on the hard sand. When the tide is out, the sand is just like a paved road for miles and miles, all the way around the Island. As they came closer, I could tell they were Mormon missionaries. Their mode of dress was distinctive and different from the native clothing."

I waited for the two missionaries to come to where I was sitting. One of the missionaries was Elder Eckland, who was the conference president for the island of Tutuila. Elder Eckland handed me a letter, with the invitation to read it immediately. He said it was from Church Headquarters on the island of Upolu."

"I remarked, 'I know the contents of this letter. Three weeks ago, I received a letter from the Mission President telling me that my mission was complete and that I would be returning home on the next boat. This would be in about 28 days from that time. I'm sure that this is my release from my mission.'"

"However, I procrastinated reading the letter, with the suggestion that I would read it while the Elders went for a swim in the big, beautiful cement swimming pool at the Mission Home. I got some towels for the Elders and followed them down to the pool. There was no one using the pool at this time. As I was walking along behind these two Elders, a feeling that I shall never forget and can hardly express now, came over me. The sensation made me feel that I was someone very important. Yet it frightened me. I sat down on the steps of the pool, while the Elders went in swimming. I read the letter that follows:

Dear Elder Nelson,

I have recently written to the First Presidency of the Church to tell them about an illness I have contacted. They have instructed me to return home on the next boat. They have given me instructions to select an Elder from the Mission to take my place until someone can come from America to take over the leadership of the Mission. After fasting and prayer and under the inspiration of the Lord, I have selected you to be my replacement.

I would like to meet you at (an appointed hour) in the Chapel at Pago Pago. There you will be set apart as President of the Samoan and Tongan Mission. I trust you will be willing to serve in this capacity and that the Lord will bless you in your efforts.

Sincerely your brother in the Gospel,

President Christian Jensen

"President Jensen had been presiding over both the Samoan and the Tongan Islands. There had been a separate mission in Tonga years previously, but because of an uprising among the natives, the First Presidency of the Church had taken the missionaries away. These Tongan saints had been presided over from Samoa. At this time, missionaries were being called to Tonga to proselyte among the people. Tonga is some 600 miles from the Samoan Islands."

"As I finished reading this letter, Elder Eckland came up to me and asked, 'How do you feel about the letter?' He already knew the contents of it, as the Mission President had shared this important message with him."

"I replied, 'I cannot accept it. Me? A humble missionary. I have spent much of my mission teaching school. I haven't had the experience necessary to take this important calling. It's impossible.

I feel so weak and humble. I am sure our Mission President has made a mistake in this assignment. Besides, I am booked to go home on the next boat, which leaves in 28 days. For me to even stay another few months longer and preside over this vast mission is more than I can think about. I'm sure I cannot accept this calling. I'm not able, I'm not willing, and I'm not worthy for this responsibility.'"

Elder Eckland consoled me and after their swim, we all three walked back to the Mission Home, there in the little town of Alao. I fixed the Elders some supper and invited them to spend the night there. My missionary companion was also there, and I told him that I would go and spend the night at the home of some of the saints, as there wasn't room for all of us at the little mission home."

The family welcomed me and provided me with a good bed. I didn't say anything to them concerning my letter. When I went to bed, I found that sleep had gone from me.

I never closed my eyes all night long. I even pinched myself to see if the Lord expected a humble young missionary, only 23 years of age, to accept this new calling, to preside over the Samoan-Tongan Mission.

Just as the sun came up the next morning, I arose and went back to the mission home."

"The first words that Elder Eckland asked of me was, 'How do you feel this morning concerning your new appointment as the President of the Samoan and Tongan Mission?'"

"I replied, 'Elder Eckland, just as the sun was coming up this morning, there was a beautiful, peaceful influence that came over me and the thought came into my mind, 'Who am I that I should refuse a special call from the Lord?' So, Elder Eckland, I have decided to accept the call, weak as I am.'"

He shook hands with me and congratulated me because of my willingness to accept the call. He offered words of encouragement and said that the Lord would bless me to become equal to the task ahead of me."

"When the appointed time came, I met with President Jensen. He had been given the power and authority from the First Presidency of the Church, because of the extenuating circumstances of his illness, to lay his hands upon my head, and set me apart as the President of the Samoan and Tongan Mission."

"A new chapter of my life was about to begin. I felt the Lord's Spirit and love with me, and humble as I was, I knew I was not called to fail in this assignment, but to succeed.'"

ELDER NELSON SET APART AS PRESIDENT

Realizing that a new temporary President of the Mission was being called to replace President Jensen, all of the Elders of the mission were called to attend an Area Conference. President Jensen took charge of the meeting. After some other mission business had been taken care of, a number of the missionaries bore their testimonies. They gave thanks to their Heavenly Father for the opportunity they had of coming to the Islands to proclaim the everlasting gospel to the Israelites, because the Samoan people truly are of the House of Israel."

At length, President Jensen arose and explained that although he had only been the Mission President for one year, he had contracted an illness that made it necessary for him to return home. He said that he had written to the First Presidency of the Church informing them of his illness. They in turn had answered his letter with the request that he come home immediately, so that his health may not be impaired to any greater extent."

He was instructed to choose an Elder from the mission to take his place as President of the Mission.

After due consideration, fasting, and prayer, he said he had selected Elder John A. Nelson as his successor.

He explained that this would be just until the First Presidency could send someone else from America to preside over the mission, perhaps a period of several months, at the most."

"I was set apart by President Christian Jensen. He had been given the authority from the Prophet of the Lord, President Joseph F. Smith. President Jensen laid his hands upon my head and gave me a blessing to lead the mission in a successful manner. I felt very humble. I felt my inability to take over and preside in the footsteps of a man as wonderful and so accomplished in every way as President Jensen.

John grew a beard to look more mature. He was quite a spectacle, since his beard was red, his hair was coal-black, his skin very fair, and his eyes were blue.

The meeting ended. President Jensen was to set sail for America the very next day.'"

NEW RESPONSIBILITIES

President Jensen had given me a letter from the First Presidency of the Church, with instructions on how to begin my labors. All of the mission records, books and history of the mission were located on the island of Upolu. The mission secretary was there, also. I immediately sailed for Upolu, arriving that night. I introduced myself to some of the members that I met there and to the secretary of the mission."

"My instructions were to go over all the mission records, reviewing the history of each missionary. Each missionary kept his money sent to sustain him while he was on his mission in a safe at the mission home. The money was to be allotted out to them, piece-meal, so to speak. This was done with the purpose in mind of cutting down on their expenses in that faraway country."

We found that there were many weeks and months that the missionaries did not need any money for food. The natives had an abundance of food, such as: bananas, coconuts, yams and all types of food that grew. Food was often wasted on the ground, because the natives did not know how to preserve it. They had no refrigeration, consequently, the natives were very free with their food when it was in plentiful supply. However, on occasion, they did experience a drought or weevil or beetle that could make the food scarce."

"Together with the mission secretary, we went over all of the records of the mission. I spent several weeks at this assignment. I became better acquainted with the missionaries. Perhaps I learned to love the missionaries with even a greater love and feeling, because of the great distance we were separated around the mission.

I had made an appointment for each one of the missionaries to come to the mission home where we could have a heart-to-heart talk. This helped me to become better acquainted with each Elder. Each previous Mission President had made it a practice to visit from island to island on a regular basis. I continued this practice and tried hard to see each Elder at least once a month. As I traveled to the various Branches, we would hold an Area Conference. It was a very spiritual two or three day get- together. It helped to build up the missionaries and gave me an opportunity to give them instructions and guidance. It was important that we shared our testimonies with each other."

'It was easy for the missionaries to get homesick. They had a difficult time with the language at first. I immediately started a language training school to help the Elders get a good start on the language. I taught them how to study correctly so that they could get a knowledge of the language. The Lord was always willing to help, but the Elders had to put forth the same effort in order to get the best results of their studies."

PERMANENT ASSIGNMENT

A month or two later, a letter came from the President of the Church, Joseph F. Smith. I thought that it was to tell me of my replacement and give me the name of the man who would be coming to take over as President of the Samoan and Tongan Islands. I had been anticipating this letter but instead of receiving my release as Acting-President, the letter was written something to this affect:

Dear Elder Nelson,

As the First Presidency of the Church, it is our privilege to extend a special calling to you. After due consideration and fasting and prayer, the Lord has made it known to us that He wishes you to continue serving as the President of the Samoan and Tongan mission for a period of three years.

We trust that you will realize that this is the will of the Lord, and that you may make the necessary arrangements to complete this important calling. If you put your trust in the Lord, we know that He will make you equal to the task. May the Lord bless you in this new assignment.

Most respectfully,

Joseph F. Smith,

President,

Church of Jesus Christ of Latter-Day Saints

HOW GREAT IS THE POWER OF THE LORD

I accepted the call, acknowledging that it had come from the Lord. I knew that He would help me to accomplish His purpose. Shortly after I was appointed and set apart to preside over the Samoan and Tongan Mission, I worried a great deal, because of my young age, how I should get along with the missionaries and with the members of the Church. There were so many new responsibilities that I was to take care of."

The Church was operating a plantation on the Islands, and the natives were paid for working there and keeping the young plants in proper care. There was a great deal of gardening, trimming the weeds, planting the coconuts and taking care of 800 acres of land owned by the Church. When the coconuts were mature, the 'popo,' as it was called, was cut and dried and shipped to many other countries. Among these countries were America, Australia, New Zealand and others. There it would be made into soap of the finest quality."

When I took over leadership of the mission, there were 142 missionaries assigned to the two islands, Samoa and Tonga. I was concerned about the spiritual progress of each of the missionaries and the members of the Church. The responsibility weighed heavily on my mind. I felt a sense of inadequacy as I realized that many of the missionaries serving were men who were old enough to be my father, and who were there on their second missions. I sensed a jealousy among some of them and a feeling, 'Why should such a young man as he, be called to preside over us?"

Many of saints were great orators; men and women who knew the Bible and the gospel of Jesus Christ, especially about the apostasy. I had over-heard conversations that were not conducive to spiritual growth, and it troubled me. I thought maybe if I grew a beard, it might make me appear older and wiser. So, this is what I did.

I am sure I was quite an unusual sight to the natives with my black hair, blue eyes and red beard, but it made me feel that I looked a little more mature."

I still felt inadequate compared to the missionaries and saints, as well. As I was pondering the situation concerning these feelings, I decided to make it a matter of prayer. I fasted and prayed to the Lord, just how I could make the missionaries and the members respect me as their Mission President, even though I was just a very young man."

"One night as I retired to my bed, (I don't know whether I was awake or whether it was a dream) but it seemed to me that I was carried away, down a beautiful road. As I walked down this road, rather heavy in heart, the weight of my position as President of the Samoan and Tongan Mission burdened me. I felt the desire to help the missionaries gain testimonies of the gospel. I wanted them to advance in their knowledge of the wonderful plan that Jesus Christ, our Lord, had established for mankind when He was upon the earth. I desired the love and respect of the Saints of those two Islands and I needed the help of the Lord, to make me a worthy leader."

"With these thoughts weighing on my mind, in this vision or dream, I noticed immediately ahead of me a large group of people. They seemed to be standing there waiting for something. As I drew nearer, I could see there was a large cement structure obstructing their progress down the road. They couldn't seem to go around the structure, nor could they climb over it. It seemed to me that as I walked through this group of people near this cement mountain, as it were, I saw a man on top of it. He reached down and extended his hand to me. I reached up and very lightly, I sprang to the top of this cement obstruction with his help."

"I looked down the other side of the obstruction and noticed steps were going down the other side of it. I seemed to be the only one who crossed over the cement obstruction and it seemed as though, when I got over, I was so happy for the help that had been given me, that I almost cried for joy."

I looked back at the large obstruction that had crossed the highway and said to myself, 'How great is the power of the Lord?'

Then the thought came to me, that all I had to do to preside over the Samoan and Tongan Mission, was to follow the instructions of the First Presidency of the Church.

They provided the steps for me to teach the missionaries and the Saints. They showed me the way to lead the Mission, as they wrote letters to me each month, advising and counseling, asking questions as to how things were going along. All I had to do to become an effective President, was to follow their instructions, and to seek the Lord in mighty prayer for guidance. These were the steps to get over the massive concrete wall. These were the steps to becoming a successful Mission President."

From that time on, as I met with the missionaries, I felt a greater power, a mantle, so to speak, of a power that seemed to be over me. I could answer their questions. I could help them in every way possible. From then on out, there seemed to be no thoughts of any jealousy among the older missionaries, or the Saints. They seemed to respect me. They seemed to honor my calling as Mission President. We got along very beautifully together from that time on."

The older members of the Church also accepted me. Many of the men were old enough to be my father but they accepted me as their

President. There was never a doubt again as to the authority that I held as President of the Samoan and Tongan Mission."[51]

THE SPIRIT OF LOVE

"While I was presiding over the Samoan and Tongan Missions, on occasion, I would ride a horse to take me across the mountains to hold conferences with the Saints. It was a 30 or 40 mile trip across the mountains on the island of Upolu. This island was oblong in shape. I was riding a little brown horse."

'As I rode along, I was contemplating what I could tell the Saints on the other side of the mountain. All of a sudden, a beautiful light appeared immediately in front of me. My horse was startled and stopped abruptly.

I dismounted from the horse and felt an urgency to pray. I stepped out into the light of this beautiful illumination and knelt down.

I poured out my heart and soul to my Heavenly Father in thanksgiving for the blessings I had received from Him. I asked Him for further guidance, that I might continue to preside over the mission with love and kindness. I prayed that I might be given the power and guidance to lead His great work here in the Polynesian Islands."

"This beautiful spirit of prayer so impressed me. I stopped praying and mounted my horse. I rode on down the mountain trail and traveled to the other side of the mountain. I felt so grateful that I was an Elder in the Church of Jesus Christ of Latter-Day Saints. I was mellow to the very core and I could not thank my Heavenly Father enough. I had a love for all mankind. I had no enemies, regardless of the religion others belonged to. I loved them all just the same. I realized that we are all children of our Father in Heaven."

I testify that if a missionary will follow the instructions of the mission religiously, he will go home with the knowledge that he has

51   Ibid 1.

110

accomplished something good. He will have taught the Plan of Salvation to the people on the earth.

So, my counsel to all missionaries, is to follow the rules of the mission, and you will be blessed."[52]

TATTOOS AND BOXING GLOVES

"While I was serving as president of the mission, two of my former missionary companions, Elder Warren Smith of Alberta, Canada and Elder Kotch from Denver, Colorado were serving as companions. Elder Smith had been in Samoa for a year or so and understood the language quite well. Elder Kotch was fairly fresh from America. He had been raised as an only child. His mother had died and his father had undertaken to raise the boy by himself. While his father worked, the boy went to school and played around and didn't always have the best friends. When he came out to us as a missionary, I received a letter from his bishop, telling me to labor with him in kindness and love, that it might be possible that he might right-about face and make a wonderful missionary."

This little story is rather jocular in a way. Elder Kotch was a big, symmetrically-built fellow, about twenty years of age and he liked boxing. In fact, the first thing he did when he got to the Islands was to send to New Zealand for a set of boxing gloves and all the instructions on how to become a good boxer. (We found that we could receive shipments from New Zealand quicker than from the United States.)"

Elder Kotch slipped away one day and went down to the harbor to the naval post exchange. He found someone to give him tattoos all up and down his arm.

Of course, when I found this out, I rebuked him as severely as I could and as kindly as I knew how. However, there was nothing I could do about the tatoos, once they had already been done."

52   John Nelson Dictaphone tape #4.

'A short time later, the boxing gloves arrived from New Zealand. Elder Kotch refused to take any instructions from his missionary companion, Elder Smith. Elder Kotch put the boxing gloves on and was giving instructions to the native boys in the fine art of boxing. There were a lot of young men his age and older who were delighted to learn the American way to box.''

"Elder Smith was a big, strapping Canadian, who had lived on a ranch all his life. He had been through the 'ins and outs' of hard work and was in very good shape physically. He was very strong and muscular.

One day he said to Elder Kotch, 'You've got to put those boxing gloves away. You are not studying the language the way you should and I insist that you put the gloves away if you are to continue as my companion.'"

Elder Smith continued, 'I'm supposed to look after you. I am to give you instructions and help you with the language and also help you with an understanding of the Gospel. The purpose we have been sent here is to teach these people. If I see you once more with those boxing gloves on, you're going to have to account to me.'"

'It went on the same way for a few days, and Elder Kotch didn't seem to pay any attention to his senior companion, Elder Smith. Elder Smith said to him, 'Now listen, you and I are going to have it out right now. I know that when I go in to the mission headquarters at our conference meetings and President Nelson finds out that you are not studying the language and that you are doing nothing but boxing, I will be the one that will get the reprimand for it, because I'm your senior companion. You and I are going to settle it right now. We're going to have a wrestling match. I'm not a boxer and you could likely beat me at a boxing match, but I don't think you could beat me when it comes to wrestling.'"

Elder Smith immediately took hold of Elder Kotch and threw him to the floor of the house where they were living. 'Now,' Elder Smith said, 'I've got hold of you and I'm going to hold you here until you promise me that you'll never pick up those boxing gloves again as long as I am your missionary companion.'"

I was later told about this event, and that it took about two or three hours before Elder Kotch would give up. He finally realized that Elder Smith was the stronger of the two and he had little choice but to promise he would hide the boxing gloves as long as he was the junior companion to Elder Smith. A week or so later, when these missionaries came into the mission headquarters for their monthly meeting with me, Elder Smith said, 'When I tell you what happened, I don't suppose you'll think very much of your old Canadian friend,' When he told me about the boxing gloves and the wrestling match, I said, 'Did you accomplish the purpose you set out to accomplish?'"

'Elder Smith said, 'Yes, Elder Kotch kept his word and he has not used the boxing gloves since.' I congratulated him and told him that sometimes we have to use manual strength to accomplish the purpose that the Lord has in store for us. I promised both of the elders that if they would work together as a team they could accomplish a great deal of good among the people of the Samoan Islands. It seemed to be the lesson that Elder Kotch needed for he did, indeed, become a wonderful missionary."[53]

FIRST VISIT TO TONGA

After I had visited each of the Island of the Samoan group, I decided it was time for me to make a visit to the Tongan Islands. As I have mentioned before, Tonga was taken back into the Samoan Mission because of an uprising with the Tongan saints. It was 600 miles away from the Samoan Islands. I was to travel on one of the big ocean-liners headed to America, the Sonoma. There were several missionaries who had just arrived from America who were to be assigned to the Tongan Islands. They traveled with me. They were not always happy to know they were going to Tonga, but as they captured the spirit of missionary work, they adjusted and felt happy about it."

53   John Nelson Dictaphone tape #47.

"There were no Conferences scheduled on the day of our arrival, as it was often impossible to know just when our ship would arrive. There was cargo to unload all along the way from Island to Island and it was hard to set a good time schedule. Our Conferences were always held the day after the Mission President arrived from Samoa."

I held meetings with the saints, but there seemed to be some discontentment about my being chosen as Mission President, because I did not have the understanding of the Tongan language. They felt that they were being discriminated against by not having their own President.

I had to speak through an interpreter. This was a great source of regret to me. We did hold some very special, spiritual meetings with the missionaries and we had our Conference with the saints just the same as in any mission. We held our meetings on Saturday night with the Priesthood and with the group of the Relief Society sisters."

[Editor's note: In the dictaphone tapes and letters John wrote from his home in Great Falls, to his daughters living away from Great Falls, he recorded the very special experience of receiving the Gift of the Tongan language. He did not record the date of this wonderful gift, only that it was about three months from his first visit to Tongan. That would make it very early in his time as Mission President. It was John's testimony. This experience is edited from a letter that John wrote to his daughters, Ruth, Verda, and Joyce.]

March 15, 1953

My Dear Daughters,

Inasmuch as you girls have written and asked me to write some of the experiences of my life, and Ruth has asked just recently, that I tell the story of receiving the Tongan language as a gift from the

Lord (which in my way of thinking is the greatest experience and testimony of my life) I will write this story to you today.

In order to give you the background why the Lord gave me the gift of speaking the Tongan language, I would like to mention a little of my work as a Missionary in the Samoan Mission up to the time of receiving this gift.

The Tongan Islands, also known as the Friendly Islands, at this time were under the direction of the Samoan Mission. There had been an uprising among the natives, which necessitated the First Presidency of the Church withdrawing the missionaries from the Tongan Mission. Later on, when the people quieted down and were not so war-like, the President of the Samoan Mission received instruction from the First Presidency to send missionaries from Samoa to preach the gospel.

The missionary work to Tonga was carried on this way for many years. The Mission President would go from Samoa every three months to hold conferences with the Tongan saints and the missionaries assigned there. Many of the Saints had remained true to the faith for many years, without any missionaries to keep them on the straight and narrow path. When the missionaries came back from Tonga, they had learned to speak the native Tongan language. However, the President of the Mission lived in Samoa, an expanse of water six hundred miles between the two groups of Islands. He did not have the time necessary to learn the Tongan language. Consequently, he would speak through an interpreter. This is a slow way of preaching the gospel to a large audience of Latter-Day Saints and investigators. There were three or four Islands in the Tongan group, where the Mission President traveled. On each Island, he would speak through an interpreter.

We used a young Tongan man, who had been educated in the college in New Zealand and who spoke both Tongan and English fluently, as our official interpreter. He was married, with several children. He was an outstanding young man, with a good knowledge of the gospel. We appreciated him very much and always felt that he interpreted as correctly as he could.

In Tonga they have, what is called, "talking men." These are men who are highly respected and hold a great deal of influence with the natives. Many of them were members of our Church. In almost every meeting, one of these men would rise at his own discretion and say something like this, "Why is it that the Tongan people cannot have a Mission President who can speak our language? Why do we have to have a man from Samoa, who must use an interpreter to speak to us?"

I felt their disapproval very keenly and understood their requests. I felt, too, that they should have their own mission. I heard this request in almost every meeting that was held that first month and a half while I was in Tonga. I felt sorry that I was not able to communicate with these fine saints, and it frustrated me that I was not able to speak their language.

Upon returning to the Mission headquarters in Apia, Upolu, Samoa, I felt impressed to dictate a letter to President Joseph F. Smith and his counselors, something to this effect:

Dear President Smith and Counselors,

I have just returned from a tour of the Friendly Islands, or the old Tongan Mission and everywhere I went, this question was put to me: Why can't we saints in Tonga have a mission of our own and a President who can speak our language?"

Sincerely your Brother,

John A. Nelson

I am sure that these brethren had been asked this question before by other Mission Presidents. In due time, an answer came back, signed by all three of the Presidency of the Church, to this effect:

Dear President Nelson,

We received your letter relative to separating the Tongan Mission from the Samoan Mission and we appreciated your concern. However, it is our *recommendation that the time is not right to divide this Mission. We want you to go back to Tonga, in the course of your travels, and the Lord will bless you. We desire you to continue handling the affairs of the Tongan Mission from your office in Samoa.

President Joseph F. Smith, Anthon H. Lund, Charles W. Penrose First Presidency, Church of Jesus Christ of Latter-Day Saints

In about three months from my first visit to Tonga, I boarded the good old steamship, Sonoma, from America. After about three days of sea-sickness, stopping here and there at small islands to unload cargo, I arrived at Vavau, the first Island of the Tongan group. It usually took from one month to six weeks to accomplish my work, according to the schedule of the boats. I had in my mind the instructions that the First Presidency had given me: "Return to Tonga and the Lord will bless you."

I felt very humble and weak as I contemplated our Conference meetings and the fact that I again had to speak through the interpreter bothered me greatly. It was very frustrating to me. I would begin with a few words, such as, "I am happy to be here this morning," then I would have to wait for the interpreter to tell them what I had said in Tongan.

As our ship pulled into the Vavau harbor, I looked down and saw three of our missionaries waiting to greet me. After a delay of several hours, while our luggage was inspected for any Samoan coconut beetle that might be carried in, I was allowed to go ashore and greet the Elders.

Elder Jaynes, one of the Elders who had come to greet me, said, "President Nelson, I have a meeting appointed on one of the little Islands about a half- mile from the Mainland. I am going out in a row boat and would like you to come and go with me."

I immediately answered, "Elder Jaynes, I would be very happy to go with you tonight, as I have no other meetings scheduled, but I understand only a very little of the Tongan language and can speak only a few sentences. I do not know enough of the language to do you any good.

When we arrived at the Mission Home, Elder Jaynes again approached me with the thought of going out to this little Island with him. I again turned him down, but it seemed as though he would not let up on the subject. Finally, I said, "Elder Jaynes, if you want me to go so much, I will, even though I cannot understand or speak the language."

Elder Jaynes had been in the Islands about three years. He was to return home to his loved ones in America in a short time. He had a very good speaking knowledge of the language and he understood the people in Tonga. He was well-versed in the scriptures on the first principles of the gospel. All-in-all, he was an excellent missionary.

It took about a half hour to row out from the Mainland to the little Island where the meeting was to be held. Elder Jaynes had been granted the privilege of holding a meeting in the chapel of the Church of England. All of the people on this Island belonged to this same church, some three hundred in all. The Minister had given his permission, perhaps with a motive in his mind. He could keep an eye on the missionaries and hear what was told to his people and he did not want the missionaries to go into the private homes to do their proselyting.

The Church was one of the long sugar-cane-thatched buildings with lattice work all around so that a person could enter the building at any point. It was much like the Salt Lake Tabernacle. The people gathered when the bell, or pate, sounded. In that country, the people all attended church. It was not long until the beautiful grass, immediately on the outside of the church, was covered with devoted members of the Church of England. The minister and a few others entered and sat in the center of the building. The remainder sat on the grass, knowing that they could hear quite well from the outside.

Elder Jaynes took a seat with me at one end of the large hall, near the only door where a person could enter standing straight up. In fact, the little bench on which we sat, was the only seat in the church. The natives always sit cross-legged on the floor, with fine mats under them. I was sitting near the door, with Elder Jaynes on my left.

The "saints" all joined in a hymn Elder Jaynes suggested. The Islanders all love to sing, especially in large groups at a church meeting. He then offered a nice prayer and while I could not understand the words, I felt the spirit of it. A second song was sung, after which Elder Jaynes gave a discourse on the first principles of the Gospel.

When he had finished his sermon, he told the people that President John A. Nelson, of the Latter-Day Saints Mission with headquarters in Apia, Samoa, was going to speak to them in the Samoan language, since he did not understand or speak Tongan. These people did not understand Samoan, any more than I understood Tongan. Since the Islands are a distance of 600 miles apart, it was very rare to see a Tongan man or woman in Samoa.

As I arose to speak, a woman appeared in the doorway to my right. I motioned for her to come inside. Since she was a Tongan woman, I assumed she had come to attend the meeting. She shook her head, indicating that she did not wish to sit down. Conse-

quently, I left her standing near me in the doorway. Elder Jaynes later said that he did not see her.

I had thought I would give a few sentences of greeting in the Tongan language and then switch to Samoan. Just as I had ended the few sentences I knew in Tongan, intending to switch to Samoan, the woman in the doorway seemed to give me the words of the Tongan language.

I did not hesitate for a single word. I continued speaking in the Tongan language. It was as though I could see the words as they came from her mouth, from her lips, to me and I grasped them and went right on speaking in Tongan.

It was a revelation to these 300 or more people who were sitting on the grass and in the chapel. Those who were sitting on the outside began to come in. They realized that I had not known the Tongan language, as Elder Jaynes had announced this fact as he introduced me.

When the Lord gives a gift, he doesn't do it haphazardly. It is given in its complete form. I was speaking the Tongan language as fluently as any native. There was no hesitancy in my speech. The natives were astonished. Elder Jaynes looked at me in great wonderment to realize that I was speaking in Tongan.

I bear my testimony to you, that I spoke to that group of people for nearly an hour, in their own language. I told them of the restored gospel. I told them of the Prophet Joseph Smith. I told them of their lineage; that they were Israelites and the Lord loves them. Because of this love, he had called missionaries to come 7,000 miles from America to teach them the great plan of salvation. This plan had been restored to the earth in these latter days, through the instrumentality of the Prophet Joseph Smith.

After the people sang one more beautiful song, Elder Jaynes closed the meeting with prayer. He thanked the Lord for our being there and for the experience we had just witnessed: the gift of tongues to a humble servant of the Lord. It is one of the greatest testimonies of my life.

After the meeting, the minister came up and congratulated me. I told him that the Church of Jesus Christ of Latter-Day Saints has all of the gifts and powers that were in the Church when Christ was upon the earth. I told him that the gift of healing and all of the other blessings enjoyed by the prophets of old, had been re-established and sent to the earth again for the benefit and blessings of mankind. He seemed to enjoy our discussion. However, I realize that people do not join the Church just because of a miracle. I never saw the woman in the doorway again. Elder Jaynes repeated that he had never seen her at all. There was a beautiful spirit and wonderful feeling of friendship and love felt and expressed by many.

The next day at our Conference, I spoke fluently in the Tongan language, not lacking for a word. I did not need an interpreter. The letter that I had received from the First Presidency of the Church, which said, "Return to Tonga, and the Lord will bless you," was certainly true. He did bless me.

As we traveled from Island to Island and from Branch to Branch, many of the people followed us. They were so eager to hear the words of their Mission President, who had been given the gift of tongues, the gift of the Tongan language. This was not only a blessing to me, but also to the Tongan people. I learned to read the Bible translated into the Tongan language and I studied so that my pronunciation would be perfected.

From that time on, I never needed an interpreter to deliver my messages to the Tongan saints. I never heard again, the request, "Why can't we have a Mission President who can speak our language?" As true as I live today, I bear testimony that the gospel of Jesus Christ, as revealed to us in this day and time, through the instrumentality of Joseph Smith, is true. It is the one and only true plan of salvation that God has revealed to the people on earth today.

When I returned again to Samoa, I wrote the First Presidency of the Church of my gift of the Tongan language, for it was indeed, a gift. I have always recognized this experience as the most precious testimony and gift that the Lord has ever given me.

There, Ruthie, is the story you have requested of the Gift of the Tongan language. I am sending Joyce and Verda a copy of this so that they can read it also and rejoice that we are all members of the Church of Jesus Christ. I know that this is the only plan God has given to His children, whereby they might be saved in His celestial kingdom.

I love you, dear daughters,

Dad

8

JOHN'S MISSION CONTINUES

LOST ON THE LAVA FIELDS

"Samoan Islanders didn't care how long you would stay at their homes, if you took care of your own needs and cooked your own food. Food was plentiful there, with bananas, breadfruits, pineapples and tropical fruits growing abundantly. There was taro out in the fields, but it took work to gather it in. However, because the natives did not have a way of preserving the food, much of it went to waste on the ground. When the breadfruit crop came on, the natives ate as much as they wanted while it lasted. Tons and tons of it spoiled and it had to be scraped out to the ocean to get rid of the terrible smell."

"As I traveled around the Mission in the year 1913, I used to take a native boy with me. He was a good husky lad, named Sapi. He seemed to enjoy traveling with me and seemed to enjoy listening to me talk to the people, holding meetings at night, and so on. He would assist the family that we were staying with by gathering in and cooking the food. We always had plenty to eat."

"On one of these trips, we went to the Island of Savaii. We traveled from the Mission Headquarters located on the Island of Upolu. We took a small launch and crossed the 40 mile channel between the two Islands. We arrived on the north side of Savaii, where there was a huge volcano. The volcano had become almost extinct with the exception of a few air holes where smoke was coming out. In order to get to the village where I had made arrangements for a conference to be held with the natives and the missionaries, it was necessary to cross this lava bed."

"The volcano had been active in the years past and the molten lava had run down from the top of the mountain for twelve miles into the sea. New red-hot lava had flowed like a river right up over the old lava beds where it stopped, cooled and formed lava mountains. It would be easy for someone trying to cross these lava beds, to become lost."

"At about four o'clock on Saturday afternoon, Sapi and I started out across this lava bed. The natives had been crossing it for several years and they had left coconut husks, pieces of boards, branches of dead trees, and numerous other markings along the way. If you understood the markings, you should be able to follow the trail without becoming lost."

"Sapi and I were not accustomed to this marking system. However, we did pretty well, until Sapi's feet got sore. The lava was too hot for him. I tied two coconut husks on his feet. This was about the only thing we could use to keep his feet off of the hot lava bed. I had on thick-soled shoes that I wore on occasions such as this, so I was all right. However, as we traveled along we soon realized that we were lost. We had, somehow, missed the markings the natives had left along the way."

Sapi was a young, inexperienced boy and I had never been over this lava bed before. When a missionary has a problem, such as this, the first thing that he does is kneel to the earth and pray to his Eternal Father in Heaven for help. This is exactly what I did. I asked for guidance, that we might find the trail and get us out of this terrible circumstance."

"We traveled along for several hours, not knowing just where we were. There was a smoky haze around us and we could not even see the sun. Then we realized that the sun had gone down beneath the horizon. It would soon be dark."

"Suddenly, we noticed fresh smoke billowing up in a different direction from the one we were traveling. We concluded that if we followed the smoke, we might find a village on the opposite side of the lava. Our supposition was correct. As we approached the village, we found several natives and we ask directions to our destination. They told us how to get there. However, they did not tell us that down the trail a little way, there would be two roads. We later found that one road led down to the coast and the other road led inland, going back up into the woods. Sapi and I didn't know which road to take, and as luck would have it, we took the wrong road."

"After we had traveled for a little way, we passed a blind woman, led by a little girl. The blind woman had a bunch of banana leaves tied on to her back. (This was a typical way of carrying the leaves from their plantations.) The trail was good for a little while. However, it soon was dark and we had lost the trail. We decided to camp there for the night, rather than become more disoriented."

"I stuck my pocketknife into a tree to show the direction we had just come. Sapi used his knife and cut some sticks and put them into the ground. It wasn't long until he had made a little hut of big banana leaves. We planned to sleep there, on the ground, until the next morning. We had only been asleep a few minutes, perhaps, when Sapi nudged me. A wild female boar with four or five little piglets was rooting around our hut. These boars are extremely dangerous, especially the female with her babies. Sapi was very frightened. He suggested that we make a fire immediately in front of our hut and keep it going the rest of the night. We decided on this plan and then we took turns, keeping the fire going and sleeping. The plan worked because boars are afraid of fire. I'm sure neither one of us got much sleep, but the boars did leave without bothering us."

"When daylight came, we retraced our steps and headed back toward the village. On the way back, three people came towards us with a basket of food. They had been sent out by the mayor of the village at the suggestion of the blind woman we had met earlier. She had told the mayor that she was sure the missionary and the boy were lost because they were going the wrong way into the bushes. We hadn't said anything to the blind woman, just passed the time of day, as we assumed we were on the right path."

"The men offered us food from their baskets and just at that moment, a pigeon cooed in a tree nearby. The natives had a gun, and with careful aim, killed the pigeon.

Almost instantly, a fire was made and we had roast pigeon and taro. We were very hungry. The men led us back to their village.

The mayor was called in and all of the chiefs of the town were called. A great council was held. They asked me questions about my work. It gave me a great opportunity to explain the gospel of Jesus Christ to all of these people."

"They then sent one of the natives along with us to help us get to our appointed location. They treated a Mormon Elder and his companion very kindly. Many people remembered the lost missionaries on their Island. I am sure that a kind Heavenly Father protected us from harm. I offered Him my thanks."[1]

---

1   John Nelson dictaphone tape #15.

APPEARANCE OF JOHN THE REVELATOR

"During the years I presided over the Island Missions, I often wondered if I was working to the full capacity of my capabilities. I often sought the Lord in mighty prayer for guidance. The education of the missionaries seemed to prey upon my thoughts as much as anything else. I wanted the missionaries to return home, after having had a full mission, with many wonderful experiences and above all, with testimonies that they knew Jesus was the Christ, the Son of God. I wanted the missionaries to be able to teach these wonderful native people the simple beauties of the Gospel of Jesus Christ. These were often my thoughts as I went about my work."

"One night as I had retired to my bed, I seemed to be carried away in vision, or what I'll never know, but I felt sure that I was not asleep. I was carried out into a beautiful church. It seemed as though there were two of my brethren with me, who having filled missions in the Islands had returned home and had passed on to their rewards. They were Elder Shepherd and Elder Ramsey. As the three of us stood in that beautiful chapel, up the walk came a very stately man. He spoke to us and said, 'Follow me.' As we followed him, Elder Shepherd said to me, 'Ask him if he is one of the Three Nephites, or John, the Revelator, the beloved apostle of the Savior who was banished to the Isle of Patmos.'"

"So I touched him on the shoulder and said, 'Will you please tell us just who you are? Are you one of the Three Nephites, or John, the beloved apostle of the Savior?' He did not speak, but it came over me, as it did the others, that he was John the Revelator, the beloved apostle of our Lord and Savior.

So we followed him. When we got outside, I could not see Elder Shepherd or Elder Ramsey, but this individual told me to follow him. We went out into a large square, where there were hundreds of people."

"This individual, who I am sure was John the Revelator, sat down on a box, resembling an apple box. He said to me, 'Listen to me.' I sat over just a little to the side of him. Immediately in front of him and all around, were many native people, who had apparently assembled to hear him talk.

The thing that impressed me more than anything else was the simplicity with which he spoke. The tenderness in his voice, the love in his eyes and the great message he seemed to have for the people. He told them of the Savior dying on the cross for the sins of the world. He told them of their forefathers, speaking very beautifully at some length, about their missions in life and what they were to do."

"This impressed me to such a great extent, that I shall never forget it. When I became aware of my surroundings, I found myself lying on my bed in the mission home, my pillow wet with tears, so great had been my experience in the visitation of this wonderful individual. My companions, who had parted, perhaps were also privileged to come with me."

"I know for a surety that my visitor was John the Revelator. I know that he is still upon the earth somewhere. He received the divine promise that he would not be taken from the earth until the Savior comes again in all His glory. Nothing will molest him or cause him trouble, neither heat nor cold nor anything of that sort. The only thing that will bring him sorrow will be the sins of the people of the world."

"I tell this story as it was a divine testimony to me, that it did build me up that time and make me a more powerful servant of the Lord. When I spoke, I seemed to speak with the authority that had been bestowed upon me when I had hands laid upon my head and set apart as President of that wonderful mission. I had been called to preside over the people and to teach them the gospel of Jesus Christ, in its simple beauty. I knew, through the power of the Holy Ghost, that this had been a divine visitation and that my visitor had been John the Revelator, the Beloved Apostle of the Master."[2]

A MIRACLE FOR A MISSION PRESIDENT

"When I was presiding over the Samoan and Tongan Mission, my chief responsibility was to travel about the mission, visiting the missionaries and the members of the Church. I was on the Island of Tutuila, the capital of American Samoa, where we had just completed a very successful quarterly conference. In our conference, the missionaries came together from the surrounding islands to report the progress of their labors. There were reports from the individual missionaries and the conference president gave a report of the overall picture. Each missionary reported on how he was getting along with the language and how he was being blessed in his assignment. The conference presidents reported on the various branches over which they presided."

John, when he was Mission President, with a group of his missionaries. John is in the middle row, fourth from the left.

2   John Nelson Dictaphone tape #18

"At the close of the conference, I was preparing to return to the Mission Headquarters, which was on the Island of Upolu, a distance of about forty miles. There were many boats traveling between these two islands, but not on a regular schedule. The large ocean-liners traveling between Australia and America would only go out of the straight course when the cargo warranted it."

Probably some of John A. Nelson's missionaries.

"The missionaries had all gone back to their various fields of labor. I had intended to visit some of them in the branches where they were working, but a feeling came over me that I should take the first boat to Apia, Upolu, a German island where the mission headquarters and mission home were located. I inquired immediately as to the first boat sailing that way and was informed that the Sonoma from Australia was due the next day about noon."

"Elder David Wilcox was being transferred from Tutuila to Upolu and consequently would travel with me. Elder Wilcox was in Samoa for the first time, even though he was a married man with a wife and three fairly-grown daughters. Although he had not as yet learned the language to a great extent, he was doing a wonderful work with the missionaries, helping them understand the gospel in their study hour. He had served a prior mission among the European people."

"The following day, as the Sonoma was about due to arrive in the Pago Pago Harbor, Elder Wilcox and I took our suitcases and set out for the wharf. Here we found the usual throngs of people who delighted in watching the movements of the big ships as they drew up to the pier. Then, too, strange people from all parts of the world would be aboard; many of them would go ashore to buy curios from the natives that lined the wharf for blocks. Many of the natives would also beg money, candy, or whatever they could get from the people who got off the ships."

"To our great disappointment, the ship did not pull up to the pier as everyone had expected, but dropped anchor almost a half mile out in the Pago Pago Harbor.

There were always ropes stretched across the pier to hold the people back until word was given by the authorities. When the word was given to remove the ropes, the people were allowed to board the ship."

"A rowboat was lowered from the ship and two men climbed into the boat and rowed ashore. The men had a bottle filled with alcohol which had a key (apparently of some importance) inside the bottle. The men shouted to the manager of the wharf that there wasn't any mail and that there could be no passengers come aboard the ship, as the ship was under strict quarantine for smallpox. There was a big sign held up stating, 'No Passengers Will Be Allowed--Boat Quarantined.' Smallpox had broken out just after they left Australia and there was a number of people with this dread disease aboard."

My hopes of going to Upolu on this large ship, was at first shattered. Even though I may have been able to go on a small cargo boat later on that week (I always got sea-sick on these small crafts), I just had the prompting of the Holy Spirit that I had to get on this particular boat."

"I wasn't thinking about the policemen with their guns and clubs standing by the ropes to keep everyone back from boarding. I said to Elder Wilcox, 'I want you to relieve me here, I am going on this ship to Upolu.'"

"Astonished, he replied, 'President Nelson, you'll get shot if you step over that rope and walk down that gang-plank.' However, without another word or any hesitation, I stepped over the rope and walked down the pier and handed my suitcase to one of the men.

Another man took my hand to steady me as I stepped into the rowboat. Under ordinary circumstances, a policeman would have either pulled me back, or shot me as I stepped over the rope before the signal was given to allow the passengers to board. (To say nothing about trying to board a quarantined ship.) "

"It was the will of the Lord that I should go to Upolu. I have always been sure that the policemen, as well as the hundreds of people standing around, did not see me. The Lord obstructed me from their view, as He had a work for me to do. I was asked no questions by the men in the rowboat. When we reached the ship, I was the first to leave the rowboat and climb the ladder attached for the purpose of boarding a ship out in the bay."

"As I stepped onto the deck of the ship, no one seemed to notice me. The two men carried my suitcase up the ladder and the ship immediately drew up its anchor. The men reported my destination to the Captain and the Captain had the ship's course changed to go to the Island Upolu. They had not even intended to stop at this Island, due to the quarantine."

"I was not asked for money to pay my fare. No one asked me for a ticket, although I didn't even think about this until much later on. After a two-hour trip, the Sonoma stopped just off the coast of Upolu, long enough to let me climb down the ladder and step into a small launch waiting to carry mail and passengers ashore. Under ordinary circumstances, the big tugboats would go out later to get the cargo, as there was no pier on this island."

"When the launch pulled along side the Sonoma, the purser shouted down to the men, 'There is no mail and only one passenger to get off.' A Mormon Elder to leave a quarantined vessel and go scot-free, with no long waiting in a quarantine station, was an unheard of occurrence.

My only thought was to do the will of the Lord and He had prepared the way before me, so that I could accomplish His righteous purpose in sending me on this trip."

"After leaving the mail launch, I took my suitcase and walked as rapidly as I could to the mission headquarters at Pesega, a distance of four to six blocks. Elders were surprised to see me, as they had received word that the boat would not dock because of the quarantine."

"There were three new Elders from America who must be appointed to their fields of labor. I appointed Elder Owen Ricks, who was from Rexburg, Idaho, to the Tongan mission. He had wanted to stay in Samoa and was a little disappointed. After I hurriedly took care of some of the other Mission business, Elder Ricks and I boarded a ship from America that was going to Tonga. It generally took three to five days for the boat to go the six hundred miles, depending on the number of stops to pick up passengers, or deliver cargo along the way."

"The average steamship could travel about three hundred knots in twenty-four hours, which was a little over three hundred miles. The steamship we were traveling on was called the Ventura. Elder Ricks and I met many interesting people from America and elsewhere, all going to Australia and New Zealand."

"Let me digress from my story long enough to tell a little story about Elder Ricks. There was a man and his wife from England on board. The woman and Elder Ricks sat at the same table while they had their meals. The lady noticed that Elder Ricks did not use tea or coffee, nor did he smoke after his meals.

She was curious about this, and asked him, 'Don't ye drink tea?' 'No,' said Elder Ricks. 'And don't ye drink beer?' 'No.' 'And don't ye smoke?' 'No,' replied Elder Ricks. 'And I know ye don't play cards, so what I want to know is what do ye do?' Then she added, 'My young man, I am sure your mother shan't have to worry about ye while ye are away from home!'"

"As we were traveling along and neared the Island of Tonga, Elder Ricks would come to me asking the meaning of a certain words in the Tongan language. Now, he had never studied the Tongan language and had never seen a book written in that language. I asked him where he had heard the various words. He replied, 'They just came to me.' This young missionary was going on his first mission, where he had to learn a new language in order to preach the Gospel of Jesus Christ for the next three years. The Lord was already beginning to bless him with his new language.[3]

---

3   John Nelson's dictaphone tape #15.

ELDERS STRICKEN WITH DEADLY DISEASE

"In due time, the ship dropped anchor at the Vavau Pier in Tonga and after so much red-tape, we were permitted to go ashore. When we arrived at the Elders' home, we found six of the seven missionaries sick in bed with the dread, black typhoid fever. This was a very severe and contagious disease. A native guard was sitting on each corner of the lot with a gun, so that not even a dog was permitted to cross the lot. There were signs up on the lot saying that the Mormon missionaries had this dread black typhoid fever. The missionaries had called the doctor and he came, but would not enter the house. He gave instructions and medicine outside the gate, but he was afraid of contacting the disease, so would not enter."

Elder Beatty, the only missionary who was not sick, had dreamed a dream. In the dream, it seemed that all seven of the Elders were running a race. All along the race course, first one and then another of his companions would sit down before reaching the goal. It seemed that he was the only one who reached the end of the racecourse. After all the Elders had become bedfast with the dread fever, Elder Beatty knew the meaning of his dream. He concluded that he would not get the fever. (He did not get sick.)"

"The day after we arrived in Tonga, I sent Elder Ricks, the new missionary who had come with me, out to visit the various branches of the Church, asking the Saints to fast and pray for the afflicted Elders. I wrote a letter in the Tongan language, with every other line in English, so Elder Ricks could understand it. I gave Elder Ricks instructions to return by Saturday night and to report how he had found the Saints."

"When he came to me on Saturday night, I found the Lord had blessed him with a good knowledge of the Tongan language. He was indeed a very humble and happy Elder. He was so grateful that he had been appointed to labor among the Tongan people and he thanked me for appointing him to the Tongan Islands."

"Elder Beatty had to act as doctor, nurse, cook, and dishwasher for his afflicted brethren. He had to keep the sickest of the Elders tied to their beds while he took care of his work and tended to the other Elders, as they would be so delirious. I was not allowed to enter the home. I had some of the native saints build me a little banana hut right by the gate. They put down posts that stuck in the ground and packed it all around with banana leaves, so that if it rained, I would not get wet."

"I sat at the gate and gave encouragement and instructions when needed by Elder Beatty. When Elder Beatty had any trouble with the sick Elders, he would call out to me for help. I would shout out instructions for him and the sick Elders seemed to obey me. Elder Beatty might say, 'President Nelson, please make Elder Jones do this, or that,' or 'He's eating too much,' or, 'He won't take his medicine.' It seemed as though, when I shouted to them from the gate, they would always do as I asked. It was a peculiar situation, but I felt I must stay there with them as long as they needed me."

"Elder Jones was one of the sickest of the group. He was a big, raw-boned fellow, six foot tall. He had only been in the islands a short time and he was homesick. He was delirious the longest. He seemed to be packing his trunk for America all of the time."

"Elder Beatty did a very marvelous work taking care of all of his sick companions. He was, indeed, a marvelous missionary. However, no one would fail to acknowledge that the Lord in Heaven had given him the strength to handle this situation. I also know that the faith and prayers of the dear saints on the Tongan Islands were answered in behalf of their missionaries. It was here that I gained a strong testimony that the Lord will take care of those who put their trust in Him."

"Even with the experience of our Elders having this dreadful black fever, I felt we had been greatly blessed during this time. I know that the Lord provided the way for me to travel on a quarantine ship so I could arrive in time to be of comfort to these sick Elders. I know that I was given inspiration and help along my way, so that I could be of comfort and assistance to the Elders under my leadership."

"All of the Elders finally regained their full health and after holding a very spiritual meeting with them and giving thanks to the Lord for his protecting care and healing influence, I sailed on to another island of the Tongan group."[4]

A TONGAN JUBILEE

"While the missionaries were so sick with the black-typhoid fever, the King of the Tongan Islands sent out a decree that he wanted to have a representative from each church in his Dominion, give a report of their organization's growth at the up-coming Jubilee. I felt that the sick Elders still needed me to be close by them, so I asked Elder Ricks to go and represent our Church."

"It would be necessary for him to make the short presentation speech and deliver a copy of the Book of Mormon to the King. I helped him memorize an appropriate speech and he went with a special blessing, the blessing of the Lord, as we both had fasted and prayed. He felt very humble and inexperienced, having only been in the Islands two weeks.

He went in power and delivered his message to the thousands of people who had assembled to pay honor to their King. How great is the power of the Lord!"

"Elder Ricks had been blessed with the gift of the Tongan language and the ability to present his message to the Tongan people assembled at the Jubilee. He gave a very good account of himself and of the Mormon Church and of the missionary program. The people clapped for him as he made his speech in the big open grandstand that had been erected for this wonderful Jubilee."

"My testimony is that the Lord helps his chosen servants. It doesn't matter what language they speak. I know that the scripture, 'And

4   John A. Nelson's Dictaphone tape #8.

they shall speak with new tongues, and they shall heal the sick and cleanse the lepers and all of those might works that they shall do' is true. I bear my solemn witness that Elder Ricks truly received the gift of the Tongan language and blessed the lives of the people of that Island."[5]

LOVE EXPRESSED FOR ELDER RANSOM

"One of my former missionary companions, Elder Ransom, had a very difficult time learning the Samoan language. He wrote words on his hands, studied them all day and the next morning, he had forgotten them. He seemed like a bright young Elder, but just couldn't master the language."

"By this time, I had been called to be the Mission President and it had been my responsibility to assign Elder Ransom to his field of labor. I appointed him to go to the Island of Savaii, the largest Island of the Samoan group.

Elder Ransom had been in the mission field for nearly two years but he could hardly speak a word of the language, nor could he understand it. He had become despondent at times, then he would 'perk up' and feel he was doing some good in helping the natives in different ways."

"We had been holding our Conference on the Island of Savaii during which time, plans were made to transfer Elder Ransom to the Island of Upolu. During the afternoon, several hundred natives came down the street. We did not know what was going on and wondered if we were going to be mobbed. They came up to our meeting place and they stopped. The head of the village and the head 'talking-man' came into the room of the building where we were meeting. The building was much like the Salt Lake Tabernacle with openings where you could enter at any spot. When it storms, it was possible

---

5   John A. Nelson's Dictaphone tape #8.

to let down lattice work and you would be securely enclosed in a good, warm place."

"The 'talking-man' spoke, 'We understand that you are moving Elder Harmosa (Elder Ransom's mission name) from our Island. We have come here today to protest against this action.

Even though this Elder does not speak our language, we love him. Many of us are not members of the Mormon Church, yet we love to have him come into our homes because he has a very beautiful, sweet spirit with him. Many times he has had the spirit of healing. He lays his hands upon our sick children and heals them. He anoints them with oil, and, in the name of Jesus Christ, they are healed. He binds our wounds when we get hurt. He is our friend. He talks to our children by motioning with his hands, even though he cannot talk to them with lips in the language of our people.'"

"The 'talking-man' continued, 'We have come to make a special request that you, the head man of the Samoan Mission, leave Elder Harmosa with us here on the Island of Savaii. We love him.

We don't say that we are going to join his Church (he hadn't been able to explain it to them) but it must be a wonderful Church because of the feelings we receive from this good missionary. Please leave him here with us.'"

"What else could we do? I turned to the missionaries and to Elder Ransom and said, 'We will leave you here for a few months longer, if you wish to stay.' He, of course, was very happy because he loved these people. He did remain and he was a wonderful missionary and did a lot of good. He opened the doors for the other missionaries. It seemed as though, wherever Elder Ransom had been, the other missionaries were welcome.[6]

---

6   John Nelson's dictaphone tapes #45 and #17

9

EXPERIENCES OF A MISSION PRESIDENT

A WINNING MORMON DEBATE

"In the year 1915, I was presiding over the Samoan and Tongan Islands as the Mission President. I received a letter, through the newspaper, from Reverend Heiner, of the Church of England. He challenged me to an open, public debate. He suggested that we debate the proposition, 'The last prophet since Jesus Christ was John the Revelator.'"

"The Reverend knew that the Church of Jesus Christ of Latter-day Saints believed that it is necessary to have prophets in this day and time for the guidance of our Church. This need is now, just as much as it was in the early rise of Christianity, or even farther back in the days of the Old Testament, when Isaiah, Daniel, Jeremiah, Ezekiel and all of the other prophets who lived and preached the gospel."

"I knew that the First Presidency did not sanction open debates, so I held the Reverend off for quite a while. Finally, it became evident that I must do something. I wrote a letter to Salt Lake City and asked the First Presidency if it would be all right if I accepted the challenge of Reverend Heiner to debate with him. I told them that the proposition was, 'Resolved, that John the Revelator, who was banished to the Isle of Patmos, was the last prophet since Jesus Christ.'

"In due time, I received a letter from the First Presidency giving me their permission to accept the challenge of Reverend Heiner.

I immediately wrote to the Reverend and told him that I would be happy to meet him and debate with him, the proposition that he had proposed.

I suggested that we should meet and cast lots to see in whose chapel we should hold the debate. He responded and the time and place was arranged. The Mormons had a big chapel at Pago Pago. However, the Church of England chapel was much larger that ours."

"On the day appointed, I met Reverend Heiner at the post office. I noticed a little boy, standing close by. I asked him to pick up two little sticks, making one longer than the other, as we were going to draw lots. I asked the young boy to step around the corner of the building to prepare the sticks. He came out with his two hands hiding behind his back, hiding the sticks. I asked the Reverend to take the first draw. The long stick would be the winner as to whose chapel the debate would be held. Reverend Heiner drew the first draw, drawing the short stick. Consequently, the debate was to be held in the chapel of the Church of Jesus Christ of Latter-day Saints."

"It was advertised in the newspaper that we were going to hold this debate. It was planned to last for six nights, starting Monday evening and going until Saturday night. We had a timekeeper. The first speaker had thirty minutes, with ten minutes rebuttal from the opponent. We decided that there would be no judges. We would leave the congregation of people assembled to be the judges and decide who brought the greatest evidence."

"For the first debate, we had the chapel filled with people, all colors, and creeds. Reverend Heiner and I sat at the front of the chapel. Our timekeeper suggested the proposition, on which we were to debate. I had a little advantage over him, perhaps, because I had fifteen or twenty missionaries who were taking notes and they helped me get the biblical references that I needed to counteract anything the Reverend might say contrary to the proposition."

"The first night went along fairly well. We each spoke for the thirty minutes and took our ten-minute rebuttal. The congregation seemed intensely interested. After the meeting, we had a good many conversations with people, who had questions concerning our beliefs.

The second evening, Reverend Heiner seemed as though he was running out of material.

He attacked me and my Church because of our belief that it was as important to have prophets in these latter days, just as in early biblical days. I had to pull his coat tail two or three times that night and say, 'Reverend Heiner, stick to the subject.'"

"We went on the third night. Reverend Heiner was even more assertive that ever. I, with the help of the Lord and the help that the missionaries were giving me, had far more evidence to prove that it was necessary to have prophets today for the guidance of the Church. Reverend Heiner was sadly loosing the debate, because he did not have the material to back up his proposition. His claim was that the heavens were closed with the printing of the Bible, and that there were no more revelations for the guidance of the Church."

"I felt that each evening was very interesting and the people seemed to become more and more curious. After the meeting, many people would stay until mid-night to discuss the topics we had been debating about. On Friday night, Reverend Heiner spoke first. The time-keeper arose and again suggested the proposition, 'Resolved, that John the Revelator, who was banished to the Isle of Patmos, was the last prophet since Jesus Christ.' Reverend Heiner apparently felt that he could not go on any more with that subject. He said, 'I know and understand that my friend, Elder Nelson, believes that it is necessary to be baptized by immersion for the remission of sins, before a person can get back into the presence of God. I take the negative and ay that sprinkling is just as authentic and that it is not absolutely necessary to baptize a person by immersion.'"

"He kept on talking on that same subject until his time was up. The bell sounded. Baptism is a pet subject of all the missionaries. I had been speaking on this for many years and even though I hadn't prepared a text, I gave the people a discourse on the authenticity of baptism by immersion. Just before I got through speaking, Reverend Heiner arose and left the building. After the meeting, those in attendance commented that it seemed as though he had run out of material."

"Saturday night, when the bell sounded, Reverend Heiner did not appear. It was quite evident that he had lost the debate. I was grateful to my Heavenly Father for the divine principles, which I understood, that are contained in the Bible."

"I bear my testimony that prophets are called to guide the affairs of the Church of Jesus Christ of Latter-Day Saints. I also bear testimony that Jesus Christ showed us the way to be baptized, when he was led into the River Jordan by John the Baptist, as he was immersed in the water. We also need to be baptized as Christ was, to fulfill all righteousness. Thus, the pattern was set, by which people should become members of His true Church. It was conceded by the congregation, that the Mormon Elder had won the debate."[7]

---

7   John Nelson dictaphone tape #26

A FACE FROM THE PAST

"While I was laboring as a missionary in the Samoan Islands and again while I presided over the Samoan and Tongan Missions, I had to travel a great deal by water. This was necessary so that I could visit the numerous islands of the two groups. I sailed in vessels of various types: gasoline-powered boats, rowboats, sailboats, big ocean liners. I did not like to sail and would often become seasick. I worried a lot about being on the ocean and was concerned that we would make our destination each time."

"One time when I was the Mission President, I was going from the Island of Savaii to Upolu, a distance of about 40 miles across the channel. I had an Elder traveling as my companion. We had booked passage on a gasoline-powered ship that was carrying a ton of cement as freight.

Just as we got to the point where we were supposed to start out across the channel, something went wrong with the engine and it stopped. At that particular place, there was a great current that was going out towards the ocean and we appeared to be caught in that current.

It was difficult for the men manning the boat to propel the boat back to shore with only the use of their oars."

"The boat had sails on it, but with as much weight as it was carrying, they were afraid to try to get across the channel just using the sails. We finally were rowed back to shore. The captain of the vessel said to my companion and me, 'You gentlemen had better go ashore and find lodging somewhere with the people. We will try to repair the motor of the ship and hopefully will be able to set sail tomorrow morning about 8 or 9 o'clock.'"

"As we walked down the coast, trying to find a place to stay the night, we came across a white man who was operating a little grocery store. He also had all kinds of native novelties for sale. He had married a native woman. He seemed very friendly as we told him our plight. He offered his home to us immediately and made us feel most welcome."

"During the conversation of the evening, I discovered that this man had lived in Canada when he was a young man. He knew my father, as well as many of my uncles and aunts. He had worked, putting up hay with the men of my family. After working in Canada for many years, he had drifted out to the Pacific Islands. He was somewhat of a roamer. He had never married until he arrived in the Islands. There he had taken a Samoan woman as his wife and they had a few good-looking children."

"I realized that night, that the world is indeed very small and we often find people we know, or who may have known our family or friends, no matter how far away from home we may be."[8]

THE FIGHT OF THE STALLIONS

"My new-found friend told us stories about my father and my uncles that I knew to be true. He told me a story of my Uncle Jasper Head that I had remembered as a young man when I was growing up on the prairie land of Alberta. It seemed that Uncle Jasper had a large beautiful stallion. He used to drive him eleven miles from his ranch into Cardston, Canada to pick up groceries and to exercise the horse."

"One day as he was going on his usual errands, a band of wild horses came riding across the Canadian prairie. There was a wild stallion leading the band.

When the wild stallion saw Uncle Jasper's stallion, he immediately engaged in a terrible battle. The buggy was kicked to pieces in just a few minutes. Uncle Jasper found himself helpless although he did have the buggy whip in his hand. Whenever he would get a chance, he would give the wild horse a hit with the whip."

---

8   John Nelson's dictaphone tape #16

"Soon the band of wild horses disappeared over the hill. Uncle Jasper was able to catch his stallion before he could follow the wild horses. Uncle Jasper gathered up what he could of the remains of the harness and put it in a heap, planning to come back later to get it. He couldn't hitch the stallion to the buggy, as it was too badly broken. The stallion had been broken to ride, so after Uncle Jasper got the horse quieted down, he mounted him and rode back to the ranch."

"It was so enjoyable to visit with this kind man and his family and I guess it made me a little homesick for my dear family and the beautiful grassland of Alberta. I have thought of this many times.

Here I was 71,000 miles away from home and to find someone who had been closely associated with my family was such a coincidence."

"We spent the night with this family, and the next morning went back to see if our boat was ready to take us to Savaii. The Captain thought that they had the problem solved, so we set sail again on the same vessel as we had started out on the day before."

A SAILOR'S CONVERSION

"We got about half-way between Upolu and Savaii when the motor stopped again on our ship. There was no wind at all. Without the wind, we were pretty well at a stand still.

For three days, all we did was bounce around out in the ocean with big swells coming up, but we were not making any headway. The sails were hoisted, but without the wind, we could make no progress."

"There was nothing to do but talk and wait for a wind to blow to carry us across the channel. The captain was curious about our activities. We explained that we were Mormon missionaries and had come 71,000 miles away from our homes to teach the gospel of Jesus Christ to the people of Samoa and Tonga. The captain was very interested. As we sat on the deck at night, we used a kerosene lantern to read to him from the Book of Mormon. We spent the next two days teaching him the gospel."

"Finally a wind came up and we were able to resume our journey and in due time, we arrived at our destination.

The Captain made the request that he come ashore with us at Savaii. He asked to be baptized into the Church of Jesus Christ of Latter-day Saints.

We had spent the past several days with him teaching him the gospel; we did not feel that we could deny him baptism. As we landed out in the bay at Upolu, he lowered a little boat and let the natives go ashore. Then he took my companion and me ashore and we went to the baptismal pond by the Mission Home. There I led the Captain into the waters of baptism and baptized him a member of the Church of Jesus Christ of Latter-day Saints. When we came out of the water, I confirmed him a member of the Church."

"He was a man of about 40 years of age. He seemed so happy and pleasant. After he left, he wrote to me many times as I remained on the Islands. He gave me his address where I could write to him. I wrote and gave him instructions where he would find members of the Church and so on. It was my hope that he would remain faithful to his new-found religion."[9]

EXTENDING THE HIGHWAY

"Our Church plantation of 800 acres was located at Soniatu which was about 30 miles down the coast and three miles inland from the Mission Headquarters at Apia. Part of the trail between the two villages was wide enough for a horse to pull a little two-wheeled cart up. However, there was a section of the trail that was so narrow, because of rocks jutting out that the cart had to be unhitched from the horse and left along the way. The horse could then walk

---

9   John Nelson's dictaphone tape #16.

along this very dangerous spot which extended for a distance of about one block."

"During all my years in the Islands, I had been desirous of seeing the trail widened, so that the carts could be pulled safely between the two villages. I knew that, with a great deal of effort, the side-hill could be dug out to make the trail wider. A month or two before I was to be released from my mission, I decided to try something. I planned to take Old Belle, our Mission horse, and the two-wheeled cart and go all of the way to Soniatu with the horse and the cart. I planned to get up early before the natives were on the trail. I got an extra long line attached to Old Belle's bridle. My plan was to walk down under the jagged cliffs and drive her. I would let one wheel of the cart remain up in the path and then I planned to take hold of the other wheel and lift it over the rocks."

"My plan worked like a charm! Old Belle was very gentle and well-trained. As we got to the dangerous, narrow place on the path, I climbed down to the rocks beneath the trail. By talking to Old Belle and lifting the wheel up over some of the larger rocks that stuck out on the seaward side of the trail, I managed to get the cart and the horse across this hazardous spot. I'm sure that it was the first cart that had crossed this particular spot on the trail."

"The natives had never thought about cutting down the hill so that they could travel the whole distance between the two villages with their carts. It would mean a great deal of saving in time if they could transport their produce: bananas, coconuts, and taro, across the trail rather than have to put it all on boats. They had done this for generations in order to get around this dangerous part of the trail."

"As I arrived in the village of Aua with my horse pulling the two-wheeled cart, people came running out to see me. I told them that I had come from Apia.

I stood up on the seat of the cart and said, 'I have a declaration to make to you people here this morning. No one but a Mormon Elder could have crossed that dangerous cliff with a two-wheel cart. I have a plan that would make it possible for all of you to cross with your carts.'"

"I continued talking, 'You must get out on that hazardous trail with your picks and shovels and your crowbars and dig the rocks out of the way. It won't take you too long before you'll have a nice wide road where you can travel just as I did this morning.'"

"They held a council meeting. All of the chiefs gathered around and circled my cart as I stood there. They asked me several questions as to how this could be accomplished. I was invited to go into the chief's home and have kava with them. Kava is the national drink of the South Pacific Islanders. It's a root that grows in the ground. It is taken and dried and then mashed up. To invite someone to share kava with them was a way of showing respect and honor to that person."

"They were very pleased and happy to even think that I, a Mormon Missionary, had traveled that dangerous road in a two-wheeled cart. No one but Old Belle and myself knew the way this had been accomplished.

For a long time, I didn't even tell the missionaries. They all were curious how I was able to get the cart across. Some said that I took the cart apart and carried it over--piece by piece. Then they thought I had taken Old Belle across and then put the cart back together again."

"Taking my suggestion, the natives of Aua began working on the new highway, digging out the hillside. Everyone who could use a shovel or roll rocks into the ocean was helping. When I left the Island, two-wheeled carts were running back and forth along this block of dangerous trail. It was a lesson to me that a little work, regardless of what effort it may take, can be accomplished with teamwork."

"Perhaps the natives of that little village will long remember the Mormon Elder, Misi Nelesona (as I was called) as the man who directed them to tear down the hill and build a wider trail for their benefit."[10]

GIFT OF SIGHT

This testimony was written in a letter to John's daughters on June 15th 1959:

My Dear Daughters:

I have been thinking about a testimony that I desire to write to you about. I have thought of it a hundred times, but have never told it in public. It is very sacred to me and I have always given the Lord the credit for the accomplishment of a very wonderful blessing bestowed upon a very faithful Samoan sister.

In the month of June 1914, while I was presiding over the Samoan and Tongan Missions, I called a Samoan man and his wife, Afatasi and Losa to go on a mission to the Tongan Islands, six-hundred miles from the Samoan group, where they had to learn a new language.

Afatasi was an Elder and a very powerful speaker in his own tongue. Losa was a wonderful mother of several children and a good Latter-day Saint. However, she was blind. We had just finished a wonderful missionary meeting in the chapel where these wonderful people were both set apart for their missions to Tonga.

I had gone upstairs to the office. The mission office and several apartments for the missionaries were on the second floor. For some reason, I arose very suddenly from my chair in the office an, I walked to the head of the stairs just as Losa was coming up feeling her way along the side of the wall. Just as she was about to take the last step up, I reached down and put the fingers of my right hand on her eyes and in the name of Jesus Christ, I commanded her to receive her sight.

---

10   Dictaphone tape #6.

The outcome of this was she went on her mission with the full vision of her eyes. She could read and write as well as any schoolgirl. She performed a wonderful work among the Tongan women and the Lord gave her another special blessing--the gift of the Tongan language, as well as the gift of her eyesight. Her dear husband was also a wonderful missionary and did a great work among the Tongan people.

I testify that I was but an agent for the Lord. It was not my power that bestowed her eyesight, but the power of Jesus Christ. I heeded the spirit's direction and I was the instrument in the Lord's hands to perform this sacred miracle.

I know that the gospel of Jesus Christ is true. I bear this testimony to you, my dear daughters, in the name of Jesus Christ, our Savior! Amen.

I love you,

Dad

A MESSAGE TO MY CHILDREN

"I caught a cold yesterday; however, I shall keep going as rapidly as I can. I wish to have pictures and stories for the benefit of my children and grandchildren, so they will read them later in life. Perhaps they will be inspired by these stories. I would like my children to read them and learn from them. I want them to have stories to tell and talk about as they go about their church duties from time to time."[11]

---

11   John's Dictaphone tape #4/ #16.

MY SUCCESSOR

"On January 1916, the time had come for me to be released as the President of the Samoan and Tongan Islands. It would soon be time for me to return to my Canadian home. I had received a letter from the First Presidency of the Church with the news that they felt the time was right for dividing the Samoan and Tongan Mission. As my successor, they had chosen President Ernest L. Wright to be the President of the Samoan Mission. He and his wife Margaret and their children: E. Lynn, Melvin B., and Fern, would be traveling to Samoa, arriving on the next boat."[12]

This is the letter John received from the First Presidency of the Church of Jesus Christ of Latter-day Saints:

Office of the First Presidency

Church of Jesus Christ of Latter-Day Saints

67 East South Temple Street

Salt Lake City, Utah

February 5, 1916

President John A. Nelson

Samoan Mission

Dear Brother Nelson:

You are hereby honorably released from further acting as President of the Samoan and Tongan Mission. Your release is to take effect as soon as the affairs of the Mission shall be transferred to your successor, Elder Ernest Wright. We have appointed Elder Wright to succeed you as President of the Samoan Mission and who, with his family, also with Elders Edward J. Wood and Joseph H. Dean, leaves today for Samoa.

---

12   John Nelson dictaphone tape #25.

Brother Wood is under a special appointment from us to make a general inspection of the affairs of the Samoan Mission and will be associated with you in the performance of this duty. He bears a letter of appointment to this effect, which he will submit to you for your perusal. When he has completed the work assigned to him, you and he will be at liberty to return home together.

Brother Dean is also under appointment from us to make a special visit to Samoa, as you will perceive from his letter of appointment.

In thus releasing you, it affords us great pleasure, indeed, to say that your labors as missionary and presiding officer are fully appreciated by us, and that we shall be glad to welcome you home again. We pray God, our Heavenly Father, to bless and preserve you and qualify you for future usefulness in His service.

We are,

Your brethren and fellow servants

(signed) Joseph F. Smith

Anthon H. Lund

Charles W. Penrose,

First Presidency of the Church of Jesus Christ of Latter-day Saints

A NEW MISSION PRESIDENT

"The First Presidency had written and asked me to choose a man who was now serving a mission in the Islands, who would be called to preside over the new Tongan Mission. No word was mentioned whether he should be from the Samoan area or from the Tongan area of the mission. In their letter, the First Presidency said that Joseph Dean, who was organizing a new Samoan hymnal, would be coming. Edward J. Wood was also coming to Samoa for a visit. He had been a former missionary and then Mission President in Samoa and was currently President of the Cardston, Alberta, Canada Stake. The Church leaders learned he was coming so they asked him to act as a special ambassador for the First Presidency and to set apart the new Tongan Mission President." [13]

"E. J. Wood and Joseph Dean would be accompanying President and Sister Wright and their family."[14]

John as Mission President, with a companion.

"I was instructed very carefully as to my responsibility in selecting the new Tongan Mission President. The First Presidency advised me to go over the eligible men, one by one, as to their qualifications, their testimony and their ability to preside. I proceeded to follow these

13 John Nelson dictaphone tape #35.
14 Samoa Apia Mission History, 1888 to 1983.

instructions very carefully. They asked me to fast and then to supplicate the Lord in might prayer, for guidance and help in selecting the man who would become President of the Tongan Mission."

"As I went over the eligible names of the missionaries, I wrote them down in a notebook, going over their qualifications very carefully. One of our Elders was Willard L. Smith, from Leavitt, Alberta, Canada. He had been teaching high school in Mapusaga, on the Island of Tutuila, in Samoa. He was a married man. His wife's name was Jennie Leavitt Smith.

Every time I came to the name of Willard Smith, it seemed as though his name stood out as the one eligible for the calling as the new Tongan Mission President."

"I was somewhat disturbed as I remembered, when I first was made Mission President, how desperately the Tongan Saints had wanted a mission of their own so they could have their own Mission President who spoke their language. I felt a great deal of compassion towards their feelings and knew that I must take their desires into consideration. I knew that Willard Smith did not have a knowledge of the Tongan language. However, there was no question in my mind that he was the choice the Lord had made and I, acting through the inspiration of the Lord, was confident that he was the man to be chosen."

"It was only a short time after this decision, that Elder Dean and Elder Wood arrived in Samoa. Immediately upon landing from the ship from Canada, Elder Wood asked me, 'Have you selected a man to be President of the Tongan Mission?'"

"I replied, 'Yes, I have.'"

"He answered back, 'Well, do I know him?'"

"I replied, 'Yes, you do. He's one of your boys from Cardston, Alberta, Canada.' Then I mentioned the name of Willard Smith. This rather surprised President Wood, because Willard Smith had only been in the Samoan Island for only about eleven months and did not speak one word of the Tongan language."

"I knew I had followed the instructions of the First Presidency of the Church very conscientiously and precisely, as to how I would choose the new President. I was sure Willard Smith was the man the Lord wanted to be President of the Tongan Mission."

"Although Elder Wood wasn't sure at first, he later confirmed my decision. Consequently, a meeting was called of all the Elders on the Island of Tutuila, for the purpose of instructing the missionaries and setting apart the new Mission President of the Tongan Islands. Willard G. Smith was set apart as President of the Tongan Mission under the hands of President E. J. Wood, of the Alberta Stake."

"At the meeting as I was speaking, I turned to Brother Smith and said, 'Brother Smith, did you have your patriarchal blessing before you came to the Islands?'"

"He said, 'Yes, I did. When I was eleven-years old, my mother took me to Patriarch Thomas Duce in Cardston, Canada.' I asked him if he might have a copy of that blessing with him. He replied that it was upstairs in his trunk. The chapel was downstairs and we had several rooms upstairs made into apartments where the missionaries lived. I asked him if he would please go up to his apartment and bring the blessing down. It was very interesting to read his blessing. It said, among other things, 'The time will come as you grow older, when you shall go to the Islands of the sea and learn the languages of the people.'"

"I stopped there and asked him if he remembered if the Patriarch really meant languages or should it have been just language?

He said that he remembered very distinctly of his mother going back to the Patriarch to see if that should be left languages? The Patriarch had instructed them to leave it as it was written."[15]

15   John Nelson dictaphone tape #35.

"Brother Smith left leave immediately to his new assignment."

From the <u>Samoa Apia History,</u> 1888 to 1983:

"This then marked the beginning of Tonga as a separate mission. As we have seen the great growth in Tonga, we realize that, truly, that land was ready for the gospel and as of this writing, some 30,000 members of the Church are there now, which is better than one quarter of the total population. The missionary work flourishes with 300 to 400 people a month flocking to the Church and joining through the waters of baptism. Tonga also has a sister temple to one being completed here in Samoa."

BLESSINGS FOR PRESIDENT WILLARD SMITH

"Some of the missionaries who spoke the Tongan language, wondered why President Smith had been selected to serve as the President of the Tongan Islands, when he did not know how to speak that language and had to speak through an interpreter. It was only a very few weeks until President Smith was able to speak, fluently, to the Tongan people in their own tongue. This was a great blessing to the people of that nation and to the Elders who were laboring as missionaries for the Church of Jesus Christ of Latter-day Saints." [16]

Willard and Jessie Smith served a total of 13 years in the Islands; one and a half years to begin in Samoa, four and a half years while he was President of the Tongan Mission, and an additional seven more years back in Samoa.[17]

The Biographical Encyclopedia, page 367, states that John Alexander Nelson, Jr. returned to report his mission to Church Headquarters in Salt Lake City. From there he went on to Cardston, Alberta, Canada where a joyful reunion was held with his family. He had been away from them for six years, three and one-half months. He returned home April 25, 1916.

---

16   John Nelson dictaphone tape #35.
17   Samoa Apia Mission History, p. 35.

ORDAINED TO OFFICE OF HIGH PRIEST

"I was ordained to the office of High Priest, October 15, 1917, by Sterling Williams at Woolford, Alberta, Canada. Sterling Williams was ordained a High Priest February 20, 1894 by John W. Taylor, who was ordained an apostle April 9, 1884 by John Taylor, who was President of the Church. President John Taylor was ordained an apostle December 19, 1838 by President Brigham Young and Heber C. Kimball. Brigham Young was ordained an apostle by Oliver Cowdery, David Whitmore and Martin Harris, who were called by revelation, through the Prophet Joseph Smith, to choose the first 12 Apostles and were blessed to do this ordaining February 14, 1835. These men received the Priesthood under the hands of Peter, James and John, who were ordained by our Savior, Jesus Christ."[18]

JOHN RETURNS HOME: A TIME OF ADJUSTMENT

During days and weeks after John's return from his mission~ he went back to Canada and back to the family farm with his parents. It was likely a difficult adjustment for him to make after having been a missionary to the South Pacific for about six and one-half years. His life had been one of total dedication to the work of the Lord and he had held a very responsible position the past three and one-half years as the President of the Samoan and Tongan Mission.

His parents and brothers and sisters had sacrificed a great deal to keep him on this mission. They felt that it was a blessing and a privilege to support John in his calling as President of the two Islands, even though it meant additional sacrifice on their part to have him stay another three and one-half more years.

John realized the sacrifices that his family had made for him and now he was anxious to be home again and to carry his share of the family work load. With the help of a supportive family, this adjustment period was made easier.

---

18   John Nelson dictaphone tape #25.

John was considered a very eligible bachelor and a little over a year after John's return from his mission, in sunny California, some events were transpiring that would have an eternal impact on John's life.

A beautiful young woman, Vera Wilcox, had received a letter from her sister, Minnie Turner. Minnie lived within a few miles of John's family home. Minnie was expecting another child and she thought it would be a wonderful idea to have her sister come and stay with her and care for the other children when the baby arrived. Vera decided that she needed a change of scenery and a little vacation from her job as a clerk in a department store, so she decided to take Minnie's offer and go to Canada. Her plans were to spend a few weeks there and return to her beloved California.

Thus begins a new chapter in the lives of John Alexander Nelson and his soon-to-be eternal companion, Martha Vera Wilcox.

HUSBAND	Samuel Allen WILCOX		Sheet #1 con't on Sheet #2		Husband	Samuel Allen WILCOX	1819
Born	21 Mar 1819	Place	Norfolk, St. Lawrence, New York		Wife	Martha Bolton PARKER	
Chr		Place			1. ?m/ms		
Mar	17 Jan 1838	Place	Mountain, Dundas, Ontario, Canada		2. LJM		
Died	7 Apr 1898	Place	Cedar Fort, Utah, Utah		Ward		
Bur	9 Apr 1898	Place	Cedar Fort, Utah, Utah		Stake or Mission	Taylorsville Central	

HUSBAND'S FATHER: Silas WILCOX
HUSBAND'S MOTHER: (2) 21 Oct 1872 Anna Christina PETERSEN
HUSBAND'S OTHER WIVES: (1) Martha Bolton PARKER

NAME & ADDRESS OF PERSON SUBMITTING SHEET
Sheila Nelson Zolman
2108 Champagne Circle
SLC, UT 84118

WIFE	(1) Martha Bolton PARKER		
Born	23 Jan 1820	Place	Mountain, Dundas, Ontario, Canada
Chr		Place	
Died	23 Jan 1912	Place	Wardboro, Bear Lake, Idaho
Bur		Place	Cedar Fort, Utah, Utah

WIFE'S FATHER: Joseph PARKER
WIFE'S MOTHER: Lucy BOYD
WIFE'S OTHER HUSBANDS:

RELATION OF ABOVE TO HUSBAND: 2 gg dau
RELATION OF ABOVE TO WIFE: 2 gg dau
FOUR GENERATION SHEET FOR FILING ONLY: YES [x] NO [ ]
DATE SUBMITTED TO GENEALOGICAL SOCIETY:

LDS ORDINANCE DATA

	BAPTIZED (Date)	ENDOWED (Date)	SEALED (to parents)	SEALED (to spouse) (Date)
HUSBAND	14 Sep 1839	6 Feb 1846		26 Jan 1869 EH
WIFE	14 Sep 1839	6 Feb 1846		///////// LG

CHILDREN

SEX	Name	WHEN BORN	WHERE BORN (TOWN)	COUNTY	STATE OR COUNTRY	DATE OF FIRST MARRIAGE / TO WHOM	WHEN DIED	BAPTIZED	ENDOWED	SEALED TO PARENTS	SEALED TO SPOUSE
F	Malinda	5 Dec 1838	Nauvoo	Hancock	Ill.	(1) Isaac PUGH	6 Jul 1888	21 Nov 1967	13 Jun 1870		3 Dec 1884 LG
F	Lucy (stillborn)	1840	"	"	"			stillborn	stillborn		do not seal LG
F	Sarah Jane	24 Oct 1841	"	"	"	7 Mar1859 (1) William ALRED	11 Mar 1931	7 Aug 1864	14 Oct 1880		3 Dec 1884 LG
M	John Dingman	23 Apr 1843	"	"	"	23 Aug 1865 Mary Theodocia SAVAGE	19 Jun 1922	7 Dec 1967	11 May 1867		3 Dec 1884 LG
F	Aseneth Viola	1 Apr 1845	"	" /	"	29 Oct 1865 William PASSEY	27 Aug 1927	21 Nov 1967	2 Feb 1869		17 Oct 1888 LG
M	Adam	11 Feb 1847	Bonapart	V-Brn	Iowa	2 Feb 1880 (1) Eunice Jane DALRYMPLE	17 Jan 1917	7 Aug 1864	1 Jul 1880		3 Dec 1884 LG
X M	Samuel Allen	9 Jan 1850	Hamburg	Fremont	"	30 Jan 1871 Julia Anne LAUGHLIN	28 Oct 1908	7 Aug 1864	8 Mar 1869		3 Dec 1884 LG
M	Joseph	29 Nov 1851	"	"	"	2 Feb 1880 Armina Abigail BALKE	22 Oct 1936	7 Aug 1864	8 Mar 1869		17 Oct 1888 LG
M	Silas McCaslin	10 Jan 1854	"	"	"	unmd	21 Jun 1917	7 Aug 1864	2 Feb 1887		17 Oct 1888 LG
F	Phoebe Roseltha	21 Mar 1857	"	"	"	20 Dec 1875 (1) John BERRY	26 May 1925	27 Aug 1864	20 Dec 1875		17 Oct 1888 LG
M	Boyd Extine	2 Sep 1859	"	"	"	4 Nov 1880 Mary Sophronia DAYTON	3 Nov 1895	16 Feb 1960	4 Nov 1880		17 Oct 1888 LG

OTHER MARRIAGES
#1 md (2) 11 May 1867 James COOK
#3 md (2) 7 Jun 1866 Newton Francis AUSTIN
#6 md (2) 8 Jun 1910 Octavia (Cesaria) CHENEY
#10 md (2) 8 Dec 1888 Lewis CHRISTIE
#12 md (2) 8 Jan 1901 Martha Sarah HANSEN

SOURCES OF INFORMATION
1. Personal Fam Rec in poss of Mrs. Jackson, Pocatello, Idaho
2. Cedar Fort Ward Rec (GS 025,566) husb, wife, child #11,12
3. Utah L3A p. 166; F Utah SIL p. 206
4. Logan Temple Sealings
5. Cedar Fort Cemetery Records
6. Idaho Vital Statistics
7. SL Slg of Lvg couples p. 245

NECESSARY EXPLANATIONS

3/80

| HUSBAND | Samuel Allen WILCOX | | Sheet #1 con't on Sheet #2 |

HUSBAND	Samuel Allen WILCOX								Husband	Samuel Allen WILCOX		1819

Born __21 Mar 1819__ Place __Norfolk, St. Lawrence, New York__
Chr. _____ Place _____
Mar. __17 Jan 1838__ Place __Mountain, Dundas, Ontario, Canada__
__7 Apr 1898__ Place __Cedar Fort, Utah, Utah__
Died __9 Apr 1898__ Place __Cedar Fort, Utah, Utah__
Bur. _____ Place _____

HUSBAND'S FATHER __Silas WILCOX__   HUSBAND'S MOTHER __Margaret Belinda ALLEN__
HUSBAND'S OTHER WIVES __(2) 21 Oct 1872 Anna Christina PETERSEN__

WIFE __(1) Martha Bolton PARKER__
Born __23 Jan 1820__ Place __Mountain, Dundas, Ontario, Canada__
Chr. _____ Place _____
Died __23 Jan 1912__ Place __Wardboro, Bear Lake, Idaho__
Bur. _____ Place __Cedar Fort, Utah, Utah__

WIFE'S FATHER __Joseph PARKER__   WIFE'S MOTHER __Lucy BOYD__
WIFE'S OTHER HUSBANDS

Husband	Samuel Allen WILCOX
Wife	Martha Bolton PARKER
Ward	1. _Jones_
Examiners	2. LJW
Stake or Mission	Taylorsville Central

RELATION OF ABOVE TO HUSBAND __2 gg dau__ RELATION OF ABOVE TO WIFE __2 gg dau__
FOUR GENERATION SHEET FOR FILING ONLY   YES [X]   NO [ ]
DATE SUBMITTED TO GENEALOGICAL SOCIETY

NAME & ADDRESS OF PERSON SUBMITTING SHEET
Sheila Nelson Zolman
2108 Champagne Circle
SLC, UT 84118

LDS ORDINANCE DATA

	BAPTIZED (Date)	ENDOWED (Date)	SEALED (Date and Temple) WIFE TO HUSBAND
HUSBAND	14 Sep 1839	6 Feb 1846	26 Jan 1869 EH
WIFE	14 Sep 1839	6 Feb 1846	SEALED (Date and Temple) CHILDREN TO PARENTS
	22 Jun 1888	17 Oct 1888	17 Oct 1888 LG

SEX M F	CHILDREN List each child (whether living or dead) in order of birth Given Names SURNAME	WHEN BORN			WHERE BORN			DATE OF FIRST MARRIAGE	WHEN DIED		
		DAY	MONTH	YEAR	TOWN	COUNTY	STATE OR COUNTRY	TO WHOM	DAY	MONTH	YEAR
1	David Almearn WILCOX	11	Oct	1862	Cedar Fort	Utah	Utah	7 Jun (1) Florence Malinda COOK	11	Nov	1884
2											
3											
4											
5											
6											
7											
8											
9											
10											
11											

SOURCES OF INFORMATION
See Sheet #1

OTHER MARRIAGES
See Sheet #1

NECESSARY EXPLANATIONS
See Sheet #1

3/80

FAMILY GROUP RECORD 1972 The Genealogical Department of The Church of Jesus Christ of Latter-day Saints
PFG50020 2-78 100M Printed in the United States of America

HUSBAND	(1) Samuel Allen WILCOX (Farmer)		Husband	Samuel Allen WILCOX
Born	21 Mar 1819	Place Norfolk, St. Lawrence, New York	Wife	Annie Christina PETERSEN	1817

Chr.		Place		Ward	1.	
Mar	21 Oct 1872	Place Salt Lake City, Salt Lake, Utah		Examiner	2.	LIN
Died	7 Apr 1898	Place Cedar Fort, Utah, Utah		State or Mission Taylorsville Central	NAME & ADDRESS OF PERSON SUBMITTING SHEET
Bur.	9 Apr 1898	Place Cedar Fort, Utah, Utah			Shelia Nelson Zolman

HUSBAND'S FATHER (1) Silas WILCOX   HUSBAND'S MOTHER Margaret Belinda ALLEN   2108 Champagne Circle   SLC, UT 84118

HUSBAND'S OTHER WIVES (2) Anna Christina PETERSEN

RELATION OF ABOVE TO HUSBAND 2 gg dau   RELATION OF ABOVE TO WIFE step 2 gg dau

WIFE	(2) Anna Christina PETERSEN		FOUR GENERATION SHEET FOR FILING ONLY YES ☒ NO ☐
Born	18 Mar 1856	Place Vridslosemagle, Sengelose, Copenhagen, Denmark
Chr.		Place	DATE SUBMITTED TO GENEALOGICAL SOCIETY
Mar		Place Lehi, Utah, Utah
Died	13 Oct 1934	Place Cedar Fort, Utah, Utah
Bur.	16 Oct 1934	Place Cedar Fort, Utah, Utah

WIFE'S FATHER Ole PEDERSEN   WIFE'S MOTHER Maren HANSEN

WIFE'S OTHER HUSBANDS

LDS ORDINANCE DATA

	BAPTIZED	ENDOWED	SEALED (Date) CHILDREN TO PARENTS
HUSBAND	14 Sep 1839	6 Feb 1846	21 Oct 1872 EH
WIFE	22 Mar 1868	21 Oct 1872	

SEX	CHILDREN List each child (whether living or dead) in order of birth Given Names	SURNAME	WHEN BORN DAY MONTH YEAR	WHERE BORN TOWN	COUNTY	STATE OR COUNTRY	DATE OF FIRST MARRIAGE TO WHOM	WHEN DIED DAY MONTH YEAR	BAPTIZED	ENDOWED	SEALED TO HUSBAND WIFE TO HUSBAND
1 F	Anna Laura	WILCOX	18 Jan 1874	Cedar Fort	Utah	Utah	4 Jan 1893 Fredrick CALTON	29 Feb 1948	6 Aug 1882	4 Jan 1893	BIC
2 F	Margaret Maren	WILCOX	11 Dec 1875	"	"	"	4 Jan 1893 John BREMS	9 Feb 1962	1 Nov 1885	4 Jan 1893	BIC
3 M	James Alfred	WILCOX	10 Oct 1877	"	"	"	1911 Beatha Agnes MATHEWS (div)	31 Aug 1949	1 Nov 1885	21 Sep 1966	BIC
4 F	Bertha Charlotta	WILCOX	8 Oct 1879	"	"	"	18 Oct 1897 (1) Samuel ANDERSON	28 Nov 1925	2 Jun 1888	1 Jun 1910	BIC
5 F	Martha Cordella	WILCOX	25 Dec 1881	"	"	"	19 Jul 1903 Joseph M. STEPHENS		14 Sep 1890		BIC
6 F	Mary Inger	WILCOX	19 Mar 1884	"	"	"	20 May 1903 (1) Eugene SABEY	10 Feb 1963	3 Apr 1893	16 Nov 1906	BIC
7 M	Ross Earnest	WILCOX	13 Apr 1886	"	"	"	unmd		30 Jul 1897	21 Sep 1966	BIC
8 F	Helen Mar	WILCOX	8 Sep 1888	"	"	"	14 Sep 1907 John Henry YATES	10 Oct 1968	30 Jul 1897	24 Mar 1971	BIC
9 M	Ole Able	WILCOX	23 Nov 1890	"	"	"	16 Sep 1914 Nellie Louisa YOUNG	16 Nov 1914	27 May 1899	3 Apr 1919	BIC
10											
11											

SOURCES OF INFORMATION
1. Cedar Fort Ward Rec (CS 025,566) husb, wife, child #1-3,5-9
2. Family rec of Mary Inger Wilcox Sabey
3. Sheet copied from Samuel Allen Wilcox Fam Bulletin #7, 1950
4. Sengelose Par Reg (GSF #8872 pt 4)
5. LDS Dec Memb F #385 child #8; #48 child #2; #65 child #1.

OTHER MARRIAGES
#6 md (2) 30 Apr 1908 Joseph CALTON
#4 md (2) 1 Jun 1910 Mathew FJELDSTED

NECESSARY EXPLANATIONS
Wife added Christina to her name la

3/80

10

VERA'S HERITAGE TO BE PROUD OF

WILCOX AND PARKER FAMILIES

Vera, like John, was "born of goodly parents." "As ye remember them . . . and . . . their works. . . ye may know that they were good.[1] Vera always spoke fondly of her heritage and felt she was blessed to have come from such good people. In learning about Vera's ancestors, one will better understand Vera.

Vera's paternal grandfather was Samuel Allen Wilcox, Sr. Hi was born March 22, 1819 in Norfolk, St. Lawrence County, New York, a son of Silas Wilcox and Margaret Belinda Allen. Little is known of Samuel's family until 1839. We do know that Samuel Allen Wilcox, Sr. crossed over the St. Lawrence River and became acquainted with Martha Parker who lived at Mountain, District of Dundas, Ontario, Canada and they were married January 17, 1838.

The Wilcox and the Parker families were highly respected, well-to-do residents of Eastern Canada. These families were religiously inclined

---

1   Helaman 5:6, <u>Book of Mormon.</u>

and had accepted the Methodist religion. Samuel and Martha tried to live as close to the Lord as they could, but they felt that there was something lacking in their lives. They thought the gospel should be the same as Christ taught when He was upon the earth and they didn't find this in the Methodist religion.

Thus, one day William Snow and Christopher Merkeley, who were Mormon missionaries, came to their homes in 1839. Samuel and Martha were ready to accept the truth of the gospel as set forth by these humble young elders. [2]

SAMUEL ALLEN WILCOX, SR. AND MARTHA PARKER

Samuel Allen Wilcox, Sr.
Vera's Paternal Grandfather

Martha Parker
Vera's Paternal Grandmother

Martha Parker wrote, "My husband, Samuel Allen Wilcox, and I were baptized into the Church [L.D.S.] 14 Oct. 1839. My father and mother and my husband's father and mother were baptized soon after. Then we had a great desire to go to the new state of Illinois and see the Prophet of God. Thus we sold our pleasant home and in company with my father and mother, Joseph Parker and Lucy Boyd and Asenath, my sister, Sam's father and mother and their other 4 children . . . 14 in all, we left for Nauvoo, then called 'Commerce.' We traveled fifteen hundred miles in our wagons, starting on the 15th day of August and reaching Commerce on the 9th day of October, 1840."[3]

As they neared Nauvoo, they met a number of people leaving. The people told them that they had better go back to their homes for

2   Wilcox Family Bulletin, 1952-1953.
3   Ibid.

Joseph Smith was a fallen prophet, and the church was falling to pieces. The Wilcox and Parker families decided to on to Nauvoo to see for themselves. When they had seen and heard the Prophet Joseph Smith speak, they were assured that he was indeed a Prophet of God and they always retained that testimony.

Martha Parker Wilcox wrote in her journal, Wardboro, Idaho, March 12, 1907, "The Saints had just had their conference and there was great rejoicing amongst them when we arrived in Nauvoo, for the Prophet of God had just revealed the law of baptism for the dead. Such rejoicing I had never seen before.

We arrived on a Friday and on the next Sabbath we went to see and hear the Prophet. He said there had to be a temple built with baptismal fonts to do this work, like Solomon had in his temple.

The Saints commenced right off to prepare for the building of the Temple at Nauvoo. When it was built, my husband and I had our endowments in that holy house."[4]

DAYS IN NAUVOO

Martha continued, "The female Relief Society was organized and I had the privilege of being a member of that first organization. The first I met with them was in the upper room of the house of the Prophet Joseph Smith. Sister Emma Smith was the President."

She also recorded, "The last time I heard the Prophet Joseph Smith speak, he asked the brethren if they would die for him. No one answered. Then he quoted the words of the Savior, when he said, 'Greater love hath no man than this: that he lay down his life for his friends.' Then Joseph asked again, 'Would you lay down your life for me?'"

"It seemed to me that the whole congregation with one voice cried, 'Yes.' 'It is well,' he said, 'then I will die for you.'" Martha wrote.

4   Ibid.

In another record, Martha recorded, "We saw the Prophet and heard his voice. Oh, how can I describe the feeling that thrilled through my soul when I heard his voice and knew I was sitting in the presence of a Prophet of God. I had often wept when I was a child to think that I could never see a Prophet of God. But now my eyes, my own eyes, could see a Prophet, yea, more a seer, a translator and a revelator, and a messenger to the nations."[5]

Martha wrote in her journal, "I was baptized by Joseph the Prophet in the Mississippi River for a renewal of my covenants and also for 20 of my dead friends."

January 1, 1881 at the age of 61, Martha wrote a wonderful letter telling of her life and experiences in Nauvoo and of her testimony of the divinity of the Church of Jesus Christ of Latter-Day Saints. This letter was sealed in a box prepared by the General Board of the Relief Society along with many other letters to be opened fifty years later. Martha instructed that after the box was opened, her letter would be delivered to her granddaughter, Martha Wilcox (Martha's namesake).

The following is from this letter:

"The spirit of Mobocracy was prevalent throughout the nations and wherever a servant of God went to preach the gospel they were greatly persecuted. Enemies took every advantage to cheat and rob those who had gathered together. Then came the terrible trials when the Prophet was killed with his brother Hyrum, Patriarch of the Church. They were holy and innocent men. Their blood stains the whole U. S. A. and will never be wiped out until the God of Heaven cleanses the earth. Our Prophet and Patriarch were slain. I saw them in their gore and the wicked and ungodly mob threatened to annihilate the whole Church. There were wolves among the members of the Church who entered into the flock of God to destroy it, but the hand of God was over us

5   Ibid.

and He raised up the twelve apostles and anointed them to lead and feed the flock of God."

"I was there when Sidney Rigdon made his claim as guardian of the Church.

I was there when Brigham Young returned from the field and preached to the Saints and was transfigured before that host of Saints. I saw it with my own eyes and sprang to my feet for I thought it was Joseph.

It soon passed and I knew it was Brigham. We were given a certain number of days to leave the state or they would burn our city. Brigham Young, who was called the 'Lion of the Lord' because he stood up boldly in defense of Israel, led us from our city."[6]

EXODUS FROM NAUVOO

Sarah Jane [Martha and Samuel Wilcox's daughter], wrote:

"During the time of the great trouble just prior to and just after the death of the Prophet, there was an understanding that at the sound of the fife and drum the men would gather at the place designated and hold a consultation and make plans for the safety of the people.

I remember seeing my father grab his hat and run and my mother turn pale and tremble so she could hardly stand.

I will never forget some of those scenes when the mob would set fire to hay or grain stacks. I would get as close to mother as I could and I felt safe if I could get hold of her dress. We left Nauvoo in 1846. President Brigham Young counseled the people to have sea-biscuits baked and the corn parched, ground and sacked so it could be carried easily. We had ten large sacks of this meal. My father had a good team and wagon and a good milk cow which he brought with him. Mother and Father had four children. Everything was left in the house except our clothes and bedding.

---

6   Samuel Allen Wilcox Bulletin, 1952-1953.

We were starting out into a wild region; we traveled through a trackless prairie. In many places the grass was so high that my father had to stand in the seat place on top of the wagon-bed in order to get his bearings."

"After crossing the river with the saints, we went to a place called Bonaparte in Van Buren Co., Iowa. Winter was upon us. We didn't have a tent or a cover for the wagon, so Father went to the timbers and got some logs and willows and set four good sized logs on the ground and as many others as were needed.

He wove willows tight and firm between the poles and then plastered it inside and out with black mud, sand and clay and then he made a fireplace out of some thick heavy sod and clay. He had a window and a door in the house. He strained the light through the window with a piece of white cloth. It was here another daughter, Asenath was born."

"When he had the family comfortable, he went in search of work. He found a man who wanted a man and team to do some hauling. In one week, after he finished his hauling, it came time to settle up. The man found out that Sam was a Mormon. He said, 'I will not pay a 'G.D. Mormon' one cent.' Father had to come home without a mouth full of anything to eat. In three or four days another man wanted some hauling done. He came and asked Father if he could do some hauling for him. Father said he would be glad to. He told this stranger that his circumstances for food were very poor and the stranger gave him a sack of flour and groceries to help him along. ; He worked until the hauling was done."[7]

"The man told Sam to take what was right. He said he should know how much he owed Sam for he had not kept account. The man said, 'Whatever you think is right, goes with me.' Sam went home and he and Martha figured it all up and the man had paid him one hundred dollars over his wages. Sam took it back to the man and the man

---

7   Ibid.

laughed and said, 'Mr. Wilcox, you are the most honest man I ever saw. There is not one in a thousand who would do that.'"[8]

A NEW HOME FOR WILCOX FAMILY

In the fall of 1847, the Wilcox family left Bonaparte and went to Ferryville, opposite winter Quarters, where Samuel Allen Sr. built a log house. There they remained until the spring of 1848. They were not yet prepared for the long journey across the plains so they went down the Missouri River and rented a farm with a small stream called Keg Creek, in Mills County, Iowa. They stayed on this farm until 1850 when they moved 35 miles down the river into Fremont County. The town was later called Hamburg.

It was here that Martha gave birth to Vera's progenitor, Samuel Allen Wilcox, Jr. on March 9, 1850. By this time, Martha had given birth to six children: Malina born Dec. 5, 1838 in Mountain, Ontario, Canada, Lucy was stillborn in Nauvoo, 1840, Sarah Jane was born in Nauvoo on October 24, 1841, John Dingman was born on April 23, 1843 in Nauvoo, Asenath Viola was born April 1, 1845 in Nauvoo, Adam was born February 10, 1845 in Bonaparte, Iowa, and then Samuel Allen, Jr., who was born in Hamburg, Iowa. Four more children were born in Hamburg: Joseph, born November 30, 1851, Silas McCaslin, born January 10, 1854, Phebe Reseltha born March 21, 1857, and Boyd Extine born September 2, 1859.[9]

Their two eldest daughters, who were married by this time, left home in Hamburg with their husbands headed for California. They had some incredible experiences as they crossed the plains.[10]

---

8   Asenath's Journal, Wilcox Family Bulletin, 1952-1953.
9   Wilcox Family Bulletin, 1952-1953.
10   Wilcox Family Bulletin, 1952.

WAR CLOUDS GATHER

Back in Hamburg, life went on much as usual except that Martha and Sam missed their two daughters. Everything went well until the Civil War clouds began to gather. One day in the winter of 1860 while on one of his freighting trips in the town of Sidney, Samuel heard the news that the South Carolina had seceded from the Union on December 20, 1860. This news brought forcibly to his mind the prophecy of Joseph Smith that there be would be a Civil War between the North and the South. When he returned home, he told his wife, "Well, Mother, we must get out of here for South Carolina has seceded just as Joseph said they would."

Then one day in the spring (probably a week or so after April 12, 1861 when the first shots of the Civil War were fired), Sam came home from one of his freighting trips to St. Joseph, Missouri, and said, "Mother, you can start packing. We are going West."

"The United States is at war. The first gun was fired at Fort Sumter, South Carolina, just as the Prophet prophesied. If we don't leave now, we may never be able to go."

They had been making some preparations, and now they sold their lovely farm, getting what cash they could and taking cattle for the remainder.

THE LONG, TIRESOME JOURNEY

The family went first to Winter Quarters where they joined the David H. Cannon Company and started across the plains. It was a long, slow journey. The boys drove the cattle, Sam drove one team and wagon, and Martha drove the other.

The long and hard trip across the plains is told about in detail in the Wilcox Family Bulletin of 1952-53. The Wilcox family arrived in Salt Lake City on October 7, 1861. Hearing there was good feed for their cattle and horses in Cedar Valley, they proceeded there and

*Samuel Allen Wilcox, Sr.
Born March 21, 1819, St. Lawrence
County, New York. Came to Utah Oct. 7,
1861, David H. Cannon Company. Missionary to Canada 1868. Farmer*

*John Dingham Wilcox
Son of Samuel Allen Wilcox and Martha
Parker. Born April 23, 1843, Nauvoo, Ill.
Came to Utah Oct. 7, 1861.*

located at Camp Floyd which had just been vacated by Johnston's Army. On the way there, they met the Army at the point of the mountain between Salt Lake Valley and Utah Valley, as the Army was on its way back East.

From the book, Pioneers and Prominent Men in Utah--1861, we found a picture of Samuel Allen Wilcox, Sr. and his son, John Dingham Wilcox, with the notations above.

At Cedar Fort, Sam and his boys owned and operated a sawmill. All the water they had was from the spring that still waters the town of Cedar Fort. They would run the water all night into a pond and then run it out over the wheel the next day to make power for the mill. Sometimes the logs, as they were hauled from the canyon and piled by the mill, would have large patches of gum on them. The children would pick the pine gum off with sticks, take it home, put it in a tin can or cup and melt it on the stove. After it was melted, one of the daughters, Phebe, would take a clean cloth and strain it while it was hot, taking all of the bark particles out. After it was cooled, it was ready for chewing. This was one of their delicacies.

Most of the fruit used in winter had to be dried in the s u m m e r. This work fell to the women, the girls, and little Joseph. They would gather the wild berries, put them in muslin bags and hang them on the clothes line or other place where the air could circulate and they had to be stirred or shaken every day to prevent molding. They raised their own popcorn and sugar cane. In the fall when the apples were ripe, they would have what they called "apple bees." The young people would gather at one place or another. Someone would be seen popping corn or making molasses candy, while the crowd was peeling apples to be dried for the winter, then all would join in pulling the candy.

The Wilcox family was happy in Cedar Fort.

Samuel Allen Wilcox, Sr. was a man of quiet disposition who never meddled in other people's affairs. His twinkling eyes were surrounded with smile wrinkles. He was a staunch and true Latter-Day Saint. He never let an opportunity go by without bearing his testimony to the truthfulness of the Gospel. He served in the bishopric for many years.

Martha Wilcox was president of the Primary for many years and did a great deal of good with the children. She was also Relief Society President for many years and many times dressed the dead. But perhaps her most outstanding work was among the Indians. She had a school for them at her home and taught them to read and write and do simple problems in arithmetic. How they did love her! When any Indian came to the village, their first act was to call on the "Big Squaw" as they called her. She always cooked a fine meal for them and treated them as honored guests.[11]

---

11   Ibid.

ANOTHER MISSION FOR SAMUEL, SR.

Samuel Allen, Sr. was ordained a High Priest on January 6, 1867. He was later called to serve a mission to Eastern Canada. He left for Canada On October 30, 1871. In the journal he kept while he was on his mission, he recorded that one evening he was very tired. He rented a room and slept. It so happened that there were gas lights in the room and they were not shut off tightly. When he awakened he was very sick. He never fully recovered from that experience during the rest of his mission.

The weather was bitter cold and so was the prejudice against the Mormons. He visited many of his relatives; brothers, sisters, aunts, uncles and cousins. When he went to Hamburg, Iowa, he visited his old home.

He said, "I looked at the sight of my old place which brought many memories of when my family lived there. The place was all one big cornfield. I said in my heart, 'What is that all worth? In my eyes, nothing at all.

I would not give up one principle of the gospel for the whole of this fine farm which I left to go west with the saints."[12]

ANNIE CHRISTINA PETERSON, SAM'S 2ND WIFE

Samuel Allen Wilcox, St. returned to Cedar Fort three days after he celebrated his 53rd birthday, March 22, 1872. On October 21, 1872, he married as a second wife, Annie Christina Peterson, daughter of Oli Peterson and Marn Hansen. Annie was only sixteen years old at the time of the marriage.

The day after Samuel and Annie were married, Martha, his first wife, left for Iowa to visit her sister Asenath. However, on page 16 of the Samuel Allen Wilcox Bulletin, 1952-53 the following is written,

---

12   Ibid.

"Martha and Annie got along very well. Sam provided a house for Annie; Martha continued living in her own home."

Many of Sam and Martha's children were already married and having children of their own when Sam and Annie began having their children. Annie and Sam were the parents of nine children. Martha and Sam were parents of eleven children.[13]

The following story is about when Annie was a baby as her family crossed the plains. Annie's parents were Oli and Marn Peterson. They joined the church in Verengle, Denmark in 1854. Annie was born March 18, 1856. One day as the family was on their way to church, they noticed some of their friends talking very excitedly. They were talking about a ship that was sailing from Liverpool, England in a month or so bound for America which had accommodations for about 550. This was an answer to Oli and Marn's prayers as they had a great desire to follow the Prophet and to join with the main body of the Church in Utah.

When the Westmoreland sailed for America in April, 1857, Oli, Marn and baby, Annie Christina, were among the 544 saints, directed by Mathias Cowley, headed for Zion. They were seven weeks in crossing.

After many delays, they joined a wagon train headed for Utah. Days passed and Oli, who was young, strong and high-spirited, never gave way to weariness, but was always ready to help and cheer others. His love for Marn and family grew deeper with each mile of hardship they so bravely endured.

Grave was the concern when the dysentery spread through the company and baby Annie was stricken. Bitter, indeed, was the afternoon when she was declared DEAD.

"Sister Peterson, the Lord giveth and the Lord taketh away," counseled the company leader. "He has called your baby home. We have been delayed too long now. We haven't time to dig a grave. Besides, if

13   Ibid

the Indians found a newly dug grave they would know how recently we had passed by here and follow us.

Wrap your baby in a blanket and place her under this heavy brush, so she cannot be seen and hurry along," commanded the leader.

The grief stricken parents did as they were bid and journeyed on. At the night camp, friends tried to console the bereaved couple who had started out with such glorious anticipation for this new land, but who since beginning the trip, had lost their newborn son, and now their loving, gentle Annie.

Poor Marn. As the camp sang the much loved song, "Come, Come Ye Saints," despair was in her heart and her voice refused to join in. "And should we die, before our journey's through, Happy Day, All is Well!"

All was not well! This kept gnawing at her soul. "But if our lives are spared again to see the Saints, their rest obtain, Oh, how we'll make this chorus swell--All is Well! All is well!" Why did the last part of the song keep running through her mind as if it was trying to tell her something?

One by one, the Saints retired to their wagons, leaving Oli and Marn still seated by the campfire. Suddenly Marn spoke, "Oli, I can't feel our baby was dead." "I know dear," said Oli gently, "we had so many plans, but she is dead, and there is nothing we can do about it now but pray that we will be able to raise a family when we settle in Zion. Come to the wagon so you will be refreshed for tomorrow's travel." Wearily Marn started for the wagon.

"Oli, listen to those wolves, and our baby is lying back there alone, not even protected by a grave. How can we stand to go on?"

"We must make up our minds to go on and trust in the Lord for the rest," he said.

"I can't, Oli." Gently, but firmly Oli took her by the arm and led her to the wagon. Sometime in the early dawn, Oli awoke. Marn's place in bed was empty. Fear grasped Oli as he sprung out of bed and ran among the camp, frantically calling, "Marn! Marn!" But no answer came. The Saints hurriedly arose and joined in the search about the camp. Finally someone shouted, "There she comes," as they looked down the long dusty road they had traveled the previous day. Marn, her baby clutched to her breast and stumbling with weariness, was coming toward the camp. Oli ran to Marn and helped her to the campfire. "Darling, why didn't you awaken me and tell me you were going back to the baby?" Oli asked. Suddenly a look of amazement spread across his face. As his eager hands reached for the baby, his words confirmed his discovery, "Our baby! She's warm! She isn't still and cold like dead babies are! She is alive!"

"Brother Peterson, this is a miracle. I was positive your baby was dead yesterday, but she is alive now and a change for the good has come over her body. Her sojourn here in life has not been completed. May God's choicest blessings descend upon her and help her to live and finish her mission here on earth," said the camp leader, then he walked humbly away to attend to the other affairs of the camp.

Eventually Salt Lake City was reached, but the Petersons followed the old stage route to Cedar Fort before their journey was completed. Annie spent her first six years in Cedar Fort and then the family moved to Lehi, where they lived in a dugout with a dirt floor. Shortly after her 9th birthday, they moved back to Cedar Fort. They never went hungry for food, but sometimes were pretty close to it. Through all their trials and hardships, Annie's parents never complained, and when asked to tell of their sad experiences, they would say they were not to be remembered. Oli and Marn were blessed with three other children. Baby Annie grew to maturity and at the age of sixteen was married for time and all eternity to Samuel Allen Wilcox, Sr. in 1872.

In her later years Annie became a healer, often traveling by night to minister to the needs of her neighbors. On her gravestone in the Cedar Fort Cemetery it is recorded how wolves would approach her during these dark errands of mercy, and would even lick the hand that held her lantern, but they never bothered her any more than they did when she was a baby, bundled under the brush by the side of the trail West.

Annie and Sam were the parents of nine children, three boys and six girls.

Samuel Allen Wilcox Sr. and his second wife, Annie Christine Peterson, and their nine children. Samuel died when he was 79 years old. Annie lived another 36 years as a widow, dying at the age of 78 on Oct. 13, 1934.

DEDICATION OF THE SALT LAKE TEMPLE

Samuel and Martha attended the dedication of the Salt Lake Temple with some of their children and grandchildren. Martha Wilcox Hacking remembered that the following members of the family were at the dedication: Grandfather and Grandmother Wilcox, Aunt Sally Austin, Samuel Allen, Jr., Boyd, Father (John Wilcox), Mother (Mary Savage Wilcox), Os (John and Mary's son), Melissa (Os's wife). "We had hired two rooms on Mercury Row and all had a jolly time there together. We bought food and ate in the rooms. We joked and laughed and even danced. Uncle Sam seized Aunt Sally by the waist and commenced waltzing with her, and Aunt Sally said, 'Why, Sammy, and you a bishop!'" [No form of dancing but square-dancing was allowed in the Church at this time.]

Concerning the dedication, Martha wrote: "I was greatly impressed by the beauty and splendor of the temple and the sacred ordinance of dedication. The day I went through the temple, Joseph F. Smith, counselor to President Woodruff, later President of the Church, gave the dedicatory prayer. I was thrilled at the opportunity of listening to it."

No doubt it was an inspirational, experience for the other family members also.[14]

DEATH COMES TO SAM

On October 7, 1898, Samuel Allen Wilcox, Sr. passed away as a result of a stroke. His sojourn on earth lasted 79 years from March 21, 1819 to April 7, 1898. His life was one of quiet dedication and devotion. He was a noble patriarch, the husband of two wives and the father of twenty children, eleven with Martha and nine with his second wife, Annie. Martha and Annie both survived him.

Annie especially missed Samuel as she was left alone to raise the five children she still had at home, the youngest, eight years old. Annie lived to be 78 years old. She died on October 13, 1934.

14   Ibid.

MARTHA PARKER WILCOX'S TESTIMONY

On June 28, 1907, which was five years before Martha's death, Martha Parker Wilcox wrote a letter of testimony to the "Liahona Magazine." The editors introduced the letter as follows:

"We are in receipt of a somewhat remarkable letter under date of Wardboro, Idaho, June 28, 1907, propounding a series of questions and adding some historical data and testimony which we think, to the reflecting person, will be sufficient answer to the queries. It is written by SISTER MARTHA PARKER WILCOX, a white-haired mother in Israel, who is well on her way to the four score and tenth milestone, and who, with trembling hand, but unabated fervor, leaves her dying testimony to all who may read. Her style is quaint and her forms of expression may not stand the test of rhetoric, but her words have the ring of truth and sincerity."

[Martha, in her letter, recounts how prophets and apostles have been persecuted down through the ages because Satan strives to destroy the work of God. She then concludes with the following witness of the restoration:]

"Now, in the dispensation of the fullness of times, God, our Heavenly Father, has raised up a holy priesthood after the order of the Son of God, which is after the order of an endless life; and commanded him to ordain elders and send them forth to all the nations of the Gentiles to warn them to repent and prepare for the coming of the Son of Man, which is drawing near, and the return of the House of Israel to build the temple that Malachi saw in vision, and which must be built before the coming of the Son of Man."

"The Lord whom ye seek, shall suddenly come to his temple; even the messenger of the covenant, whom ye delight in. That glorious day is now dawning for all Israel.

O! Glorious day which prophets long foretold. I cannot live to see the gathering of the House of Israel, but I remember when our beloved Prophet sent Apostle Orson Hyde to Jerusalem with power from on high to dedicate the land of Jerusalem for the gathering of the House of Israel, in the last days for the last time.

They have been gathering ever since, just as the Prophet Isaiah said they would, one by one, until there are now many thousands of them in Jerusalem, and they are still gathering, but they are very sorely persecuted by the Gentiles on account of the death of the Savior. The Gentiles forget that they nailed Him to the cross, and that a Gentile pierced his side with a spear."

"Dear 'Liahona,' I hope you will forgive my poor writing and all mistakes, for my hand trembles, and I am now in my eighty-seventh year, and am failing. But I know that Joseph Smith was a true prophet of God and like all the holy prophets he was hated without cause, and persecuted to the death. All the believing Saints loved him as they loved their own lives, and he loved them for the love of God filled his soul; and he died pure and unspotted.

The last time I heard him preach, he said to the brethren: 'Will you die for me?' No response. He talked on a little while and then said, 'Would you be willing to die for me?' The whole congregation cried out, 'Yes.' 'Tis well,' he said, 'Then I will die for you.'"

"Before he was martyred, after the Saints had been driven from their homes, and a small town of two hundred houses had been burned down, and many of the Saints had died of hunger and exposure, and quite a few had apostatized, so that some of the quorums of the Priesthood had become disorganized, Joseph filled up the quorums and set the Church in order. He said, 'Now, I have got this Church properly organized. All earth and hell combined can never overthrow it. If they kill the First Presidency, there comes the Twelve next and if they kill the Twelve then the Seventies.'

"Dear 'Liahona,' If you cannot read this, throw it in the waste basket, but I felt as though I loved the name of Liahona and hope it will prosper and do a mighty work in its day."

Your friend and well wisher, MARTHA WILCOX[15]

MARTHA DIES

Martha, Samuel's first wife, lived for fourteen years after Samuel died. She died January 23, 1912, the night of her 92nd birthday. In Martha's patriarchal blessing, she was promised that she would live as long as she wanted to. The night of her death she gathered her family around her, blessed them and read a verse from the Bible, turned her face toward the wall and went to sleep. She went off so easily, the family hardly knew when she breathed her last breath, which was shortly after midnight January 23, 1912.[16]

DAVID SAUNDERS LAUGHLIN

David Saunders Laughlin was Vera's maternal grandfather. He was born on April 28, 1816 in New Hampshire, probably in or near Hillsborough County, since the 1790 census shows four families by the name of Laughlin residing in that county of New Hampshire, and only in that county in the year 1790.

He joined the Church of Jesus Christ of Latter-Day Saints at an early age in Kirtland, Ohio. David experienced the persecutions that attended those who dared to espouse the new religion called "MORMONISM" and accepted Joseph Smith as the prophet of God. He was with the saints who were driven from Kirtland and who settled in Far West, Missouri.

It was during this time that he met and married Mary Clark, who was born in April of 1821. They moved to Nauvoo, Illinois with the Saints, where Mary passed away, July 14, 1845 at the age of 24

---

15   Ibid.
16   Ibid.

years, 2 months and 3 days of fever (according to the newspaper, "Nauvoo Neighbor," July 16, 1845).

David Laughlin was with the Saints when they were driven from Nauvoo by the mobs. On July 16, 1846, he enlisted in the Mormon Battalion as a private in Company "D" with Nelson Higgins as Captain. Illness overtook David during the long, arduous march of the Battalion and at Santa Fe he was transferred to Captain James Brown's sick Detachment that was sent to Pueblo for the winter. David suffered severe hardships with the Mormon Battalion. His name is listed on the Mormon Battalion Monument on the Utah State Capitol grounds.

Of the Pueblo detachment's movement back to Utah from their winter's quarters, John Steele stated, "We are now 145 miles from Pueblo, and we are informed that Sergeant Shelton has lost all of his horses. We passed four trading houses and found a six pound cannon there. June 5th they crossed over the Platte, came nine more miles and camped on its banks. Sergeant picked up ten head of cows and sold them, one to David Saunders Laughlin for $20.00 and one to Captain Brown for $13.50."

On August 26, 1847, David Saunders Laughlin was with the large party, many of them members of the Mormon Battalion, which was headed by President Brigham Young and the Apostles, and which to left Salt Lake Valley to return to Winter Quarters.

He left Winter Quarters as a missionary to Ohio, and it was while he was on this mission that he met Julia Ann Rocker Knapp.

She was living in Cleveland, Ohio at the time and had recently been deserted by her husband, Martin Knapp, a man many years her senior in age. Julia Ann had one daughter with Martin Knapp, He Louisa Knapp, who was only about a year old, having been born on March 4, 1846.

David Saunders Laughlin converted Julia Ann Rocker Knapp to the gospel and they were married in April 1849 in Cleveland, Cuyogha

County, Ohio. Tragedy struck the family, when in January 1851, twin boys, Jacob and Joseph, were born to live only a few hours and then pass away. The following March 7, 1852, John Saunders Laughlin was born. David and Julia immediately prepared to come to Utah. Like all of the pioneers, they passed through many trials and hardships before reaching Utah. They came across the plains in a wagon train with an ox team.

After settling in the Cottonwood area, Brigham Young sent David back for supplies and the immigrants who were arriving to join the Saints in their land of refuge.[17]

Julia Ann Rocker Laughlin Cook,
Vera's Maternal Grandmother

It was in Cottonwood that Vera's mother was born, September 19, 1853. She was given the name of Julia Ann Laughlin. The small family then moved to Cedar Valley where Harriette was born on July 3, 1855.

David's health was failing rapidly and on December 5, 1856, after a long illness, he passed away, being only 40 years of age. Before his death, he made Julia Ann, his devoted wife, promise to marry Bishop Henry Cook in order that Bishop Cook could care for her and their four small children, for David counted young Louisa Knapp (by Julia's first marriage) as one of his own.

Throughout his life, which was one of hardship, persecution, tragedy, and illness, David still maintained his devotion to the Gospel and to his testimony of it's truthfulness.

---

17   History of David Saunders Laughlin, by Lillian Myrle Roberts, January, 1958.

Before Julia Ann's marriage to Bishop Cook as his second wife, which was solemnized March 12, 1857, she was sealed to David Saunders Laughlin with Bishop Cook standing as proxy for the sealing.[18]

JULIA ANN ROCKER

It was in a little town in lower Canada, probably in the French speaking city of Quebec, that in the spring of 1828 a dark-haired, dark-eyed little girl was born to Francis Rocker and Mary White Rocker. She was the sixth child and only girl in the family. While she was still a small child, the family moved to Cleveland, Ohio.

There were hard times for the family and Julia was trained very early in her life to do all the things pertaining to the duties of homemaking. She was an accomplished seamstress and made a man's suit by hand for $15.00.

When she was fourteen years of age, she went to work for a fine lady. This lady thought so much of Julia that she felt the best was none too good for such a worthy girl. She, therefore, used her influence on Julia's behalf. She was quite influential in the town and knew a great many people. Among them was a promising young man by the name of Martin Knapp. He had a good position and fine prospects to go far. Mr. Knapp was fifteen years older than Julia, but at sixteen Julia was very mature, lovely, refined, and very attractive, so it did not take much managing on the part of Julia's benefactress to get him to propose to her. Because Julia had been made to feel that it was the only thing to do, she accepted him. They were very happy the first year and a little girl was born to them. They named her Lida (Louisa).

Mr. Knapp was untrue to Julia from the first, but she was unaware of it until Lida was one year old.

Then, through her benefactress, who had been instrumental in their marriage, Julia learned that her husband and another woman, with

---

18   Ibid.

a baby the same of age as Lida, were planning to run away and take the children with them.

Not because Mr. Knapp cared for Lida, but because the other woman would not leave her baby, he planned to take Lida to get even with the other woman for taking her child along. Because Julia's friend had overheard the plans, she took Julia and the baby and hid them for a week, during which time Mr. Knapp gave up hunting for them and left. Julia later secured a divorce from him for desertion.

After David Saunders Laughlin had returned with the Mormon Battalion to Salt Lake City, he was sent on a mission to Ohio. It was here that he met Julia Ann, converting her to the Mormon faith. They were married in April, 1849. In January, 1851, twin sons, Jacob and Joseph, were born to David and Julia. They lived only a few hours.

Another son was born to them, John Saunders Laughlin, on March 7, 1852, probably in Cleveland. It was their desire to join the main body of the church in Utah, so with others having this same desire, they joined with a wagon-train headed for "Zion."

Julia Ann received her patriarchal blessing in which she was told she would be "an angel" among her sisters and that her mother would be there to meet her by the hand when she died.

They settled in the Cottonwood, Salt Lake County, Utah, and it was here that Vera's mother, Julia Ann Laughlin, was born September 19, 1853. Within a year, they moved to Cedar Valley where Harriette Ann Laughlin was born on July 3, 1855.

David's health had been deteriorating and he passed away December 5, 1856. Before he died, he expressed the desire for Julia Ann to marry Bishop Henry Freeman Cook, so Bishop Cook could take care of her and their little children. Julia married Henry Freeman Cook on March 12, 1857 in a polygamous marriage. Four children were born to Julia and Henry, namely, Henry, Frank, Milinda (called Minnie) and Ada.

At that time, there were few doctors in Utah and no one to care for the sick. Julia Ann was called to go to Salt Lake City to take training as a midwife. She received her training under Mrs. Connley. Julia Ann brought many babies into the world. It was recorded that she delivered over 500 babies into the world and never lost a mother or a baby, but always gave the credit to a loving Father in Heaven. She was a very humble person and she never went out on a case without first kneeling in prayer. She said that she always carried a prayer in her heart that the Lord would be with her in her efforts. She took care of the mother and baby, and in many cases did the work for ten days to three weeks as the case needed her. Her fee was $5.00.

Julia was also called in for all other sicknesses, no matter what the nature, contagious diseases and all, and never a cent was paid for these services. She was called by the people of Cedar Fort "An Angel of Mercy." Up until ten years before she died, she prepared every person who died in Cedar Fort for burial, even her own family. She donated these services to her friends and neighbors although many people would send her flour and meat and various other things to help her.

When the Civil War broke out in 1861, all five of Julia's brothers went to fight. During the whole four years of the war, she was never able to receive any word from her family in Cleveland, Ohio. These hardships were especially hard for her to bear. For years following the war, she tried in every way possible to get word of them, but was unsuccessful. She had lost complete track of her parents.

It was always supposed that her brothers were all killed in the war and that her parents had died during that time. Julia could never stand to talk of her family after that without crying, therefore the children never broached the subject with her.

Among the deaths she could never quite get over were those of two boys by the names of Weeks, who were dear friends of hers. The boys went up into Pole Canyon to get wood. The neighbors warned

FAMILY GROUP RECORD

HUSBAND (2) David Saunders LAUGHLIN (Member Mormon Battalion)

Born	26 Apr 1814	Place: Dunbarton, Merrimack, New Hampshire
Mar	11 Apr 1849	Place: Ohio City, Cuyahoga, Ohio
Died	5 Dec 1856	Place: Cedar Fort, Utah, Utah
Bur		Place: Cedar Fort, Utah, Utah

HUSBAND'S FATHER: David LAUGHLIN — HUSBAND'S MOTHER:
HUSBAND'S OTHER WIVES: (1) Mary Bell CLARK, sealed EH 27 Sept 1861

WIFE (2) Julia Ann ROCKER

Born	19 May 1828	Place: Lower Canada
Chr		Place:
Died	22 Jan 1891	Place: Cedar Fort, Utah, Utah
Bur		Place:

WIFE'S FATHER: Francis ROCKER* or Franklin ROCKER or BERCIER (div) md 26 Jun 1845
WIFE'S MOTHER: Mary WHITE
WIFE'S OTHER HUSBANDS: (1) Martin KNAPP   (3) 12 Mar 1857 Henry Freeman COOK

Husband	Hyrum Utah North
Wife 1	
Ward Examiners 2	

Name & address of person submitting sheet: Ruth Nelson Miller, 280 No 2nd West, Hyrum, Utah 84319

RELATION OF ABOVE TO HUSBAND: gg-dau   RELATION OF ABOVE TO WIFE: gg-dau
FOUR GENERATION SHEET FOR FILING ONLY: NO ☐
DATE SUBMITTED TO GENEALOGICAL SOCIETY: 30 June 1981

LDS ORDINANCE DATA

	BAPTIZED (Date)	ENDOWED (Date)	SEALED TO PARENTS
HUSBAND	17 Oct 1852	27 Sep 1861	
WIFE	(4)	(6)	27 Sep 1861 LE / 12 Mar 1857

CHILDREN

	SEX	Children Given Names / SURNAME	WHEN BORN Day Month Year	WHERE BORN Town	County	State or Country	DATE OF FIRST MARRIAGE / TO WHOM	WHEN DIED Day Month Year	BAPTIZED	ENDOWED	SEALED TO PARENTS
1	F	Mary Louisa KNAPP	4 Mar 1846	Cleveland	Cyhg	Ohio	2 Feb 1869 / Thomas Kimball MESSERSMITH		22 Sep 1861	27 Sep 1861	27 Sep 1861
2	M	Jacob (twin) LAUGHLIN	2 Jan 1851	Cleveland	Cyhg	Ohio		2 Jan 1851	27 Feb 1894	2 Feb 1869	*
3	M	Joseph (twin) LAUGHLIN	2 Jan 1851 (3)	Cleveland	Cyhg	Ohio		2 Jan 1851	CHILD	CHILD	*
4	M	John Sanders LAUGHLIN	7 Mar 1852 (5)	Cottonwood	Salt Lake	Utah		17 Jul 1864	CHILD	CHILD	(5)
5	F	Julia Ann LAUGHLIN	19 Sep 1853	Cottonwood		"	28 Jan 1871 / Samuel Allen WILCOX, Jr.	13 Nov 1913	*	EH 12 Jul 1939	13 Jul 1939 AL
6	F	Harriet Ann LAUGHLIN	3 Jul 1855 (5)	Cedar Fort		Utah	1 Apr 1872 / Dana Ossian WALTON	13 Apr 1893	22 Sep 1861	30 Jan 1871 EH	13 Jul 1929 AL
									27 Aug 1864	12 Jul 1939 AL	12 Jul 1929 AL

SOURCES OF INFORMATION:
1. 1850 Census, Cuyahoga, Ohio (GS 020, 221)
2. Marr Rec Cuyahego, Ohio (GS 877, 913)
3. Memb rec Big Cottonwood Ward (GS 002,041)
4. TIB wife
5. Sealing Film #170, 745 Alberta, Canada
6. Sealing Film #183, 395 - Proxy by Henry F. Cook

OTHER MARRIAGES: (1) Wife died 14 Jul 1845 Nauvoo, Illinois - in the Nauvoo Neighbor 16 Jul 1845
7. #35 Quorum of 70's Bk B Pg 259
8. Julia A Laughlin Cedar Fort, Utah Cemetery
9. Mary Clark - End H. #3914 B G Slg p574   #660 B C S18 Pg 105

NECESSARY EXPLANATIONS: * Ord in proces:
#1 Child Mary Louisa KNAPP adopted
End House Rec 1444 Bk G Pg 47 Loui
Endowed herself, lists David as fa
Husband: re-end 15 Oct 1890
Wife: re-end 12 Jul 1939 AL
Wife: re-sealed 12 Jul 1939 AL

PFGS0029 2/78 100M Printed in the United States of America
©1972 The Genealogical Department of The Church of Jesus Christ of Latter-day Saints

FAMILY GROUP RECORD

HUSBAND (3) Henry Freeman COOK (Farmer & stockman)

Born	12 Jan 1815	Place Homer, Cortland, New York
Chr.		Place
Mar	12 Mar 1857	Place Cedar Fort, Utah, Utah
Died	14 Apr 1882	Place Cedar Fort, Utah, Utah
Bur.	Apr 1882	Place Cedar Fort, Utah, Utah

HUSBAND'S FATHER William COOK HUSBAND'S MOTHER Lucy CHAPMAN

HUSBAND'S OTHER WIVES (1) 9 Apr 1837 Sophronia STROWBRIDGE

WIFE (2) Julia Anne ROCKER

Born	19 May 1828	Place Lower Canada/Quebec
Chr.		Place
Died	22 Jan 1891	Place Cedar Fort, Utah, Utah
Bur.		Place

WIFE'S FATHER Francis ROCKER WIFE'S MOTHER Mary WHITE

WIFE'S OTHER HUSBANDS (1) 26 Jun 1845 Martin KNAPP (div) (2) 11 Apr 1849 David Sanders LAUGHLIN (sld 12 Mar 1857 EH)

Husband Henry Freeman COOK
Wife Julia Anne ROCKER
1815

Ward/Examiner 1. 2.
Stake or Mission Hyrum Utah North

NAME & ADDRESS OF PERSON SUBMITTING SHEET
Ruth Nelson Miller
280 North 2nd West
Hyrum, Utah 84319

RELATION OF ABOVE TO HUSBAND Step gg-dau RELATION OF ABOVE TO WIFE gg-dau
FOUR GENERATION SHEET FOR FILING ONLY YES [X] NO [ ]
DATE SUBMITTED TO GENEALOGICAL SOCIETY 30 June 1981

LDS ORDINANCE DATA

	BAPTIZED	ENDOWED	SEALED (to parents / to husband)
HUSBAND	13 May 1843	27 Sep 1861	do not seal
WIFE	*	27 Sep 1861	[SEALED TO PARENTS]

CHILDREN

Sex	Given Names / Surname	WHEN BORN (DAY MONTH YEAR)	WHERE BORN (TOWN)	COUNTY	STATE OR COUNTRY	DATE OF FIRST MARRIAGE / TO WHOM	WHEN DIED (DAY MONTH YEAR)	BAPTIZED	ENDOWED	SEALED
1 M	David Franklin COOK	9 Jan 1858/59	Cedar Fort	Utah	Utah	29 Mar 1878 Maria Louisa SMITH	7 Jun 1887	22 Mar 1868	13 Sep 1878	*
2 M	George Henry COOK	18 Feb 1860	"	"	"	25 Oct 1883 Elizabeth Hannah NATE	12 May 1912	22 Mar 1868	25 Oct 1883	*
3 M	Florence Malinda COOK	11 May 1862	"	"	"	David Almearn WILCOX	28 Feb 1899	22 Jul 1895	17 Oct 1895	*
4 M	Ada COOK	9 Dec 1866	"	"	"	27 Sep 1884 Marvin Lyman COOK	7 Nov 1941	3 Oct 1875	5 Nov 1942	CL

OTHER MARRIAGES

SOURCES OF INFORMATION
1. Fam rec in poss of Fam Rep Mrs. Gertrude C. Jackson, Pocatello ID
2. CFI for child #4

NECESSARY EXPLANATIONS
* - Ordinance in process
CL - cleared for ordinance work
Husb & wife sld for time only
Wife sld to husb (2) David Sanders
LAUGHLIN 12 Mar 1857
Wife aka BERCIER

FAMILY GROUP RECORD 1972 The Genealogical Department of The Church of Jesus Christ of Latter-day Saints
PBGS0099 8/79 10M/Pub. Printed in USA
5/80

them that the Indians were in a very bad mood, but they said that they would be back early.

When they did not come, three men went to see what was wrong, and right at the mouth of the Canyon, they came upon a tribe of Indians dancing around with the boys scalps on poles. They had cut the boys hearts out and eaten them.

The said the boys were very brave and died well, so they ate their hearts as a token of bravery.

To give the boy's bodies any semblance of decent look was very difficult, and it was months before Julia recovered from the horrible experience of preparing their bodies for burial.

Julia was of such a sympathetic nature that other people's troubles, as well as her own (and she had many), worked a hardship on her. Bishop Cook died in 1881, leaving her a widow again.

Minnie Turner, Julia's granddaughter, recalled that Julia Ann was a French woman who spoke little English. She added that Martha Parker Wilcox (who was Vera's grandmother on her father's side) and Julia Ann Rocker Laughlin were friends in Quebec and both later settled in Cedar Fort where they renewed their friendship.

Julia Ann was a very resourceful person. She had her own spinning wheel, and spun cloth for her family and for many others. She was an accomplished dressmaker, having served most of her life for those who were well enough off to hire sewing done. It would take as long as two weeks to make one dress, as the fashions were in those days, and for years they were all done by hand.

Later Julia bought a Howe sewing machine, the first one, and for many years, the only one in Cedar Fort. She knitted all her own family's stockings and socks, besides making them for others. She made hats from straw and did all the other things pioneer women were forced to do through necessity.

One of the greatest compliments she was paid was that she was considered one of the Cook family's best friends. The oldest daughter, Hannah, who was about the same age as Julia, said that they lost the best friend that they ever had when Julia died. The two families were always very closely associated and if any of them had sickness or troubles, they always sent for "Grandma Laughlin" as quickly as did anyone else.

Julia was not well for two or three years before she died in 1891 at the age of 63, thus ending the life of a wonderful wife, mother, friend, and neighbor.[19]

19   Ibid.

11

SAMUEL ALLEN WILCOX, JR. AND JULIA ANN LAUGHLIN

EARLY YEARS

Samuel Allen Wilcox, Jr., who was Vera's father, was born on March 9,1850. His parents, Samuel Allen Wilcox, Sr., and Martha Parker Wilcox had been with the saints when they were driven from Nauvoo, Illinois in 1846. They had settled in Hamburg, Fremont County, Iowa and made a temporary home until they could raise means for the westward journey across the plains to Utah.

In 1861, when Sammy, as he was called, was eleven years old, the family sold their farm and taking part of the pay in cattle, they started on the long journey across the plains. The boy, Sammy, no doubt helped to drive the cattle over many weary miles in the westward trek. They traveled in Captain Cannon's Company, arriving in Salt Lake City, October 7, 1861. On inquiring where they would find feed for their cattle, they were directed to go to Cedar Valley. Samuel Allen's boyhood and young manhood were spent in Cedar Valley.

It was in Cedar Valley that Samuel met Julia Ann Laughlin. Vera's mother, Julia Ann Laughlin was born September 17, 1853 in Cottonwood, Utah. Young Julia Ann's father, David Sanders Laughlin, had died when Julia Ann was only three years old leaving her mother, who was also named Julia Ann Laughlin, a young widow of twenty-nine years old with four little children, the youngest only a year and a half old.

SAMUEL ALLEN WILCOX, JR. AND JULIA LAUGHLIN

Samuel Allen Wilcox, Jr.
Vera's Father

Julia Laughlin
Vera's Mother

Realizing his impending death would leave his wife with a young family to raise alone, young Julia Ann's father, David S. Laughlin, expressed his wish that upon his death his wife would marry Henry Freeman Cook in a polygamous marriage. After David's death, this wish was carried out. Henry was many years older than his new wife, but she found him to be a kind and loving husband and father.

At an early age, young Julia Ann became skilled in the art of homemaking. Her mother had a spinning wheel and Julia Ann helped her spin cloth to make clothing not only for their own family, but for Bishop Cook's family of ten children. Her mother was an accomplished dressmaker and no doubt taught her daughters to sew, which served Julia Ann well when she had daughters of her own. Her mother bought the first sewing machine in Cedar Fort, but it is not known whether she permitted her daughter, Julia Ann, to use it or not.

FAMILY GROUP RECORD

HUSBAND Samuel Allen WILCOX, Jr.
Born: 9 March 1850 — Place: Hamburg, Fremont, Iowa, known as Austin, or Franklin, Iowa
Chr.:
Mar.: 28 Jan 1871 — Place: Salt Lake City, Salt Lake, Utah (Endowment House)
Died: 29 Oct 1908 — Place: Desert, Tehama, California
Bur.: 6 Nov 1908 — Place: Cedar Fort, Utah, Utah
Husband's Father: Samuel Allen WILCOX, Sr. — Husband's Mother: Martha Parker

WIFE Julia Ann LAUGHLIN
Born: 19 Sept 1853 — Place: Cottonwood, Salt Lake, Utah
Chr.:
Died: 5 Nov 1913 — Place: Gridley, Butte, California
Bur.: 2 Nov 1913 — Place: Gridley, Butte, California
Wife's Father: David Saunders LAUGHLIN
Wife's Mother: Julia Ann ROCKER/BERCIER

Samuel Allen WILCOX, Jr. 1850
Julia Anne LAUGHLIN

Name & address of person submitting sheet: Ruth Nelson Miller, 280 No. 2nd West, Hyrum, Utah 84319
Relation of above to husband: gr-dau — Relation of above to wife: gr-dau
Four generation sheet for filing only: YES ☑ NO ☐

SEX	CHILDREN — Given Names	SURNAME	WHEN BORN DAY	MONTH	YEAR	TOWN	WHERE BORN — COUNTY	STATE OR COUNTRY	DATE OF FIRST MARRIAGE / TO WHOM	WHEN DIED DAY	MONTH	YEAR
1 M	David Adrian	WILCOX	25	Oct	1871	Cedar Fort	Utah	Utah	2 Jan 1900 Agnes Abigail SOUTHWORTH	22 Aug 1915		
2 M	Samuel Franklin	WILCOX	2	Mar	1874	Cedar Fort	Utah	Utah	17 Nov 1909 Luella Evans VANDAM	8 Oct 1946		
3 F	Olive Chloe	WILCOX	28	Sep	1876	Cedar Fort	Utah	Utah	4 Oct 1898 James Alfred ROBISON	13 Nov 1937		
4 M	Joseph Orrin	WILCOX	29	Sep	1878	Dingle	Bear Lake	Idaho	5 Oct 1909 Alameda A. JOHNSON	19 Sept 1915		
5 F	Scina Malinda*	WILCOX	8	Mar	1881	"	"	"	15 June 1898 James F. TURNER	23 Feb 1968		
6 F	Julia Maud	WILCOX	12	Oct	1883	"	"	"	21 Dec 1901 Laurence Calvin SQUIRES	17 Oct 1924		
7 F	Ada	WILCOX	29	Apr	1887	Lyman	Fremont	"	29 Jun 1914 Leroy SMITH	31 Mar 1934		
8 F	Martha Vera	WILCOX	25	Mar	1889	Lyman	Fremont	"	1 Jan 1912 John Alexander NELSON, Jr.	29 Nov 1972		
9 F	Hazel Elva	WILCOX	15	Jul	1891	Lyman	"	"		6 Aug 1900		
10 M	Lorin Elmo	WILCOX	13	May	1895	Lyman	"	Y	31 Dec 1935 (1) Mary Placeda GRIDLEY	23 Sept 1974		
11												

LDS ORDINANCE DATA

	BAPTIZED	ENDOWED	SEALED (children to parents)
WIFE	7 Aug 1864	8 Mar 1869	30 Jan 1871
HUSBAND	22 Sep 1861	30 Jan 1871	
1	7 May 1880	26 Jun 1895	BIC
2	7 May 1882	12 Jun 1902	"
3	1 Aug 1885	26 Oct 1898	"
4	9 Oct 1887	17 May 1900	"
5	5 Jun 1890	16 Jan 1906	"
6	4 Aug 1892	8 Jan 1902	"
7	3 May 1895	27 May 1971	"
8	6 Jun 1897	23 Nov 1923	"
9	29 Jul 1930	30 Jul 1980	"
10	12 Jun 1903	24 Aug 1950	"

NECESSARY EXPLANATIONS
**#5 Scina Malinda called Minnie

OTHER MARRIAGES
#2 Samuel Franklin civil divorce
#10 Lorin Elmo md (2) Lucy R. STOTT 5 May 1950

SOURCES OF INFORMATION
All documents listed in possession of Ruth Nelson Miller, 280 No. 2nd West, Hyrum, Utah
Documentation on back of sheet

FAMILY GROUP RECORD 1973 The Genealogical Department of The Church of Jesus Christ of Latter-day Saints PFG50029 7/73 100M Printed in the United States of America

With young Julia Ann's mother spending a week to ten days away from home as a midwife caring for maternity cases, much responsibility for the care of the home and of younger children fell on young Julia Ann's capable shoulders. Young Julia Ann had great love and respect for her mother and she tried every way she could to lighten the load at home for her mother.

Young Julia Ann was a beautiful women with large blue eyes and coal black hair. She was a small woman never weighing more than one hundred pounds except during her pregnancies.

She loved to dance as a young woman. Julia Ann had but one pair of shoes a year, so she would walk to the dances bare-footed and then put her shoes on when she arrived at the dances.

She was a beautiful dancer and had lots of suitors. She fell in love with Samuel Allen Wilcox, Jr. and they were married January 18, 1871 in the Salt Lake Temple when she was eighteen years old and Samuel was twenty-one. They made their home in Cedar Fort where two sons and a daughter were born to them, David Adrian (Adrian), Samuel Frank (Frank), and Olive Chloe (known as Chloe). Shortly after Chloe's birth, Sam and Julia moved their family to Dingle, Bear Lake County, Idaho. Four more children were added to the family, Joseph Orrin (Orrin), Scina Malinda (Minnie) and Julia Maude (known as Maude), and Ada.

THE FAMILY MOVE TO BEAR LAKE

When Sam and Julia moved to Bear Lake, they took Grandfather Samuel Allen Wilcox, Sr.'s cattle and their own cattle with them. They bought a ranch in the river bottom with a lot of hay. Julia Ann developed hay fever and suffered with it a great deal. Samuel would leave Bear Lake in the winter to find work and Julia was left with the responsibility of tending the cattle, calves and children. To supplement her income, she made butter and sold it.

Two years after their arrival in the Bear Lake area, Samuel Allen was called to be Bishop. He presided in that capacity from 1879 until 1886. Vera recalled her father, Bishop Wilcox, had his own Welfare Program and felt it was his responsibility to take care of the poor and widows in his ward with his own means.

Whenever he would kill a beef or a pig, he made the rounds to the homes of the poor. He had his own smoke house and would cure hams and mutton and Julia Ann, his wife, always added eggs and fresh churned butter, fragrant loaves of fresh baked bread and jams and jelly to those in need.

Samuel Allen Wilcox, Jr. Family in 1895.
Front row left: Vera, Ada, Hazel, Samuel, Julia Ann, Lorin
Back row left: Maude, Minnie, Chloe, Frank, Adrian and Orrin

THE FAMILY MOVE TO LYMAN, IDAHO

When Ada was six weeks old they moved out of the Bear Lake area to Lyman, Fremont County, Idaho up on the Snake River because of Julia's severe hay-fever. As soon as they were settled in their new home, Samuel was called to be Bishop of the Lyman Ward and was ordained August 21, 1887 by Lorenzo Snow. He took a leading part in getting an irrigation system of canals into operation. This system is now known as the Sunnydale Irrigation Company. He seemed to know what needed to be done. His happy, cheerful disposition made him many friends both old and young. He was an obedient son and loving husband and father.

Three more children were born to them in Lyman, Idaho: Martha Vera (Vera) on March 25, 1889, Hazel Elva on July 15, 1891, and Lorin Elmo on May 13, 1895.48

Vera Wilcox Nelson recorded, "During an epidemic of diphtheria in Lyman about the year 1893, my father spent night after night ministering to the sick and dressing the dead. I was only a small child and I can remember the Relief Society sisters sewing night and day at our home to make the burial clothing for those who had passed away."

When Samuel was Bishop of Lyman, it was the rule of the Church that only two round dances (with a partner) should be allowed in one evening, the rest should be quadrilles or square dances. A nearby dance hall, which was close to a saloon, was enticing Bishop Wilcox's ward young people. It was not properly operated and little restraint was put on the dancers. With dismay, Bishop Wilcox saw many of the young people of his ward flocking to this place. He knew something had to be done about this problem, so he proceeded to make the ward dances more enticing.

Later upon visiting Samuel's home, Stake President Ricks said, "By the way, Bishop Wilcox, are you enforcing the rules on round-dancing in your ward?" "Oh, yes, President Ricks, and we are getting along fine. But you see, I changed the rule a little. Now we have at least two square dances during the evening and the rest are round dances," Bishop wilcox responded.[20]

Vera told that during her growing-up years her friends loved to visit the Wilcox home because they always had so much fun there.

Vera recalled, "My father and mother were always such good sports in those days. I confess they were a bit foolish, but 'Chinese Weddings,' and 'Falling in the Well,' and 'Post Office' were all the rage.

I hate to say they were just kissing games, but Dad and Mother were as popular as anyone. I can still see them now in the row, sitting on the floor in a 'Chinese Wedding.' Mother was never too tired to see that there were loads of sandwiches, cakes, cookies, and lemonade and lots of homemade ice cream. More than once she fried oysters for the group after a dance."

Vera reminisced about her mother, "I can see my mother's pantry shelves always stocked with cookies, doughnuts, and mince pies. Her cooking, to my mind, has never been equaled. Our big rock cellar was filled with fruits and preserves, chow and pickles in stone jars, unsealed! I wonder, was it the vinegar or was there some faith we lack today? Mother always had a crowd to feed and there was her marvelous 'smoke house' with hams, bacon, and dried deer meat. There was homemade cheese and butter, too. I wonder how Mother ever found time to do it all?"

Mother's laundry soap was always made in late summer. She washed and corded all the wool for every bit of their bedding. The girls would have to tear rags to make one new carpet each year. Straw ticks had to be emptied and filled again with fresh clean straw twice each year, at housecleaning time. What a job that was! Carpets had to be taken up and beaten and shook. Straw was swept up and clean straw brought in to put under carpets on freshly scrubbed flours.

---

20   Vera Wilcox Nelson Life Story.

All the walls had to be whitewashed. Mother always saw to it that she made her five daughters new dresses for the Fourth of July and Christmas. Petticoats and panties were made of flour sacks."[21]

ON THE MOVE AGAIN

Samuel Allen Wilcox was released as Bishop of the Lyman Ward on December 24, 1898. He moved his family into Rexburg, Idaho in order to give his family better scholastic advantages. In the spring of 1899 he was chosen as a member of the High Council. In Rexburg, their 8 year old daughter, Hazel, passed away.

In the spring of 1902, Samuel Allen, Jr. and his entire family, except his eldest daughter Chloe Wilcox Robison and family, moved to Raymond, Alberta, Canada. Several of his children were married and had small families of their own, so they made quite a company.

On the organization of the Taylor Stake in Raymond in 1904, Samuel was chosen a member of the High Council.[22]

Samuel Allen, Jr. had been in the Sheep business in Idaho for quite some time, but upon visiting Alberta, Canada in the early winter, he was told that the cattle business was much better than sheep in that country. So, Samuel sold all of his sheep and bought cattle, and his sons Adrian and Orrin and others drove the cattle and horses to Canada. They had only been in Canada a short time when Samuel found the cattle business was not an easy one, and being well acquainted with the sheep business, decided to sell the cattle and go back to sheep.[23]

---

21   Journal of Vera Wilcox, compiled in Wilcox Bulletin, 1981, by Peggy Massey.
22   Ibid.
23   Ibid.

LOST IN A CANADIAN BLIZZARD

All went well the first fall and winter, but in May of 1903 during the lambing season, Vera recorded, "My father and mother went to take supplies to the sheep camp some thirty miles way from the town of Raymond where the family was living."

"They had only just arrived at the first camp when Father noticed a storm coming in from the north. He called to the herder, Frank Bates of Raymond, to come with him and head the ewes toward the big coulee. My father had battled a severe attack of yellow jaundice in the month of March and mother was concerned to have him out in the storm.

She called to him to take his big fur coat. He laughed and said he would soon be back. Mother ran and gave the coat to Frank. Father said in his jocular way, 'Dudie' (his pet name for mother), 'if you didn't worry so much you would live much longer.'

That was about four o'clock on the afternoon of Thursday and it was Saturday about one o'clock before the storm subsided and help came."

"I think no one ever really saw a blizzard unless they have lived in Canada. The wind and snow together came so fast and furiously that no one could see even three feet away, and so all night and all day and all the next night they (Frank and Father) wandered around in hopes of stumbling onto camp but of no avail. Poor mother watched and called with a lighted lantern in her hand. She dared not leave the wagon, but kept the tongue so she could stand on it. As I think of her sensitive nature, I often wonder how she stood the terror of it all. My baby brother, Lorin, a child of six years was with her and we all are still thankful that he was as she might otherwise have been tempted to leave the wagon and try to find father."

"Saturday about noon, father was exhausted and begged Frank Bates, who had loyally stayed by his side, to save himself as father was absolutely tired out, and could go no farther.

I have heard my father tell with tears in his eyes, how Frank knelt in the snow up to his waist and prayed to God for strength and help to save my Dad.

In a little while, the storm subsided and Frank saw an old charred stump, the only one in the coulee. He was able to locate himself and mustered all his strength and another prayer that God would watch over the kindest and best man who ever lived. He stooped and kissed my father's forehead and told him help was not far off."

"I have talked to Frank Bates and he told me he often wondered just how he made his way to the Garrick ranch house which was over a mile away, in snow up to his waist. He tore his shirt in shreds and tied it to the tree stump in case the storm should rage again. Frank said he walked with ease and was at the door of the ranch house before he realized it. He found my brother Adrian there also. Adrian had been out in all the storm but he had a horse and was in good health. The body of the horse had protected him. He was eating a bite, the first since Thursday noon. There were fresh horses in the barn so all three men, Mr. Garrick, and Adrian and our good shepherd, Frank, were not long in retracing Frank's steps and soon had my father on a horse and then into bed and some warm broth in his stomach."

"One of the other herders, Caldwell Southworth, came to the ranch, he too, having battled the storm. Adrian asked Call if he thought he could find mother and told him to say to her that all of them were well and safe. My other brother, Orrin, was still unaccounted for, but Adrian said Orrin had a good horse and he knew he would be safe. Well, Call found the camp without too much trouble and was ready and willing to tell a little white lie, but as he stuck his head in the

Julia Ann Wilcox, with three of her daughters, left to right: Maude, Ada, and Vera

camp door who should he see but Orrin, eating a much needed meal. Call said, 'Well, you have kept me from telling a damn big lie.'"

"Mother insisted on going to the ranch where father was, so she mounted Call's horse and went to my Dad. She found him in a much better condition than she had hoped and with her fine nursing he was soon able to be up again."

"I've forgotten now how many thousand sheep were lost, but my Dad said as long as every one of the family was alive it didn't matter."[24]

SAMUEL GOES INTO THE COAL BUSINESS

The next fall they sold all the sheep and moved to Taber, Alberta, Canada where they purchased a Hudson Bay section of land. With this section, the mineral rights were also purchased. Samuel Allen sunk a shaft 100 feet and found a vein of coal ten to twelve feet thick. From 1904 to 1907, he operated this coal mine and also ran cattle.

CALIFORNIA, HERE WE COME

Feeling a need for a milder climate and to find some relief from the hay-fever which continued to bother Julia Ann, they decided to move to California. Samuel's daughter, Minnie Wilcox Turner, reported that when they moved from Canada, they were able to realize a good profit from the sale of the coal mine. With the proceeds from this sale, they purchased a tract of land, which was a fruit ranch of 1200 acres at Vina, close to Chico, California.

The move was wonderful for Julia for she never had a touch of hay-fever again. When they first arrived in Vina, Julia and her girls, Ada and Vera, were so homesick that they wanted to run away. Instead they pitched their tents under a big fruit shed with peach pits six inches deep all over the ground.

Shortly after they got settled, malaria infested mosquitoes brought death and fever to the valley. There were days when there weren't enough well people to care for the sick ones. Samuel Allen had again been called to serve as the Bishop of this new area.

24   Ibid.

He had suffered from yellow jaundice on previous occasions and he contacted it again. This time, with his kidneys being weakened, he succumbed to the fever and died November 18, 1908.

A newspaper clipping telling of his death, October 19, 1908 stated,

> *"The little colony of Mormons located near Vina, California, suffered a severe loss in the death of Samuel Allen Wilcox, one of the founders of the colony and one of its strongest supporters."*

It then gave a brief sketch of his life and continued,

> *"In 1907 he was removed from Canada to Vina and was unanimously sustained as presiding officer until the branch was organized when he was honorably released and his eldest son was called to the position of presiding elder. Mr. Wilcox's life has been filled with energy and activity. Early in life he manifested those sterling qualities of manhood that have made him one of God's noblemen and he leaves behind him a family and a record which are a solace and satisfaction to those who are bereft of his love and society."*[25]

After his death, Samuel's wife, Julia Ann, made her home in Gridley, California with her unmarried daughters Ada and Vera. Her son Frank lived near her. They were happy together in Gridley but five years to the month after her beloved Sam died, Julia Ann was permitted to follow him. Following an illness that lasted several weeks, she passed away at her home surrounded by her children. Before Julia died, her daughter, Maude Wilcox Squires, traveled with Maude's six month old baby daughter from Archer, Idaho to California to help care for her mother, Julia, and to help her sisters. Maude remained in California until after Julia's death on November 13, 1913.[26]

At her request, Julia was buried in Gridley, California because she realized the trauma it had been to take her husband's body back to Cedar Fort for burial. She said, "Sam and I will be together in the

25   Journal of Vera Wilcox Nelson
26   Memories of Peggy Squires Massey.

resurrection anyway, so it doesn't matter where we are buried." Her children complied with her request.[27]

---

27   Ibid.

12

BRINGING TWO LIVES TOGETHER

VERA TELLS OF EARLY YEARS

"I was born March 25, 1889 in a little log house on the Snake River at Sunnyvale, Fremont County, Idaho. My father, Samuel Allen Wilcox, Jr., was a pioneer in that country, having moved from Dingle, Idaho in the spring of 1886 to the Snake River Country. I was the eighth child in the family. My brothers were Adrian, Frank, and Orrin. My sisters were Chloe, Minnie, Maud, and Ada. It seems my earliest recollections were when our ninth baby was born. A sweet, black-eyed girl, named Hazel. How I loved that little girl. I was two in March and she was born in July of 1891. Then four years later came our baby brother Lorin. I would gladly stay at home from a ball game or anything else, if I could just hold him all alone in my little rocking chair."

"My childhood days were spent in a log house at Lyman, Idaho, just about seven miles north of where I was born. Ours was a happy home. Sunday morning I was always up and trotted to Sunday

School with my father ahead of the rest of the family. He was the Bishop and there were no telephones in those days, so he was always at church early to see that the big stove was hot and the building was nice and warm for the crowd. The church was just a large one-room building, separated by curtains for classes. Sometimes the Deacons were there and had a fire, but my Pa could make the best fires of anyone in the world. He was one grand man and loved by everyone, large and small."

"I think my first teacher in Sunday School was Effie Robison. I can still remember the pretty little cards we used to take home with a nice little verse on them for us to learn. Effie was also my first grade teacher. I had a good memory and knew many stories and recitations. I didn't start first grade until I was eight years old. (Imagine not letting a child go to school until she was eight years old!)"

I can remember visiting the school and my brother-in-law, Fred Robinson, had taught me a poem and gave me five cents if I would say it for the class. Here is the poem:

> Oh, Lord of love, look from above,
> And pity us poor scholars,
> They've hired a fool,
> To teach our school,
> And paid him twenty-five dollars.

"Needless to say, my big sisters and brothers were greatly shocked. (Ha! Ha! Uncle Fred!)"

"I can remember Theo Osborn (our friend 'Aunt' Jean Miller's niece). She was deaf and could not talk, but on testimony day she loved to get up and make gestures and try to talk. Some of the kids laughed at her and I felt so sorry for her. I got up and stood by her and held her hand and tears streamed down my cheeks.

It seemed like that sort of shamed the class. Theo always loved me and I loved her too. She visited Jean Miller in 1936 and I had occasion to see her. It was such a happy reunion. She had learned to talk but was still deaf. Her mother was always 'Aunt Rosella,' to me."

"I was really my father's best 'boy.' You see, there were five girls in a row, so I used to ride a horse and get the cows at night and run the calves away from the cows after they had their share of the milk.

My father had a large farm and he had sheep. The sheep were kept in the foothills in the summer and the ewes and lambs brought to the farm for the winter. I used to herd the sheep to keep them off the alfalfa. I was paid five cents a day. My dad used to tell me I'd die poor because when the sheep behaved well, I used to feel I hadn't earned my money. I used to sit in the shade of a tree or straw stack and play make-believe. Sometimes I was a poor little rich girl who had no friends and sometimes I was a fairy princess. I was never lonely because I used to make believe I was a nice princess and had many beaus [boyfriends]."

"There is a story in my life I am rather ashamed of, but here it is: My sister Ada, three years older than I, was never very well. The doctors couldn't tell what her trouble was, but she spent much of her childhood days at home ill. Mother and Daddy would take her to Rexburg, which was five miles north and bring home a big bottle of bitter-root or some other 'junk' for her to take. Well, they always bought some nice gift for her to bribe her to take this medicine. Of course, I didn't understand this and one day they brought her the cutest little blue lamp. Well, the green-eyed monster got turned loose. I cried and got myself into such a state, I really thought I was going to die."

"No one seemed to know why I was so naughty. My sister, Chloe, who was always my very best friend, let me sleep with her and so some way I let her know what the matter was. She made me understand for the first time just how wonderful it was to be well. I am sure she helped me conquer jealousy, but I was at least fourteen years old before I can say I was cured. The rest of my life, I spent in trying to make up to the sick, little sister, Ada, for some of the mean feelings I had suffered against her."

"When I was ten years old, Hazel [age eight] and I both had diphtheria. Hazel was much sicker that I. I can remember so well the night before she was really bedfast.

I was out to the barn, stripping my favorite cow, and Hazel came limping toward me using a broomstick to help steady her. I asked her, what was the matter. She said, 'If you won't tell ma, I'll show you.'

She showed me her legs and private parts. She looked as if she had been burned. I screamed and ran and told mother. She brought Hazel in the house and put her in a tub of warm water."

"After that, Hazel just seemed to sleep herself away. She wouldn't try to gargle her throat and there were no doctors, except thirty miles away. When the doctor did come, he just called it 'diphtheria.' We lost our sweet baby sister from that dread disease. I am very grateful for the medical knowledge that has come into the world in this day and age. I have seen many wonderful changes in my life."

"Mother never seemed to get over Hazel's death. We all used to tell Mother that Hazel was just too good for this world."[1]

GOOD MEMORIES FOREVER

Vera wrote, "I can remember the wonderful times we used to have every summer. The family and all the friends would "hi" away to the mountains to pick huckleberries. Oh, what a wonderful time we had. The food cooked over the campfire and the songs and stories by the big fire at night and then to sleep in the back of the white-topped buggy on a feather bed. The women and children had the wagons and buggies and the men slept on pine-bows. I used to think that

---

1   Life Story by Vera Wilcox Nelson

was the best time of the year. My ma used to brag on me and say, 'What a good little berry- picker you are.'"

"Once when we went for huckleberries, Lillian Young, just my age, was asleep after dinner. The family just let her sleep in the wagon, thinking that she would probably sleep at least two hours. She woke up when she was startled by a panther crying.

Someone ran to the sound and killed the panther. That was a scary night, but someone kept the campfire burning brightly all night so we were safe.

In those days, the mountains were the home of many wild animals: bears, mountain lions, panthers, wild cats, etc. Now, most of those same lands are under cultivation."

Father bought a home in Rexburg, Idaho so that his family could attend schools there. This was very important to him, to see that

Vera (holding ball) as captain of the girls basketball team in Canada

211

his family had every opportunity available to get a good education. Maude, Orrin, Frank and I attended school in Rexburg. The farm home was about seven miles away in Lyman, Idaho and close enough so that we could get supplies from home once a week. Mother often came and stayed with us during the week and cooked and helped us with our lessons."

"From here, my family moved to Canada and [as recorded in the previous chapter] Father purchased land and mined for coal. It was very successful, but Mother was not well here either."

Friends told Mother and Father if they would move to California, they thought mother's health would improve and she would not be troubled with hay fever. Consequently, Father sold the coal mine and moved his family to California."[2]

CALIFORNIA, THE BEAUTIFUL

The Wilcox family moved to Vina, Tehama, California and bought fruit orchards there. There was quite a little Mormon colony there. Many of Samuel and Julia Ann's brothers and sisters and their families and other friends had all moved along with them. It was like a bit of heaven in Vina for them.

Julia Ann did not suffer from hay fever any more. They loved the warm climate and the beautiful fruit orchards. The Wilcox family was happy there until tragedy struck and malaria infested mosquitoes brought death and fever to the beautiful valley. Samuel Allen, Wilcox, Jr., Vera's father, died.

In just a few years Vera's mother, Julia Ann, also passed away. Vera went to work in the big department stores in San Francisco. She lived with one of her brothers and their families part of the time. She loved California. She loved the neat little yards of green-velvet grass. There was a wonderful group of Latter-Day Saints there and she was very happy to be a part of such a special group. There were lots of young people and she had her share of dates and nice experi-

2   Ibid.

Californians through and through: from left, Ada, Vera, Minnie and Lorin.

ences. Vera had lots of suitors, and proposals of marriage, but she had met no one she felt she could love and was willing to share her life with.[3]

DESTINY TAKES OVER

By Verda Nelson Jensen

Vera's sister Minnie Wilcox Turner was married and living in Canada. She had written and asked Vera to come and stay with her and help her out when her new baby was born. Vera decided that she

3   Ibid.

needed a change of scenery and a little vacation from clerking, so decided to accept Minnie's offer and go to Canada. Her plans were to just spend a few weeks there and then to go back to her beloved California.

After the baby was born and Minnie was getting along all right, Vera had a job offer that changed her life. A dear friend of the Wilcox family, Aunt Nell Johansen, wanted Vera to come and help her cook while the "threshers" were at their farm. The threshers" were a big group of men who traveled from one farm to another, trashing the wheat, using the big, expensive, thrashing machines. It took a lot of food to feed this big crew and having good meals for them was part of the contract. Vera thought, "I am enjoying being in Canada again, and what difference would it make if I stayed for another few weeks?"

Vera enjoyed being around old friends once more. Besides, Aunt Nell Johansen had a special man in mind that she wanted Vera to meet.

Nell told Vera that he had been a missionary for six and one-half years to the Samoan and Tongan mission, that he and Vera were just about the same age [27 years old] and that he was a very handsome and desirable fellow. Vera had laughed at her because she had heard this kind of talk before. However, Vera privately admitted that she was very interested, although she didn't want Aunt Nell to know that she was. So many people had tried to play "cupid" with her life that she was a little leery of the matchmakers.

Perhaps the reason Vera had never married, although by this time she was considered an "Old Maid," was because of a special dream she had. She had always been a very prayerful person. She knew that she was a daughter of a kind Father in Heaven and she felt that He would provide the appropriate companion for her. She had dreamed of the man who was to be her "eternal companion." In the dream, she had seen a tall, black-haired, handsome man whom she recognized as the man she would marry.

Vera related, "One Sunday morning, at our Sunday School meeting I nearly fell off of my chair, as the man who I had seen in my dream, walked into the class.

I had chills go over my body. It was almost as if I was stricken 'dumb.' Aunt Nell was sitting by my side and noticed my concern. She asked if I was alright. I replied, 'Nell, that is the man I have told you about, the one who has been in my dream as the man I am going to marry.' "

Aunt Nell laughed, "Vera, this is the man I have been telling you about, the one I have been trying to get you to meet. This is John Nelson, the missionary who just recently returned from his mission to Samoa and Tonga."

John and Vera became good friends. They compared notes and found that they had lived within a 30 mile area of each other when the Wilcox family lived in Canada before moving to California. They discovered that they knew a lot of the same people. They became sweethearts and Vera realized that she was in love with John. John felt the same way and soon asked her to marry him.

Vera related, "I loved him, I was sure of that. However, I hated the winters of Canada and did not like the idea of giving up my beautiful California to become a Canadian again. I hated the blizzards, the wind, the snow and storms of the Canadian prairie. All of these bad memories came to me and I just felt that I could not move back to Canada. I wanted to become John's wife. I wanted to be his 'eternal companion.' I tried to talk John into moving to California, where we could have a good life. But he had the security of a little land in Canada and thought sure that we would starve in California, a new area foreign to him, so he won out."

The following two letters were found in John and Vera's treasures. They are included just as they were written. The ink is so light, that they would not copy, or the original letters would have been photographed to be included.

Raymond, Alberta

November 28, 1916

Dearest John,

I intended to come home last night [back to Cardston] but-well, I simply talked too long and missed the train. I really think it was a "put-up job." Emma told me the clock was fast and Lo! It was not. So I just came home tonight and found your letter of the 23rd instead. Honestly, I was glad it was here.

I had a very nice time in Lethbridge visiting my California friends. By the way, they know you. You know, they used to live in Kimball. I was just a wee bit puzzled as-to whether or not to come up to help Sister Johansen again. I really do not want to come just now, but I will if they really need me. Did you know that I phoned? I wrote to them, but have not heard back from them. I am glad you are enjoying your missionary [Sunday School] work. I truly hope that you will arouse the people to a realization of the benefits of the Sunday School.

Really, I am sorry I was so much of a monopoly of the few short hours we spent together. If you were here tonight,--well I'm sure I'd be willing to just sit and look at you and never say one word. Anyway, I'll try to do better in the future than I have in the past. No fooling, though, I really do want to hear all about your experiences and maybe you can teach me to sing some of your favorite love songs.

The wind is simply howling and all the folks are in bed for the hour is eleven o'clock, but you see, I have been in the city for the last few nights and have the habit of sitting up, so I'll just imagine that I am visiting with you.

You asked me how Brother Tanner was. Well, I haven't seen him since a week ago Sunday in Sunday School. He was all smiles, but he was very busy with a lady-friend, so really, there is no news on that score. I am wondering if you do not receive my letters for, really, I have written real often.

You didn't tell me yet if Cleve had decided what he was going to do. I think I had better say "Good- night" for I feel quite poetic and may say something foolish. So Aura Vous and write soon. Regards to your folks...

As Ever,

Vera

Cardston, Via Raymond December 14, 1916

My Dear Vera,

It is just midnight but I feel it is my duty besides being my pleasure to write you before retiring. Had I come to Cardston a little earlier and know what I know now, you no doubt would be here with me.

You know tomorrow is Seth's wedding day and a grand time is being expected at the Hansen's ranch. Seth wanted you to come, but Hazel told him that you had gone to California, so of course he thought it was all off between us. Consequently he did not send you an invitation. When I came to the city and straightened things out, it was rather late in the day.

If you remember, on leaving the car the last night you were here, you told Hazel and Rae, "Good-bye," and said that you were leaving for California?

Do you remember the story about the boy and the wolf? All joking aside, I wish you were here.

I'm at the Post Office, the day after the night before. I stopped writing during the night to think and my thoughts put me to sleep.

Today is all excitement and I must post a word to you so you will get it in the morning.

I intended to write a lot of things last night, but you know how that is. Will and Rae and myself were going to Lethbridge, but Will took sick. I will be in Raymond on Saturday before Christmas, so LOOK OUT! It would be a joke if we were married Christmas Eve. Just a thought renewed!

Well, be good, little girl and remember that I love you forever. I will write again.

P.S. Brother Johansen's car just came to town bearing Ray, who got hurt this morning. One of the older boys hit him with a tin can.

Yours 'til the end of the chapter, JOHN

On January 1st, 1917, one and one-half years after his return from the mission field, John and Vera were married by President Garnett Allred, Cardston Stake President.

JOHN AND VERA, NEWLYWEDS

Excerpts taken from Vera's journal:

"The wedding was much to be desired. We had planned to be married a few days earlier, but John forgot the license and had to return to Cardston to get it. Brother Allred had come to the chapel in Woolford, Alberta, Canada where we were to be married. He said to us, 'Well, you're both old enough to know what you are doing. I now pronounce you man and wife.' We both wondered if it was a good enough ceremony to make it legal."

[At the time Vera and John were contemplating marriage the Canadian temple had not been built. However, soon after the temple in Cardston, Canada was completed in 1923, John and Vera were among the first people to go to be sealed and have their three little children sealed to them.[4]]

---

4   Vera Nelsons Journal and Family Group Sheets.

John and Vera's first home on the Canadian Frontier, 1917.

"John was building a little home in Woolford, so until it was completed, we moved in with his parents in Cardston. I loved them both as my own parents. They were wonderful people. My own parents had both died by this time, and I had grieved over their deaths many times and the fact that they did not get to know John and know our darling children. I always felt, however, that they did know them beyond the grave and that I had their sanction and love in the choice of my beloved companion."

Grandma Ella Nelson was such a special woman. She had been a midwife and traveled all over Alberta, delivering babies and caring for the sick. She had a special gift from our Heavenly Father, in that she always knew when and where she was needed. This was without the aid of telephone or modern conveniences.

Many times she would tell her husband, 'Please hitch up the buggy for me as Sister So and So needs me over in Magrath, or Woolford, or where ever.' She would always arrive just in time to deliver the baby and care for the mother. "

"I felt a special love from John's father. He always called me 'Auntie' and there was a bond of love between the two of us. He seemed to understand me and I felt of this love."

Our first house was a two-roomed, wooden house. No water in the house, or any plumbing for that matter. Water had to be carried from the town pump in barrels on a wagon. We used coal oil lamps, a nice big coal stove for cooking and a pot-bellied stove to heat the rest of the house. We had a buggy and a nice team. I had worked in the stores in California for quite a few years before I married and had bought some furniture. I had a lovely green carpet, with flowers

John and Vera's first parade: Pioneer Day, July 24th, 1917. Woolford, Alberta, Canada.

in the center, a bedroom set, and some lovely dishes. So, although a two-roomed house, when you had outdoor plumbing and had to haul your own water, might sound kind of primitive now-a-days, to us it was a mansion, and we were very comfortable and happy."

A GROWING FAMILY

Vera continued writing:

"As the children arrived, more rooms were added and they were always comfortable. The winters were long and hard, but many of John's brothers and sisters and families lived close by and there was a wonderful closeness between us. There was also a special bond of love between the members of the Church. We had many wonderful times and formed friendships that have lasted throughout the years. We depended upon each other for our fun and good times and we shared in each other's joys and sorrows."

"Lovell was born November 6, 1917 in Woolford. He was born at home, with a doctor in attendance. Grandma Ella Nelson was good to help out all she could. Lovell was a beautiful child, with dark eyes and black curly hair. He was truly the 'apple' of his father's eye. He was a healthy, beautiful child and was adored by all the family."

"Bruce Allen was born October 17, 1919, on his Grandfather Nelson's birthday. Bruce was so tiny. I had been sick most of my pregnancy. At the delivery, the placenta presented first and I hemorrhaged. The doctor became excited and felt that my life was in danger.

He said that he could not save both the mother and the child. John ran and got his father and they administered to me with the consecrated oil and a miracle happened.

Little Bruce was born soon after the administration. Dr. Stackpook told me later that I was the first case he had ever seen where both the mother and the baby lived under that type of circumstances. Bruce has always been very dear to us."

"John was kind and a gentle, loving husband. He worked hard and the year 1917 we had a good crop. The next seven years that we stayed in Woolford, however, were like a nightmare to us. How we lived through those hard days, I'll never know. The winters were so severe. In the summers, hail wiped out several of our crops. At other times, the crops wouldn't grow because of such severe drought conditions."

"We struggled along, with all of the other farmers in the same dire conditions. We all had put up with the crop failures and the trials of hail and drought. Often there was barely enough wheat or grain to use as seed for the following season. When Bruce was three weeks old, John left for Rockyford in Northern Alberta, with all of the FHA horses. I was to go to the ranch house with John's parents and his brothers, Wren and Darrell. The hay went up to $65.00 a ton and we had a nice herd of cattle to feed. One bale of hay every other day was all we could get. The cattle got so poor and thin. We lost so heavily that winter. Sixteen of our cows died one morning. Oh, me! Those were sad days. Still we borrowed money and planted again with hail robbing us, then an early frost, no gardens and despair seemed to engulf us.[5]

KITTY SAVES JOHN'S LIFE

By Bruce A. Nelson

Although I was just a baby when the incident occurred, I grew up hearing about one of the family horses, that I consider to be a hero. A prolonged and severe drought had ravaged Southern Alberta during the year of 1919. There was very little hay put up that year and no grass was growing in the fields that fall. An association of farmers and ranchers, knowing that crops had been better in Northern Alberta, contracted with my dad to have him take a trainload of horses to Northern Alberta. The idea was for Dad to get the horses through the winter by purchasing straw in the straw stacks and grazing rights in the grain fields where the stubble stood from that year's crops. The alternative was to lose many of the horses in the coming winter from the stark reality of starvation.

After arriving near Rockyford, north and east of Calgary, Dad made arrangements to stay at a farmhouse with some friendly people. The horses that he brought with him were soon dispersed in the stubble fields within a few miles of the ranch buildings where he was staying.

5   Vera Nelson's Journal.

Gordon McOmber, Lovell and Cal McOmber in Canada.

The horses were in very poor condition from lack of good feed and occasionally a horse would get down and expire from the cold weather and the conditions they had to endure. Dad skinned these horses and salvaged the hides, as the hides could be sold.

One morning Dad was skinning one of the fallen horses out in the fields. He became overheated by this extreme physical exertion although the temperature had dropped to considerably below zero. He got back on his horse, Kitty, to go check the other horses, but because of the extremely cold weather, hypothermia overtook him.

Dad realized what was happening to him and tied himself on his saddle with his lariat. He headed Kitty homeward, soon losing consciousness.

Now most horses, in a case like this, having to pass other horses in the fields, would have stopped to eat or browse through the stubble or the straw stack for food. Kitty, however, seemed to sense something was wrong and instead of being drawn to the other horses, stayed on course, headed for the farm house. She kept a slow walk and stopped in front of the gate at the farm house.

Fortunately, the people were home and seeing the problem, went out, untied and carried Father into the house. They revived and took care of him. They all joined in praising the faithful friend, Kitty, for saving his life.

CANADIAN MEMORIES

Bruce, Lovell, Cal and Gordon McOmber.

By Lovell Nelson

In the years we were in Canada in the winter of 1919, when Bruce was a baby and when dad went up north with all of the horses, and the cattle to winter them, I can remember Mother crying. I was only two years old, but I can remember she cried all day long. We had a horse named "Old Chappy" and he backed up against the house to get away from a storm. As he did, he broke a window and I guess that was one of the first words I ever said, Chappy broke the window." Of course, Grandpa Nelson came over and hung a blanket to the window and stuffed it up and that was the way the winter was spent with the blanket over the broken window.

Of course it was very cold. If someone dropped water on the floor, it would turn to ice. We always wore our overshoes in the house.

Cold was something we lived with in those days. I am sure our children would hardly believe any of these stories.

I did not go to school at all in Canada. We left there in 1923. I can remember our family going to the Cardston Temple before we left. I can remember the cattle holding up the baptismal font. It made a very vivid impression on my mind. Years later when I went to the Canadian Temple with my darling wife, Margaret, I saw those same impressive cattle and it brought back the memories of those early days, as though I had just seen them yesterday.

THE BRANDING OF BABY BRUCE AND OTHER MEMORIES

By Bruce Allen Nelson

[This event happened in about 1921 or 1922 in the house on the hill at Woolford, Canada.]

Dad had been branding cattle that day. When he and mother left for a short time, John Lorin Lovell and Melba Lamb became my baby sitters. John Lorin was just past four and Melba was close to his age. I was not quite three.

John with his two sons, Lovell and Bruce.

Lovell had been told, that very day, that the reason Dad branded cattle, was to keep them from getting lost and to keep them from being stolen by others. These fates worried his mind; at all costs, he wanted to keep from them from happening to little Brucie Allen Baby Boy, as his Father called the object of his concern on that fall day so many years ago.

It was only natural that the branding idea burst into Lovell's mind when he put two more sticks of wood into the old kitchen range and saw the stove poker with the nice spring stainless steel handle on it. He knew that he had the means at hand to forever protect his younger brother from being lost or stolen. So being a young, impressionable farm lad who loved his baby brother, Lovell took what he considered a very necessary step when he decided to brand me. Melba was very cooperative. She soon succumbed to the charm and good sense of her cousin, Lovell, who she adored and agreed with him that a good branding, for the cause of protecting her little cousin, was a wise and commendable thing to do.

I was the object of their love. I remember well the light from the kitchen stove, as it threw dancing lights across the ceiling. I had little trepidation as the front lid to the range was partly opened and the poker was put into the burning coals....just like Dad had done. Truly, the realization of those dancing lights and the heating of the poker were forever emblazoned on my mind.

As the evening progressed, I was tied to the kitchen chair, so that the brand could be clean and not at all smeared and so that my left hip would forever afterwards carry proof positive of whose little boy I was.

And so it is, that even to this day, when I see an old kitchen range and a charming old-time poker, a warm feeling comes to both my heart for the love shown me that night and to my left hip, where the proof of that love resides and which will identify me to the end of my days.

RUTH MAUREEN MAKES AN ANXIOUS ARRIVAL

John gives the story of the birth of their first daughter, Ruth Maureen, born Dec. 4, 1921 in Cardston, Alberta, Canada.

"We were living at Woolford, Alberta, Canada. We had two sons, Lovell and Bruce. We were expecting another child the first part of December. Our home was twelve miles away from Cardston. The weather was not too cold, but the wind had been blowing and there were deep snowdrifts all along the road. I knew a sleigh would be the best way to travel over the drifted roads. I had planned to borrow my brother-in-law's sleigh to take Vera to the hospital when her due time came. The day of the 3rd of December, Vera kept coaxing me to

Likely John and Vera, Bruce, Ruth and Lovell on the horse.

take her into town as she felt that the baby would soon be born."

"I had a nice team that I kept in the barn all of the time. It just so happened on this particular night, the team did not return to the barn, but stayed out in the field. Vera was nervous and kept coaxing me to go get the team and have them ready in the barn in case we needed them. I procrastinated, feeling that there was no hurry, as I didn't feel that the baby would be born yet."

'About midnight, Vera woke me up, saying that she felt we must get into the hospital. I went out and got the team by putting some oats into a pan and rattling the pan. The team came running and I harnessed them up. I ran for the sleigh and also took the boys over to my brother-in-law's to be tended."

"I got Vera all bundled up and started out for the twelve miles ride. Ordinarily my team could travel the twelve miles in less than an hour. The snow was drifting because of the fierce wind that was howling. Vera pulled the quilts over top of her as she lay in the bottom of the sleigh."

"We got along okay, until we crossed the St. Mary's River, within about two and one-half miles from Cardston. The snow was drifting so rapidly that I could not see the road or even tell if I was on the road or not. All of a sudden, with my right front runner, I hit a rock and it broke the runner of the sleigh. I didn't know what to do. We still had a long ways to go. I thought it would be best if I got out of the sleigh, thinking if I rode it would make it hard on the team and impossible to continue on. "

"I held the reins on my team very tightly. I ran along side of the sleigh, holding up the one broken runner as we traveled. I had a difficult time trying to keep up with the horses. I would get out of breath and then I would jump on the sleigh to ride a little ways. I don't know how long it took us to go that last two and one-half miles with the broken sleigh runner. All the time Vera was screaming with the pains of child birth."

"After what seemed like an eternity, we arrived at the hospital. Vera was chilled and nearly hysterical. Within just a very few minutes after we arrived at the hospital, our first little girl was born. The doctor said that it was a good thing that we had arrived, as Vera had to have help with the delivery and had she tried to have the baby in the sleigh, in that blinding blizzard, we may have lost both the mother and the child."

"We are grateful that Ruth was born well and healthy. I learned a hard lesson that night. I learned to be more compassionate and understanding of Vera's requests. I realized that I came close to losing the most precious thing in my life, my darling Vera, because of not taking her counsel when she knew it was close to her delivery time. I have always been sorry about this and have asked Vera's forgiveness many times."[6]

Vera recorded in her journal: "Ruth was born on December 4, 1921 in the hospital in Cardston. We were living out at Woolford, Alberta, Canada. I had felt all the day before that I was ready to deliver the baby and should get in to the doctor in Cardston. The snow was so deep, but I foolishly let John talk me out of going that day. About midnight, I took sick and we had one wild ride. I screamed most of the way and at the river bridge, two and one-half miles east of Cardston, the runner on the small sleigh broke. John had to walk and hold up the sleigh on the side of the broken runner. The doctor told me later that as no pioneer woman had a worse experience that I did that cold and windy December night.[7]

BRUCE REMEMBERS

Bruce continues his memories of Canadian days: "I also remember as a young lad, going with Dad to load the family's round, water tank in the St. Mary's River. Dad would stand on the side of the wagon and fill the tank with a bucket; he'd let me hold the reins as the team would pull the tank from the river, up the slope, and towards home."

"I remember what a great love my Dad had for horses. He had a natural ability with horses and could take the wild out of a five-year old stallion, who had never seen a man before, in a in matter of thirty or forty minutes. He would have them so well-trained that he could remove the lariat and crawl under the horse's belly."

"There were times when he would break the horses by hitching a couple of broncos up to his well-trained team of horses, Rodg and

6   John Nelson Dictaphone tape #31.
7   Vera Nelsons Journal

229

Cap. He would then take them out on a wagon through plowed fields and bring the broncos back responding to his commands. A big hired man and a good set of trip ropes, using kind but firm manner by both his old team and himself, brought the broncos to accept what was demanded of them and they would fall into obedience."

"There was a small saddle horse that Dad loved, called Old Buttons. Dad would let all of the kids from the neighborhood get on the horse, all together. He was just a good old, slow pony and he made a great kid-pony. Sometimes Dad would take Old Buttons out with him when he went hunting. He used to hide behind Old Buttons as he slowly moved towards the geese or the ducks he was stalking."

THOUGHTS OF MOVING TO GREENER PASTURES

With Peggy Squires Massey's permission, the next paragraph is included from her Mother and Father's life story:

"Two men came and talked to my parents far into the night. They were representing the Great Northern Railroad and trying to get eight families to go to Montana to settle the Chestnut Valley. So began another chapter in our lives--Montana! What a beautiful place it was that April, 1922. Chestnut Valley was nestled up against the mountains, green with grass and pines, with the Missouri River winding lazily through the valley. That first winter was mild, compared to the cold winters of Idaho."[8]

From Vera's journal: "My sister, Maude Squires and her husband, Lawrence, had moved to the Chestnut Valley in Montana. This was just about 30 miles south of Great Falls. Maude and Lawrence had been living in Idaho when they had the opportunity to move to Montana to settle the Chestnut Valley. In 1922, Maude and Lawrence wrote to us, telling us of their move to Montana, to the Chestnut Valley and encouraging us to join them there. In October, I persuaded John to take a trip down to Montana and look over the prospects of our moving there also. He returned with good reports

---

8   Maude and Lawrence Squires Life, by Peggy Massey.

and felt there were opportunities for our family. After a lot of concern and prayerful moments, we decided to make the move."

"Thus we began a new chapter of our lives. We had decided to move to Montana. There was a great deal of sadness, however, as we knew we would miss the close relationship of John's parents and his brothers and sisters and their families who stayed in Canada. However, it was exciting to think that I would finally be living close to some of my family again."[9]

---

9   Vera Wilcox Nelsons Journal.

13

OUR MOVE TO MONTANA

CHESTNUT VALLEY, HERE WE COME

At Vera's insistence, John went down to look over the Chestnut Valley. He liked what he found there. It was a beautiful valley, but it was in a depressed condition. The ditches had been neglected. The previous owners had not paid their water assessments, their ditch assessments, or their taxes. Because of this, the land had gone into litigation. The Spokane Eastern Trust Company held the mortgages on the whole valley, some five thousand acres.

A group from the Great Northern Railroad, comprised of citizens from the town of Cascade, had sent a man down to Idaho, to try and recruit Mormon families to move to the valley and settle the land. The idea was that there would be money in the bank, up to $20,000, for these settlers to draw on to help them get started. It would be a loan to them to help them get established. The settlers would be required to pay back the money they borrowed within a two or three year period.

The man who was recruiting among the Mormons, in Idaho, found eight families who were preparing to move to California. They had their equipment, horses, machinery and nearly everything they owned already loaded on the freight cars. After meeting with these families and explaining the proposition to them, he induced them to about-face; instead of going to the south, they traveled north and arrived in Cascade, Montana with all of their equipment. This was a time when not all of the people of Cascade knew much about the Mormons. The Mormons were a matter of curiosity when they arrived. People wondered just what kind of neighbors they would be.[1]

This was the reason that the Squires family had left Idaho and moved into the Chestnut Valley. Because of their invitation and Vera's insistence, John made his first trip down to the Chestnut Valley. It was a beautiful place. The potatoes were large and the corn was beautiful. The alfalfa seemed to be wonderful and it was apparent that a fanner wouldn't need as much land to farm as he needed in Canada.

John and Vera had experienced many failures and trials in the seven years they had lived in Canada because of the drought conditions, the hail and the freezing cold winters. This new adventure of moving to Montana to join the Mormons in this area looked good to them.

Consequently, they decided to leave Woolford, Canada and move to Montana.

After disposing of their home, land, stock and everything they had, with the exception of what they could take on a trail wagon, they set out for a new adventure in the big state of Montana.

Bruce wrote a few memories of this occurrence: "I remember Dad being on his wagon, hitched up and ready to start for Montana when I suddenly remembered that the 'stick horse' my cousin. Glen Turner, had made for me was not on the load, but down across the

---
1   John Nelson's Journal

lake from Uncle Rents house. I learned patience as my Father waited for me to run all the way and find my most valuable possession and bring it back to put on the load, headed for Montana. I remember the warm feeling I had, knowing my Father had taken the time to wait for me, when he had so very far to drive his two wagons, loaded with all our worldly possessions. I remember the excitement of the trip on the train with Mother, Lovell and little sister, Ruthie."[2]

THE LONG, HARD JOURNEY

John wrote some of the experiences he had while moving his family from Woolford, to Cascade, in a letter to his children dated:

Great Falls, Montana July 13, 1951

To my dear family away from Great Falls,

I promised you another story about my trip to Montana in the year 1923. It was in the fall, the month of November.

The night before I left Woolford, in a Bishop's Council Meeting, the Bishop asked Brother J. E. Steed to offer a special prayer for my benefit, while I was traveling to Montana. Brother Steed asked the Lord to protect me from harm, to protect my family while we were apart and to provide a place for me to stop each night, while I was on the way.

As we made plans to move to Cascade, I knew the hardest part would be getting our belongings moved from Canada. I sent Vera and the three children ahead on the train from Lethbridge. Vera's sister, Maude and her husband, Lawrence Squires, met them in Cascade. While Vera and the children stayed with the Squires family on their farm in Cascade, I drove my two teams of horses, as they pulled a big wagon and a trailer, which were loaded with our furniture and other belongings. I also trailed my other two horses. This long, rugged, November journey covered a distance of 160 miles to Cascade.

---

2   Letter from Bruce Nelson to his sister Verda Jensen dated April 3, 1989.

My brother, Wren, was traveling with me. The second night out we stayed at a big cattle ranch. The foreman was very kind to us. We each had a bunk to sleep on and our horses fared equally well in a big barn. The next morning, I asked the boss, what the charges were for the night's lodgings. He answered, "Not a thing," and we were on our way again.

The next stop was at Sweetgrass, where I had to get my horses inspected for glanders, a contagious disease peculiar to horses. I had to lay over there for three days waiting for the inspector to arrive. Wren left me here and took the train back to Woolford. Leaving Sweetgrass, I had to travel part way to Cut Bank about 15 miles back towards Canada, as that was the best road. Along in the later afternoon, as I passed different farmhouses and men along the way, I inquired if there was a ranch or farm that I might reach by about six o'clock that evening. I was told that there were two ranches along that road that I would reach about that time of night.

I was informed that the people of the first ranch would probably welcome me, but the folks at the second ranch would not let strangers in, under any circumstances. They had become bitter toward all mankind and people knew it all along the road.

That's why I was instructed that I would be welcomed anywhere I might stop but this one place.

About six o'clock, I reached the first ranch and finding no one at home, I decided to take my chances at the second ranch. I found no one at home there, either. However, I decided to pull into the yard and unhitch my tired horses. The yard was large, with a fence around it. There was an old granary in the southeast corner and I camped there. I always carried an extra bale of hay, in case of emergency and circumstances occurred that I could not buy any hay along the way.

Just as I was giving my horses some hay, I noticed a man getting out of his two-horse buggy to open the gate. I shouted that I would open it for him. He drove on through and I walked over to help him unharness his team. I was talking all the time, in an apologetic manner, but the man did not say a word.

He went into the house and returned with a milk bucket.

I stood as close as I dared and kept talking, watching any moment for the bucket to come whirling through the air at me.

About this time, a car drove up and a woman, I assumed to be the man's wife, got out and went into the house. I later found out the neighbors had brought her home from some function, while the husband had returned early to do the chores.

It was getting dark and I hated to make my bed under the wagon, without first making friends with the owners of the farm where I had been so bold as to stop for the evening. I took a little pail, to see if I could buy a little milk, and knocked on the back door. The man's wife answered and invited me in.

I made as nice a speech as I could, mentioning the fact I disliked to camp out on the prairie so late in the season because the hazard of blizzards. Storms often came upon us so suddenly, that I might have been frozen to death. The lady of the house warmed up to me, immediately and gave me some milk, refusing any money for it. Her husband spoke for the first time, saying I could make my bed in the granary.

Just as I had my blankets and canvas spread out on the granary floor, the man came to the door and said they would like to have me come into the house for a little while. I accepted his invitation and went with him into the house. The three of us had a very wonderful evening. I found out that she was a former schoolteacher. I told her of my experiences teaching school in the South

Sea Islands. From there, we were well on our way to developing a sudden friendship.

These dear people told me that they had been soured on the public, especially strangers, because they had been short-changed many times in the sale of their farm produce. They had made a little, road-side stand and they would let the people help themselves to buy their goods. Most of their customers were their neighbors and they were always treated honestly by these neighbors. However, often strangers would come and steal some of their produce.

I explained where I was going. I told them all about my little family and how much I missed them, even for the few short days that I was away from them. I told about sending them all ahead on the train. I told them about my being a Mormon Missionary in far-away Samoa and Tonga for over six years. This brought many questions regarding my religious beliefs. Nearly twelve o'clock, as I arose to go back to my bed on the granary floor, they both begged me to sleep in the house, in their spare room. I refused, saying that I wanted to get an early start in the morning and I did not want to disturb them.

The next morning they insisted that I come in the house before I left and have breakfast with them, which I did. They gave me hay and grain for my horses. They would take no money for their kind hospitality. When I pulled my wagon and team out of their yard, my newfound friend opened the gate for me with his wife standing nearby, wishing me "God Speed." They made me promise that I would write to them and let them know how I got along on my trip to Cascade.

I wrote them a letter when I got settled and thanked them again for their kind hospitality. In my life I have never found many mean people; I find when people really know the intent of your heart and what you are doing, there's a streak of kindness and love and generosity within their souls. And that's what I found on this trip, all the way along. I was really taken care of. The prayer that Brother J. E. Steed offered for me was certainly answered in my behalf all the way along.

There, my dear family, is a start on my trip to Montana. I will continue writing at another time. I love you all,

Daddy

FAIRFIELD, MONTANA

On John's dictaphone tape he recorded:

"As previously arranged, Lyle Squires, Vera's nephew, met me when I arrived at Fairfield, Montana. I was happy to have him join me to help me drive the horses as I continued on to Cascade where Vera and the children would be waiting for me."

"I always kept my horses in good shape and they were powerful. My lead team weighed 1400 pounds and my wheel team 1600. One of my stallions in my lead team had lost a shoe and to keep him from going lame, I took him to the blacksmith at Fairfield. The blacksmith agreed to shoe him, only if I would help to nail the shoe on.

The blacksmith said, 'I'll make the shoe if you'll hold up the stallion's foot. That's one type of animal that I draw the line on shoeing.

So you'll have to nail the shoe on him yourself while I frame the shoe and shape it to his foot.' I agreed that I would help."

"He was a mean, ornery horse to shoe. I didn't realize that before, but I found it out. He was so big and powerful and I perspired so freely that after it was over, I caught cold. The next day, I let Lyle drive as I tried to recuperate. I put on two or three heavy coats and did the best I could to keep the cold November wind from blowing through my clothes. We were without any protection from the elements as we were just sitting on the spring seat of the wagon."[3]

---

3   John's dictaphone tape #39.

A WILD INTRODUCTION TO CASCADE

"We had traveled forty miles from Fairfield to Cascade that day. My horses were tired from pulling such a heavy load. As we were going up the main street of Cascade, a train came along the track in front of us.

My horses were not used to trains as we had lived quite a ways from the railroad. My lead team was startled the minute they saw the train, and I could do nothing with them.

A group of men ran out and grabbed my horses by their bits and held on to them while the train stopped for a few minutes and continued holding on to them until the train went on. If it hadn't been for this group of men standing in front of the store, I suppose my two wagons and all my household effects and all that I owned would have been strewn all over the streets of Cascade. I was always grateful to those men who came to my rescue."[4]

"After we left Cascade, we drove about nine miles to the Squires' farm where Vera and the children were waiting for me. We stayed with them for a few days until I rented a little two-room house from a young man by the name of John Kelly. This was only temporary until 1 could buy a place and get located."[5]

THE INFAMOUS MR. BROWN

"We felt fortunate to find a little house where we could once again be a family. It also had a place for my horses. I purchased two cows to give us milk for the children. Now, I needed to find some hay to buy. Lawrence said that he had some extra that he would sell me. The only problem was that he lived nine miles away and so I had to haul it that distance."

"One day, a man came across the field where I was working. He said, 'My name is William Brown. I live over in the house you see yonder.

4   John's dictaphone tape #39.
5 Ibid.

I noticed that you are hauling your hay from quite a distance. I have extra hay over in the field close by. I put it up here, so if you wish to buy some, I'd be happy to sell it to you; then you won't have to go so far to get your hay. I'll sell it to you for a reasonable price. You can cut off of either end that you want. I'll come over one of these first days and measure it in the stack and you can just pay according to what you use.'"

"Well, I thought this seemed like a good idea. I wouldn't have to haul my hay from such a long ways away. It didn't matter to Lawrence. He was just trying to accommodate me by selling it to me. When I needed more hay, I got up on the top of the stack and took my hay knife and cut down into the stack of hay that Mr. Brown had showed me belonged to him. I had been using the hay for three or four days when Mr. Kelly, my landlord, came along. He said, 'Mr. Nelson, I see that it must be you who has cut into my hay stack.'"

"I replied, 'Mr. Kelly, I was informed by a Mr. William Brown that the hay stack belonged to him. He said that I could cut from either end of the stack and I would pay him accordingly, after we measured the stack.'"

"'Well,' said Mr. Kelly. 'I see that Mr. Brown is up to his old tricks again. He has nothing, whatsoever, to do with the haystack. The land that the stack is on is mine. This is my hay. I put it up myself with my men and Mr. Brown has nothing to do with it. He does not own any of it.'"

"I said, 'Well, I am awfully sorry about the problem.'"

"He replied, 'Well, that is all right. I want to sell some of the hay any way, so you go ahead and use what you wish and I'11 come along and measure the stack so I'll know what to charge you.'"

"I said, 'That will be fine, but I don't feel good about my experience with Mr. Brown. Why would he come and tell me that the hay was his? I want to meet him and see what he has to say for himself.'"

"In a few days, they were having an auction up the other end of the valley. Mr. Chris Wareheim was selling his farm equipment. I got on one of my horses and rode up five or six miles to the auction sale. Mr. Brown and Mr. Kelly had both come to attend the sale."

"I arranged to get both of them together and I said, 'Now I would like a statement from both of you as to who owns the hay that I have purchased. There seems to be a misunderstanding as to who the rightful owner is. Mr. Brown has given me permission to cut from either end, saying the hay is his. Mr. Kelly tells me that the haystack is on his land and that it belongs to him. Now, please tell me which of you owns the hay."

"Mr. Brown walked over to me very bold and brazen-like and spoke up, 'Oh, you can pay Mr. Kelly for that hay, that's perfectly all right with me.' The matter seemed to be settled. But that was only the beginning of my encounters with the infamous MR. BROWN."[6]

MR. BROWN STRIKES AGAIN

"Here's another experience with my friend Mr. Brown. A little later, in the spring of the year, Mr. Brown came over to my farm and made a proposition to me. He had learned that I was experienced at breaking' horses. (This is the process of teaching a horse to wear a bridle and a saddle and in a way becoming tame enough to be of use.) He had found eight or ten head of wild horses and was desirous of having them broke to lead."

"He said, 'If you'll help me, I'd really appreciate it and I'll pay you accordingly.' I must admit that I was a bit skeptical, but since I had some free time, I told him that I would come up to his place and see what I could do."

"He asked me if I had any halters we could use. He said that he didn't have any, but that he would go into Cascade and buy some. I told him that I had five or six halters that I had the harness-maker

---

6   John's dictaphone tape #39.

make for me in Canada. They were made especially strong and I called them my bronco halters."

"I told him, 'I'll go on over to your place and catch one or two of the horses. If you're not there, I'll put my halter on them and when you come, we'll exchange.' He liked the idea. So he went on in to Cascade and I rode over to his ranch. The horses were in the corral. I roped the first horse and snubbed him up and broke him to lead. I put on one of my halters. Mr. Brown had not returned from Cascade, so I tied the horse up to the post of the corral and caught another horse, and after breaking him to lead, I put another one of my halters on him. Then Mr. Brown arrived."

"He said, 'You know, I have looked all over town for some good strong halters, but couldn't find a one. Now if you'll let me use your halters for a few days, until I can get these horses broken to lead, I have some old harnesses that I think will do.'"

"I should not have trusted him, but I was not even thinking that this was just another of his stories. So I agreed to his proposal.

Well, I was sorry that I had ever suggested that I had the harnesses to begin with. That was the last time I ever saw the halters. I caught the rest of the horses and put all of my five or six good halters on the horses and tied the horses up. He promised to return them in a few days."

"Every time I would see Mr. Brown, I'd ask about my halters. He would make some excuse, 'Oh, I meant to bring those halters down to you, but I just forgot,' or he would say, 'They are still on my horses. I haven't been able to replace them.' I went to his place several times to get the halters and he wasn't home. What he did with the halters, I'll never know. He apparently took them off of his horses and decided they were such nice halters that he just couldn't live without them. I never saw them again. I decided that Mr. Brown was one man I just couldn't trust. I learned my lesson the hard way!"[7]

---

7   John's dictaphone tape #12.

A NEW HOME FOR THE FAMILY

"We were able to purchase an eighty-acre plot of ground that had been previously assigned to another family. This family had decided to return to Idaho and given up the idea of building a home on the land. It was necessary for me to purchase a house and move it onto the land. All of the Mormon families in the valley came to help. As there was not always a road to travel on, we had to get permission from many of the families to tear their fences down, in order to bring the house we were moving across their land. We had fifteen teams of horses, moving straight through the fields for a distance of about 15 miles. What a wonderful day it was when we had this little home and were able to move our belongings into it."[8]

MEMORIES OF CASCADE

Bruce Allen Nelson wrote a letter to his sister, Ruth, on February 14, 1979. Memories included in this letter follow:

"We moved a house, or part of a house, from over where the Stoddards lived using teams of horses. I suspect it was the backroom where J. Lovell and I slept without heat those many years. The winter was so cold. I slept on the north side and he on the south; both on our right side mainly, so to this day, parts of both of us tend to bear a little right from a position of true norm."

"We had water in the house from the well, by bucket. The well was Within 20 feet of the house. The faithful and wonderful little house was about 20 feet beyond that to the south. The farm was a square 80 acres with land to the north across the lane. Beets, wheat, oats, spuds were some of the crops we raised."

"I remember one Christmas in Cascade when our good Father, John Alexander, Jr. handled his lack of funds with his Solomon-like wisdom. Lovell and I had long been plagued with wet feet in the spring. As the snow melted making the corral and the inside of the barn a quagmire, I remember how wet we would get doing our chores. We

8   John's dictaphone tape #39.

thought that the best Christmas gift we could get was for each of us to have a pair of gum boots and a slicker."

> **"Much to our disappointment, Santa left not two pair of boots and two slickers, but just one pair of boots and one slicker. I recall when spring came, we traded-off keeping either our feet, or our backs dry, never both at the same time."**

"The school bus picked us up down at the north end of Mormon Lane, which is also where it dropped us off at night. We walked to the bus stop and waited for the bus as a general rule. I guess I did have the reputation of being a show-off with the girls. One cold spring day I did a foolish thing. I went swimming in the canal. [I left my long underwear on.] Then I rode my horse all the way home with the wet underwear still on. Pneumonia was the result; double! Poor Mother and Father had to care for me while I was out of my head with fever and I was cussing, too!"

A GRAND OLD TEAM

John's dictaphone tape continued:

"After we got settled in our new home, I wanted to go to the mountains to get poles and posts to use for the fences and to build up my property. I took as my companion, Lyle Squires, my nephew. We started out with my team, old Cap and Roge, a team of bay geldings that weighed about 1600 pounds. They were good workers and had been trained to work in the mountains. We came to a place where there had been a fire and there were many straight, dry poles. As we proceeded down the road, we met two men with a wagon and four head of horses tied to the wagon. These men too, were cutting poles."

"I asked Lyle if he knew the men. He replied, 'The one man is Mr. Tom James, a man who doesn't like the Mormons very much. I suppose the other man is his hired helper. We went on down the road, perhaps a mile or more and there we found a good spot where we could very easily cut the poles and load what we needed. Lyle was a strong young man and a good worker and we were able to load what we wanted in a short time. We had our load as high on the wagon as we possibly could."

"There was only one road leading out of the mountains. That was, of course, the wagon road that people had made through the years to come up over the hill and then down on the other side of the mountain, into the valley. After we secured the load with chains, we started out. When we got up to the place we had met Mr. James and his friend, we found that they had a big load on their wagon and were getting ready to pull out. I had made the remark as we came into the forest, 'He must be planning on getting a big load, as he has four horses to pull it out.'"

"As we came up behind, Mr. James called to us, saying that they were having some trouble getting the horses to pull the load. He said, 'Would you consider taking your team off your wagon and put on the lead of my wheel team, just to start them, then we could take it up the hill quite easily. My four horses will not start the load up the hill.'"

"I suggested that maybe Lyle and I could roll on a wheel and see if we could get them started that way. But this did not work. The horses would not work together to get the load started. Again, Mr. James suggested that I hook my team on to his wheel team, thinking this would get his teams started. I said, 'No, but I'll tell you what I will do, Mr. James. You take all four of your horses off your wagon and I'll let my team pull your load to the top of the hill, then certainly your horses will take it down the hill on the other side of the mountain.'"

"'Oh,' he said, 'I wouldn't think of asking you to pull this big load with your team up the hill.' I told him that was the only way I would do it. 'If you won't take your horses off, so I can pull it up with my team alone, Lyle and I will have to cut some of those trees down and go around you to get back on the road.'"

"Mr. James would not agree, so Lyle and I began cutting down some of the trees to get out around them. Mr. James came up and said, 'Do you really think your team can pull my load?'"

"I said that I felt sure they could. Mr. James unhooked his horses and they were driven up the hill.

As I saw them going up the hill, I thought, 'What a pity, those powerful animals are unwilling to pull the load of the master. They are unwilling to do their duty. They would have been willing to go home empty-handed, so to speak, and even leave the loaded wagon on the mountain."

"I helped Mr. James hook my horses on to his wagon and told him all he would have to do with my horses would be to pick up a pretty good-sized stick and put it behind the hind wheel as they stopped to rest. After they had rested, they would start themselves. 'You won't have to say a word until they get to the top of the hill. They will not hurt themselves, because they are trained for mountain work,' I told him."

"Lyle wrapped the lines up around the log and took a good-sized stick, almost as big as your body, to drop behind a wheel on this steep hill after the team got their breath. With Lyle driving, the horses started out and took the load, little by little and finally, after a good many stops, they reached the top."

"Mr. James came and sat down by me on a log just opposite my wagon and he asked, 'Mr. Nelson, do you think your team could have pulled your big load out around my wagon and then back on to the road?'"

"I replied, 'Mr. James, my horses will pull every time I ask them. They would never stop. They would pull all day. They may get a wheel up against a big rock and we'd have to move the rock, but when the rock was moved, they would pull and pull. Yes, I am sure they could have pulled this big load back on the road to get around you if I'd have asked.'"

"Mr. James said, 'I'd give anything in the world if I had one team on my ranch that would even start a load like you have here. But, it seems, all of my horses are balky. They have not been properly trained. They have been spoiled by poor drivers and even with the four that I had here today, they would not even attempt to start the load.'"

"I have thought of this experience many times. I have likened it to the Master, Jesus Christ, who has asked me as an Elder in His Church, to pull the load, to start it, and do all that I could to help get to the top of the hill.

I realize that I have a responsibility to carry whatever load has been assigned to me and as members of His Church, we must work together in harmony and love and pull together to get the end re-sult."

"Many years later, I met Mr. James in a local store. He said, 'Mr. Nelson, you are one man I will never forget. I will always remember that wonderful team you had that was so willing to pull for you.'"[9]

MR. BROWN'S QUESTIONABLE ROAD TO REPENTANCE

"I was serving as the Second Counselor to Branch President, George Barlow, in the branch at Cascade, Montana. We had quite a few people whose names were on our branch records, but who were to-tally inactive. We had some members attending whose names were not on our church records but who were holding responsible posi-tions in the Branch. Under the procedure, as directed by the Church Headquarters, it was our responsibility to determine the status of all the membership of the branch. We needed to get the membership records brought up-to-date. For example, it was necessary to write to some of the former wards or branches of our members to get the baptism records, or the priesthood ordination records before temple recommends could be issued."

9   John's dictaphone tape #44.

"My 'friend,' Mr. Brown, fell into the category of being active in the branch, but there were no records at all that he had ever been baptized, or that any priesthood ordinations had been performed. 'Brother' Brown had been called to be the Sunday School Superintendent, but he was causing a great deal of trouble and bad feelings among the saints, because of his belligerent attitude and his superiority complex."

"It was my responsibility to get 'Brother' Brown's church records current. I spoke to him, 'Brother Brown, we are trying to establish the recommends of all of our members here. It is necessary that I write to your former ward to get your records up-to-date. We want to get you baptism records and your priesthood ordinations in our branch records. We have nothing to show that you are a baptized member.'" (We later learned that we should have written to the Church Headquarters in Salt Lake City in the first place, to receive this information.)

I wrote to a Bishop in Idaho and soon received the information that 'Brother' Brown had never been baptized. The Bishop further stated that 'Brother' Brown had married a Mormon woman, but as far as this Bishop could tell, had never joined the Church."

I went back to 'Brother' Brown with this information. He flew into a rage and said, 'What is the matter with that Bishop? He knows that I was a member.' '

Brother' Brown gave me the name of another Bishop with the instructions to write to him and I'd be sure to get the information that I needed."

"I wrote to the second Mormon Bishop, with the same response. By then, we decided to write to the Church Headquarters in Salt Lake with the same request. Neither had any records of 'Brother' Brown's affiliation with the Mormon Church. I took this information to President Barlow, with the suggestion that we should talk to 'Brother' Brown about the problem."

"We called 'Brother' Brown into President Barlow's home. We went upstairs into a bedroom. I sat on a trunk. They were both sitting on chairs. President Barlow let me do the talking. I didn't mince matters at all. I said, 'Brother Brown, we are surprised that you would try to put one over on us when you have never been baptized into the Church of Jesus Christ of Latter-day Saints. It is not possible for you to hold an office in the Branch unless you are a baptized member. You have caused a lot of dissension in the Branch. You have embarrassed your counselors in the Sunday School by becoming angry if they start the Sunday School meeting without you, even if you are late in coming. What do you have to say for yourself?'"

"He hung his head in shame. He said, 'Well I guess you have me trapped. As far as I know, I never was baptized into the Church. But, what is the difference?

I've joined, all but being baptized. I attend all of the meetings. I've been asked to speak and I do everything any Elder in the Church could do; only I have never been baptized, or ordained an Elder.'"

"We explained to him that there were certain steps that he must take to be worthy for baptism. We encouraged him to prepare himself to take these necessary steps, of repentance and seeking the Spirit of the Lord in his life. It was necessary for us to release him as Sunday School Superintendent."

"He made an effort to become a member. He attended all of the meetings and seemed to be sincere about his repentance. One day, he and Brother Barlow were talking and 'Brother' Brown lost control of himself and hit Brother Barlow, knocking him down. Brother Barlow was a big man, both in stature and in spirit. He was a very forgiving man, a wonderful leader, who would do anything for his brother in the gospel. He had the Spirit of the Lord with him. He was not one to hold a grudge and would willingly forgive a man who had made a mistake, if the man came to him in true repentance."

"Shortly after this occasion, 'Brother' Brown came to President Barlow. He said, 'If you think I am worthy, I would like to be baptized into your Church.' President Barlow took him out into the canal that ran from the Missouri River down through the valley. There was a deep hole there and President Barlow baptized him and confirmed him a member of the Church of Jesus Christ of Latter-day Saints. He grew in the gospel and was a good Bible scholar. From all outward indications, he had truly repented of his sins."

"However, his old habits were deeply ingrained in him and it was not long before he was up to his old tricks again. He was just like J. Golden Kimball once said, 'You might just as well baptize a sack of sand, as a man who doesn't truly repent. It won't be any more effective, than baptizing that sack of sand.'"[10]

RUTH'S MEMORIES OF CASCADE, MONTANA

By Ruth Nelson Miller

I can remember going out with a little broom dad bought me, when I was about four or five years old, and sweeping the dooryard. It was just plain old, Cascade dirt and made a lot of dust, but I had to make it look good. I also remember carrying in water from the well and helping mother wash the dishes as I stood on a little stool by the table. One day I went to help Aunt Maude with her dishes and then I swept her dooryard to make it look better--and she said she wished Peggy would sweep as good as I did. Peggy was older than I and I felt like such a big lady. I was about five then, but now I realize that Aunt Maude was just saying this to make me feel good.

I went to Aunt Minnie's a lot and how I loved to go there to visit my dear cousins. I idolized Ada and Thirza Jean. They were my special "big cousins". We always made homemade ice cream and I remember Glen and Marvin were such teases, but at the same time, they would play with the younger cousins and we all had

---

10   John's dictaphone tape #12.

such fun. They would turn the freezer and when it got hard to turn, they would have all the cousins take a couple of turns to get it just right. And just right it was! Yummy! I can taste that real-cream, ice cream now!

Aunt Maude's family lived the closest to us and it seems we spent a lot of time together. Peggy was our special baby tender and the only girl cousin in the Squires family. The boys were all just like our own brothers and they spent a lot of time at our house. I remember once when our older boys were sick, with either the chicken pox or measles, Mother kept Jack, along with our kids, as he was the only one who had the disease in the Squires family. He and Lee were pals and jumped all over the beds. I don't think they were very sick. Mother had beds made in the front room and I can still see those beds, with kids who were supposed to be quiet.

MY MEMORIES OF UNCLE JOHN AND AUNT VERA

By Peggy Squires Massey

As I think of Aunt Vera and Uncle John, my memory goes back many years to the happy times when they moved from Woolford, I Canada to Cascade. Longer than I can remember, my family had lived in Idaho, where we were surrounded by aunts, uncles, and many cousins. Then we left them all behind and moved to far-away Montana, where we had to "go it alone." That is why we eleven were so happy when Aunt Vera and Uncle John Nelson's family and later Aunt Minnie and Uncle James Turner's family joined us in Chestnut Valley, Montana. Now we were a family again--a family of uncles, aunts and cousins and what great times we had together.

We started school in September of 1922. We rode to school in a school bus that stopped at our gate and took us to Cascade. The school was a two story red brick building. The elementary grades met on the first level and the four high school grades big were relegated to the top floor. There were no junior high grades then. My first teacher was Miss Nellie Simes. I loved her dearly for she didn't seem to mind a bit that I was a Mormon. It was funny to us that so many of the kids at school really did think Mormons had horns.

The Nelsons moved to the valley shortly before Thanksgiving in 1923. They had three children then, Lovell, Bruce and baby girl, Ruth, who was two-years old. I remember how thrilled I was to have a little girl cousin. All we had in our family were boys. John Lovell Nelson was about six-years old. He was such a handsome little boy. We were very proud to take him to school with us on the school bus.

Whenever anyone would ask his name, he would say, "I'm John Lorin Lovell Alexander Wilcox Nelson, Jr. That's my name!" He had added a few names to his own, but he liked the extra prestige of the longer name and we always chuckled because that was quite a mouthful for such a little boy.

When the eight Mormon families from Idaho arrived in Chestnut Valley, the men cast lots for their farms. Ours was located in what was known as the Upper Valley near the mountains. Later, my father acquired a farm adjoining Uncle John's farm in the lower valley, so that we would be closer to school, town, and church activities.

It was during these years of growing up together, that we were like one big family that kept growing with the addition of Lee, Verda, Joyce and Robert. How excited and happy I was when Aunt Vera, knowing how disappointed I was because I never had a little sister, told me I could choose the name for their new baby girl. Joyce, I hope you have liked the name I chose for you. It seemed to fit you.

Uncle John kept us in haircuts and stories. Aunt Vera was always a joy to be with. We loved to hear her give readings and no one could ever do "Naughty Briar Rose" like she could. When I was twelve-years old, my father and I went down to Brigham City to see my Grandma Squires, who I hadn't seen since I was three-years old. Aunt Vera had a bright yellow dress that I liked very much. She gave it to me to take on the trip and also a pair of silk stockings. That was really something! How I loved my Aunt Vera!

I believe it was Keith (one account says it was Jack) who had the measles or the chicken pox the same time some of the Nelson children had them too, so Aunt Vera took him and cared for him with her own.

Back in those days, our chief recreation was house parties. Families, friends and neighbors would gather at different homes each week for an evening of fun and games and of course, good food!

I recall Uncle John falling for the "The Farmer Shears His Sheep" trick every time. When the sheep put his head back and said, "Baa--aa," he would get his mouth filled with salt. Poor Aunt Vera would be so embarrassed because he never learned to avoid the punishment.

Aunt Vera took parts in several plays my father directed. She was a wonderful actress. I especially remember her role as Gyp, the Heiress. She also sang a solo in that production. She had a beautiful contralto voice.

One vivid memory of Uncle John was going over to the Indian tepee in the evenings. There were a large number of Blackfeet Indians from Browning who came down to work in Uncle John's beet fields. He always had a great affinity for Indians and I am afraid that I do, too. One evening, he took me with him and as we sat around a fire in the center of the wigwam, the Indians passed around a peace pipe. When it came to me, I was horrified and didn't know what to do. I didn't have the stomach for puffing on that pipe, after all those Indians had. Besides, I didn't smoke! Uncle John solved the situation for me as he gently took the peace pipe from my hand and passed it on.

Uncle John and R. D. Merrill borrowed some of the beautiful trappings from the Indians and wore them to a big masquerade ball in Cascade. What a handsome pair of Indian Chiefs they were and they certainly won the prize for the most beautiful costumes.

One evening I went to Great Falls with Aunt Vera and Uncle John when a group of South Sea Islanders were putting on a show there. Some young men were walking down the street ahead of us and Uncle John recognized some Samoan words they were using. He called to them in Samoan. Imagine their surprise to hear someone in Montana speaking their own language. They invited us back stage after the show. Uncle John was so happy to meet with them that night. If I remember correctly, he had

A favorite picture of a special cousin, Peggy Squires Massey

taught some of their parents in school when he was there on a mission.

I especially remember our trips to the mountains to pick huckleberries. Our first Thanksgiving in Montana, Aunt Vera and Uncle John and their children were with us. We ate dinner with the door open and had fresh strawberries from our garden. After the cold winters we had experienced in Idaho and Canada, we thought we had found a Garden of Eden. Then March moved in with all its fury. That winter we experienced our first Chinook when a warm wind came in from the south and in a short time, snow melted and water ran off the eves of the houses. Life and Times of Peggy Squires Massey, used by permission.)

MEMORIES OF BY-GONE DAYS

By Bruce Nelson

We had great times in those years with the tight-knit group of Latter-day Saints in the Cascade Ward. Mother and Uncle Lawrence Squires were ringleaders in the cultural arts and put on plays and programs. Her acting ability was genuine and moving.

Uncle Lawrence was gifted both as an actor and as a very capable stagehand and producer. He did things with a flourish. I can still see him painting the scenery, so artistically and beautifully. The older he became, the more he flourished in his actions. He was a fantastic dancer and the greatest "swooper" I ever saw. Only a few ladies could give rein to his fabulous dancing. These he would "swoop" until their noses and their hair would alternately seem to touch the ground. I'm sure he must be up in heaven now, livening things up in that great dance hall in the sky. I loved him very much, because of his exciting optimism and his love of life.

Our coal came from the Carlyle or the Kluse mines which were near Smith River. It was high adventure for me at age six to eight to go with my father to get the yearly supply of coal. Dad would hitch up four good horses and I'd sit on the high seat by him as we drove 12 to 14 miles on a crisp fall morning.

Dad had great, well-trained horses. They would really dig in and pull together when we'd come up the steep hills with our load of coal. Other teams would seesaw under such heavy loads. Dad's wagon had to be "braked-down" so it would not run into the horses when they were going down steep grades. The horses' harnesses were also hooked to the tongue of the wagon to help control the pull of gravity when the wagon would roll free and fast down hills. These are happy memories in a family where love" was the greatest asset.

SHAKE THE GRATES

By Bruce A. Nelson

When I was a little boy, we lived on a farm in Chestnut Valley, Cascade, Montana. The main heat source in our house was a big, old majestic kitchen range. This lovely old stove was the very center of our lives. During the cold Montana winters, it gave comfort and warmth to all the family, cooked our food and provided us with hot water. In the spring of the year when baby calves, pigs, or even sheep were born, the cold winds of springtime in Montana would sometimes chill them clear through. My father would gently enfold these fragile, shivering bodies in a little blanket and bring them into the kitchen. He would put them in a big box behind the stove. When they warmed-up and were strong enough to nurse, he would return them to their mothers in the old straw shed.

My brother Lovell and I slept out in the cold back room." I think that Lovell and I got our great love of literature from that back room as the only insulation was newspapers which my Mother and Father pasted between the studs on the wall. From these pages we would read of the wonders of Eddy's Pan Dandy Bread and the stories of Mary Roberts Rhinehard and of Doan's Little Liver Pills and the grandness of a Ranger bicycle and of a Packard auto, etc. OH FOR THE GOOD OLD DAYS--Who likes thermostats anyway?

We hated to get into our cold bed even though my father taught us to take heated flat irons (used for ironing clothes) off the old coal-burning stove to bed with us to heat the covers up a bit. When the temperatures were way below zero, we learned to keep the covers around our heads and to only have a little breathing opening for our noses.

I still like to sleep with the covers around my head with just a little breathing hole when it's cold outside.

Early every morning my father would get up to shake the grates and get the fires started in the stoves. I knew that even though my room was cold, I'd soon be able to get up and take my clothes in by the warm stove to dress. This warm memory of security and love stayed with me throughout my life.

RUTHIE'S WILD RIDE

By Bruce A. Nelson

Old Babe was a sly horse. She was not given to the love of being caught and she thought any command was to be disobeyed. One day when we lived on the farm in Cascade, someone set little Ruthie on Old Babes' back and dropped the reins.

Old Babe knew that here as her chance to run because the baby couldn't pull the reins to stop her. So, she bolted in a southwesterly direction, quickly and unfettered with little Ruthie, a strong and persistent little cowgirl, hanging on for dear life.

The entire Nelson family followed behind for a half-mile or so. We spread out across the field to corner Babe and her brave little rider in a corner of a plowed field. Once Old Babe knew she was cornered, she became gentle and subservient and allowed the family to retrieve precious little Ruthie. I remember Mother crying and hugging her baby as Lovell and I rode back to the house on the runaway mare.

MEMORIES, MEMORIES

By Lovell Nelson

Before Bob was born, while we were living in Cascade, we were a struggling young family with six children to be fed and clothed. I was about nine or ten years old. We used to get about eight or ten bum lambs from the Grimes sheep ranch every year to raise. When we had these lambs all fattened up, we would sell them. This cash would help out with family expenses.

Dad had talked with the butcher in Great Falls and told him that the lambs were getting fattened up, ready to kill. The butcher said that he would come out to our farm and take a look at the lambs and give Dad a price for what he thought they were worth.

One day, when no one was at home, someone came to our farm and stole our lambs. It was obvious that the lambs had been killed and loaded into a truck and driven off.

Dad was suspicious that it was likely the butcher who had taken our nice fat lambs. Dad went into town and confronted the butcher. However, because there was not enough evidence and the butcher denied knowing anything about the theft, nothing was ever solved. Although Dad felt quite sure that the butcher had taken the lambs, he did not harbor any hate for him, but was forgiving. We just had to accept the fact that someone had stolen our lambs.

It was a great loss because these lambs were really needed for cash, which was an item that was in really short supply in the household of the John A. Nelson family in those years.

In the early times, when we lived in Cascade, we always had a missionary or two live with us. These missionaries were given the full run of our home. They all became really close to Mother and Dad. There was one missionary who came from the Navajo reservation. When his mission was over, to repay Mother and Dad for their kindness, he sent them a beautiful Navajo rug. It was about six by nine feet in size. It was on our living-room floor for many years, even after we moved to Great Falls. It was considered a family treasure.

Among some of the other family treasures were things that Dad had brought back with him from his mission to the Samoan and Tongan islands. These special souvenirs were kept upstairs in the attic. One time we came home from a trip and discovered all of Dad's precious Samoan treasures were gone and even the Navajo rug was taken off our floor. The thieves had also backed a truck next to the basement window and loaded up all of the canned fruits and vegetables that Mother had spent so many hours canning for our winter food supply. She didn't know what was worse, loosing the Samoan treasures and the Navajo rug, or all of the food that had taken such effort to preserve. Mom cried for many, many days over that loss.

In the late 1920's, Dad was selling stock for the Merrill Mortuary Company. It was necessary for him to spend the week in Great Falls, as it was too far to go home to Cascade every night. Consequently, he would always keep a room in the Parkview Hotel where he'd stay during the week, and then come home on weekends.

One time Dad came home from Great Falls with about 20 cases of Tokay grapes. There was going to be a big Boy Scout meeting in the

Wadsworth Hall in Cascade. He put the grapes out on the banquet tables for the boy scouts and the leaders to enjoy. What a treat! Beautiful Tokay grapes covered the tables—enough for everyone to get their fill. When Mother heard about it, she was very cross with Dad because he had spent money buying the grapes with money that was needed for family expenses. The Samoan life of generosity, and hospitality had been so deeply ingrained in him while he was on his mission, that it seemed like a natural thing to do for him to share this treat with the Boy Scouts.

Dad had a corral built that was about 14 feet high. Well, maybe it wasn't fourteen-feet high--it seemed about fourteen-feet high to me, maybe it was about eight-feet high. When we were kids, we used to lie out there and watch Dad rope horses because he had a snubbin' post in the middle of the corral. Around the foothills of Cascade there were many wild horses. They were considered pests and were not worth having around, because they were eating up the pasture and the grass that the ranchers needed for their domestic sheep and cattle. Anyone who wanted these mangy, wild horses could round them up and use them for whatever purpose they wished.

Dad and Vivian Squires rounded up a bunch of these loathsome, wild horses and kept them in a pasture at our ranch. Then Dad and Vivian would buy a bunch of pigs, kill some of these despised, wild horses, skin them, and then just leave their carcasses in the corral and let the pigs eat the meat. The pigs would actually get all of the meat off the bones. The bones were white when they got done and were bleached out in the sun. Dad and Vivian would just pile the bones over in the corner and later haul them out of the corral and pile them in a field.

Later on, it was decided that the bones were valuable, so Dad and Vivian would go out and gather up the bones off of all the land so they could be ground up and used for fertilizer.

There was one nice, little wild horse that got gathered up with the other wild horses. Dad and Vivian were going to shoot this horse, as they did with the other wild horses they used, but Bruce cried and begged them to let him keep it. The horse had great big bugs on its back; it was really a scabby-looking thing. But because of Bruce's coaxing, they took the horse out of the corral and gave it to him as his very own pony. Bruce took the horse and tended to its sores and cared for it tenderly. He named it "Old Flash" and it became his special riding pony. "Old Flash" was a real runner and was Bruce's pet for many years. Because of Bruce's tender heart and his persuasive nature, "Old Flash" was saved from the bone pile.

THE CAVE-IN

By Bruce A. Nelson

In 1929, Dad was working for the Merrill Mortuary Company, selling stock in the company to make ends meet on the farm. During this time, an incident occurred that I have never forgotten. Dad had assigned Lovell and I the chores of milking the cows, separating the milk, feeding the pigs and the calves, turning the cows out to pasture and handling other jobs around the small farm, "poverty flats," in Chestnut Valley. Being full of energy and having time on our hands, we decided that the old root cellar, which was about 50 feet south of the house, would be the sight of our attention in our spare time. Some of the boys in the area were "cave-diggers" and we had caught the fever from them. You must remember that this was in the days when Dad would cut ice from the river or from ponds and put it in the "ice house," where the ice was stored. We insulated the ice in the ice house with sawdust, and then dug it out as we needed it in the summer and put it in the ice box in the house.

This root cellar had been dug by fresno and slips (horse drawn) and was great to store potatoes and other vegetables for our use during the winter. The cellar was about 20 feet wide, and 30 feet long and was about 4 feet below the surface of the ground. The ground on both sides was not disturbed.

Well, Lovell and I thought it would be a good idea if we both dug down under the four foot bank of dirt and went down deeper to really have a couple of fine caves. We were energetic and worked on the caves during our spare time for several weekends, after school and when the chores were finished. We carried the dirt out of the two caves and spread it out on the floor of the cellar so that we would not have a big pile of dirt to bother anyone and maybe so my father wouldn't notice the new dirt we had added.

Finally, we had completed two, nice, little cave-rooms, safe, so far, under the big earth bank. One Saturday morning the big excitement occurred when we decided it was now time to join our caves together. Lovell dug to the north and I dug to the south and we had just broken through the space between the two rooms.

I still remember very vividly the impulse that came upon me to leave the cave and take my lantern and go get it filled up. As I recall, it was still one-half full, but I obeyed the feeling and was just crawling out of my cave, when the entire bank above both our caves gave way.

With a swishing sound, I was pinned from the knees down into the entrance to my cave. I was able to free myself with some effort and immediately looked for Lovell, who was buried under at least two feet of the bank.

Lovell, meanwhile, just seconds before the cave-in, received a sudden and strong impulse for him to stand up in his cave. It was only this action and his immediate response to that impulse or prompting that saved his life. This allowed the sand to fall past him and settle around him, leaving his head close enough to the surface that his very muffled sounds allowed me to locate his head and to free him so that he could breathe. Hearing his muffled sounds I knew where I had to start digging to begin the rescue efforts.

I was able to find his head and to free the sand from around him so that he could breathe. His arms and his entire body were well packed in the remains of his cave, to the point that the only things he could move were his ears. (He had always had this ability and would thrill the ladies, both in his youth and later in life at church socials and other special occasions, with this talent.)

Knowing that the bank above Lovell looked like it might cave-in more at any moment and cover him completely and being a practical little fellow, I spotted an old wash tub over in the corner of the cellar, quickly retrieved the tub and placed it over Lovell's head. I told him not to worry because if it caved more, he would have a tub full of air, until I could dig him out again. I am sure he was thrilled to have me add that worry to his mind and to have a tub over his head. (There have been times when I may have desired such control over an older Brother.)

Lovell took the darkness and the waiting without a whimper. I yelled as loudly as I could, but no one could hear me. I was afraid to leave him for fear the big, ominous bank might let go any moment. Finally, Mother came out to throw some dish water out in the yard. (If we had had indoor plumbing, we might be there yet.)

I posted Mother to watch the bank, while I ran one-fourth of a mile up the hill to the east and got a couple of the Squires boys (our cousins) to bring their shovels and rescue the older of the "cave-diggers." To this day Lovell and I cry when we tell this story; the great emotion, which swells up in us, is partly from the love we share and partly from our gratefulness to the good Lord that our lives were spared to dig another cave another day. Our next cave, with Father's advice, had boards on top and was much closer to the surface of the good earth. Lovell and I have been gratefully digging caves and experiencing other adventures for around 60 years since that nearly tragic day.

MORE MEMORIES

By Lovell Nelson

When we lived in Cascade, one of the first things Dad did was build a big root cellar. It was to put the spuds and vegetables in. It was in a very sandy area and was close to the house. Then he put a roof on it and put dirt back on and it was a really good root cellar. One day Bruce and I decided we should make a cave down in this root cellar. It was really easy to dig because it was sand and all we needed were some little coal shovels and buckets.

So we started digging this cave. As we got back farther and farther, we decided to make two rooms because we each wanted our own room. Each one of us had a lantern and we'd dig in the cave and haul the dirt out of the root cellar. One day we had been in the cave for quite awhile and Bruce had to go to get some more oil for his lantern.

For some unknown reason, I had a feeling that I should straighten up. Just as I stood up in my cave room, the wall caved in.

My head was completely buried and Bruce didn't know where I was. He started crying and hollering and I could just barely hear him. Somehow, he was able to find where my head was and he dug around my head so I could breathe. By then mother was there. I don't remember that she was even crying. I'm sure that seems a little unusual, but I think she was in shock so much that she couldn't cry, as I had expected her to. So then Bruce ran to get help from some of our cousins, the Squires, who lived about a half a mile away up the hill. He was able to recruit Vivian and Boyd. Vivian was a little older than the others. They came back down to help dig me out. It took them a long time to dig me out. There were no paramedics or emergency to call in those days.

I was really in shock. I couldn't stop shaking. My rescuers built a big fire in the stove to try to warm me up, but it still didn't help me.

Vera goes to visit her sister, Ada in beautiful sunny California.
Baby Lee is the only other person Vera takes along.

However I finally got over it. I've always figured that the Lord saved both Bruce and I for some things he had planned for us in the later part of our lives.

After we moved to Great Falls, we lived by some people named June and Tommy Chauncy. They lived with their grandmother. Their name was Sloan, but at that time they went by the name of Chauncy. They were quite spoiled as children as they had a lot of things in their lives. One time our family was going to go to the temple (it was quite a journey in those days). We had to go and usually stay over night in Simms, Montana or someplace along the road. We would pick up a group of other Mormons there also going to the temple. Often we would make another stop at Bynum overnight and then we'd make the final leg of our journey going into Canada.

Anyway, June Chauncy wanted to go and she had quite a new car. It was a Model-A Ford coupe. She coaxed to go and Dad told her, "The roads up there are all gravel, so you'll have to get new tires because I don't want to have to change any tires on this trip." She didn't plan on going to the temple, but she just wanted to go along just to be going with us. Anyway, she prepared for the trip by getting all new tires for her car. Well, everything went along pretty well, until June had one blowout on her car. However, before we got to Canada, she had four flat tires on her car. I remember Dad saying, "You see how the devil works to make it hard on us, as June really had no business going as she really wasn't supposed to be in with that group."

14

FAMILY LIFE IN CASCADE, MONTANA

FAMILY HAPPENINGS

In the year 1924, Cleve Nelson and his wife, Luella, moved into the Chestnut Valley. Cleve was John's younger brother. Their oldest son, Frank, was the same age as John's daughter Ruth. Also their son, Heber, and John's son, Lee, were the same age and such good friends. Their daughter, Ella Mae, was just a year younger than Verda; Ella Mae was such a special cousin to both Verda and Joyce. Several years later, Vilate was born to Cleve and Luella. It was fun having another little girl cousin to play with and share good times. Later, as the Nelson families moved into Great Falls, many more interesting experiences occurred.

LEE ARRIVES ON THE SCENE

By Verda Jensen

Lee Carl Nelson was born in Cascade on March 11, 1924. He brought such happiness to the entire family. He was such a pleasant, rugged little fellow. He was a favorite of many of the cousins, aunts and uncles. He was known, to many, by the name of "Sockie." This name seemed to have stuck with him because of an incident where someone asked him his name. He replied, "I 'tat say 'EE' but I 'tan say 'Sockee.'"

Several times when Lee was just a little boy, six or seven years old, he spent the summers in Utah with Aunt Rae and Uncle Will Woolford. Aunt Rae was John's sister and they had been unable to have any children of their own. Rumor has it that when Lee arrived home from his visits to Utah, he was a pretty spoiled little kid and even talked baby-talk.

Rae and Will fell in love with this rough and tumble little man and wanted to adopt him as their own son. Aunt Rae said, "Vera, you have so many other children. Won't you share with Will and I and let us adopt Lee? We love him so much and would be such good parents to him? We could provide so many opportunities for him that you and John may never be able to afford. Please, Vera, let us have him!"

Vera, of course, refused their kind offer. With tears in her eyes, she said, "I can not give up one of my babies.

I know that you and Will would be good parents, but what kind of a mother would I be if I gave up one of my children? My love for this little darling is too deep to even consider such a thing."[1]

Ruth Nelson Miller, John and Vera's daughter related: "I remember one year when Uncle Will and Aunt Rae brought Lee home from spending the summer with them in Smithfield, Utah. He had all sorts of toys, but he had one big ball we all wanted to play with. He took the ball and then ran out and climbed up on a haystack and said, 'YOU KIDS STAY AWAY FROM ME!'"

"Aunt Rae and Uncle Will wanted to adopt Lee and he really loved them. They coaxed Mother to let them keep him, but for some

1   Vera Wilcox Nelson journal

Wouldn't it be fun to know who all of these people are? It looks like Uncle Darrell and Aunt Mary and family, with Vera and John, and for sure Grandpa John Nelson, Sr. at far right.

reason, (which we all know) Mother and Dad couldn't let him go. Mother and Dad continued struggling to feed and clothe their big family of seven children. I think they did a pretty good job, too."

BABY SISTERS, AT LAST AND OTHER MEMORIES

By Ruth Nelson Miller

Verda Cloe Nelson, was born on June 23, 1926. Doctor Vanetta came to our house to deliver the baby. Aunt Chloe Robinson, Mother's sister, came from Idaho to help Mother. Aunt Chloe had always been an idol of Mother's and it was special to have her come. By this time, both of Mother's parents had died. It was a beautiful June day. All of the older kids were outside when the doctor came. We all thought we saw black hair sticking out of his black doctor's bag.

Well, Verda was born with lots and lots of coal black hair, so long in fact, that Daddy cut it out of her eyes with his barber scissors, the first day or so. What fun this was to have a baby sister after three brothers. I remember thinking she was actually my baby and loving to hold her and rock her in the old rocking chair by the window. Mother said that she looked like a little papoose.

One of Aunt Chloe's daughters had the name of "La Verda." Mother thought it was a pretty name, but decided to drop the "La" and call her "Verda Cloe." Verda has mentioned that she always liked her name and although she never knew Aunt Chloe very well, she thought it was an honor to carry her name.

When I was six and a half years old, I started first grade. A short time before school started in the fall, I was standing up on the little stool by the stove, watching Mother scald a chicken in order to more easily pluck the feathers off it before it was cooked. Lovell came running in with baby Verda. The baby was holding her breath and going limp. Lovell thought she was going to die, so he was screaming for Mother to get her.

Mother dropped the chicken with a big splash into the scalding hot water, to take the baby from Lovell. The splash ended up down my neck and onto my chest, giving me a third degree burn.

Well, I started screaming from the burn and it took a little while for Mother to figure out that I wasn't just crying because the baby was going to 'die.' The baby didn't die, but I had to miss the first two weeks of first grade, with the bad burns I had received from the hot scalding water.

Joyce Ione Nelson was born March 30, 1929. She was always such a sweet little girl. It was fun to have another baby sister. I remember the day Bruce decided to cut her long braids. She had been crying because it took so long for mother to braid her hair every morning. The braids were so pretty and went way down her back. Mother loved them even though Joyce was not too keen on having them combed. Well, one day after school, Bruce said, "Would you like me to cut those long braids off?"

Would she ever! So, Bruce said, "Well, sit over here and I'll oblige you." He pulled up the braids and with one whack of the scissors, off one came, right next to her head. Well after the first one was off, he realized what he had done, but couldn't stop then, so off came the other one.

When he tried to comb the hair down, it wouldn't come. It was not there! Joyce started crying! I started crying! Bruce started cutting more to "even it up"! Well, by the time he had "evened it up," it was way above her ears.

About then, Mother came home and I wish we could have had a movie of her expression. She started to cry too, and poor Bruce! I think he wanted to cry. Joyce refused to go to school for a week and then Mother bought her a little hat that covered the back of her bald head. She wore it for a long time! But, thank goodness, hair does grow back and somehow we did forgive and forget, or did you ever, Joyce?

I remember Mother telling Aunt Maude about a drugstore in Cascade that was giving free chicken dinners; she thought they should all go get one. So, Mother and all her children dressed up in "Sunday Best" along with Aunt Maude and all of her younger children and went in for the free chicken dinner. When they got there, the found out it was a free chicken dinner alright--a free candy bar named, "CHICKEN DINNER." Mother and Aunt Maude always laughed about that and thought it was a good joke on all of them!

I remember the "BIG ANIMAL FARM" out under the lofty cottonwood trees. The Nelson boys and the Squires boys had collected different-sized bones from the dead cows Dad used to kill for meat and they had made the bones into an animal farm. It was quite impressive!

THE OPEN GATE

By Lee C. Nelson

Back in the year 1929, when the country still ran on horsepower, I was five years old and was my dad's side-kick. Since horses were the muscle that made the farm run smoothly, my dad was very careful to see that they received the best of care. Nothing was too good for them. Because Dad was a lover of horses, he was very proud of his horses. Dad had rented a pasture (I don't know from whom) just north of the cemetery. This was east and north of our house on the road just below Wareheim Hill (seven miles east of Cascade).

We had a neighbor by the name of Swedblom, who was a very difficult man. He was not of our faith and he felt threatened by all who were. He was richer than most of the neighbors, (which didn't take much). He treated everyone else as far below him. Being somewhat jealous of Dad's good horseflesh did not help matters. Well, Dad had six or eight head of horses in this rented pasture and he checked them often when they were not being worked.

He took me with him in the wagon and team one day to check on them. As we neared the pasture, we could see the open gate lying on the ground and guess who was just leaving the scene of the crime? Swedblom! We drove on down the lane and Dad pulled the wagon across the narrow road, which had a barbwire fence on each side, leaving no room for Swedblom to pass. Swedblom was in a one-horse surrey. Our wagon was pulled by a team, took much more room than his.

Dad alighted from the wagon and waited. When Swedblom's horse came close enough. Dad grabbed the reins and stopped the forward progression. (I must divert my thoughts for a moment to explain that I have no recollection of anger in Dad's life, either with his fellow man or beast. This was the only exception I can recall.)

White with anger, speaking with blazing eyes and a fury he could not contain, Dad exploded by shouting, "Swedblom, you have opened my gates for the last time. I am tired of having to round up my stock because of your actions.

If I were not a peace-loving man, you and I would be rolling in the dirt this very minute. Now, I'm telling you, Swedblom, that the next time this happens, that's exactly where we will be."

With that, Dad majestically released Swedblom's horse, stalked to the wagon, turned the team around and slowly drove past Swedblom, where he closed the open gate.

Meanwhile, our good "neighbor" had slapped the reins on his horse and hauled his buggy (with him inside) on home.

THE WAR-WHOOP HITCH

By Lee C. Nelson

(Lee C. Nelson letter dated March 24, 1989.)

I was the first child born to John and Vera Nelson in the Chestnut Valley, Cascade, Montana. Val, Bruce and Ruth were all born in Canada and were older than I. After me came Verda, Joyce and Bob.

There was a herd of wild horses that ran free in the foothills south and east of Cascade. If you caught them, you owned them. When I was five years old, in the year 1929, I was given one of these wild mares. I named her "Ginger." Now she was well broke and very tame, but young. I recall that my cousin, Boyd Squires, was one of the cowboys who worked for "Hi" Anderson, our neighbor. "Hi" took a liking to the runt of the family, freckled-face Lee. I suppose Boyd had a hand in the breaking of the greatest pet I ever owned.

I want you to understand about the wild herd. The ranchers would sometimes get enough mounted men together to drive these animals into their corrals or other areas, where they could be caught. Uncle James Turner had a ranch in the foothills and some of his kids were real "cowboys." Alan used to ride bucking broncos at the Cascade

273

rodeo and I remember one time that another cowboy taunted Alan saying that Alan couldn't even ride the cowboy's saddle horse. Of course, Alan didn't know that even though the owner could handle this horse, it was a trained bucker.

Alan accepted the dare and threw a foot in the stirrup. Before he could land on leather, the horse commenced bucking and he could buck! Well, Alan picked himself up off the ground with a broken arm. That was quite a memory for me as a little kid.

Uncle James had one of these wild horses in his corral. This particular one was large, mean and a five-year old buckskin stallion. Now, maybe you don't know, but stallions are really tough to handle. They have a mind of their own and have been known to kill men. This one had never been touched by human hands, and everyone was leery of him.

Now, Dad had broken horses, professionally, when he was a young man in Canada. His secret weapon was the "War Whoop Hitch." He was probably the best man to use three, hard-twist lariats of any man in the West. When he and I went to break this stallion, it was an eye-opener to a young seven-year-old boy.

Here is how Dad proceeded. Ready for war, Dad entered the corral with his tack, which included: tight leather gloves, the three, hard-twist lariats, a couple of gunny sacks and his boots, hat, and rough pants were the only tools of his trade.

Step 1. The horse circled the round corral, rolling his eyes at Dad. In the center of the ring was the snubbin' post [a rough post set deep in the ground, sticking above the ground about five feet.] As the horse ran by, Dad flipped (one time toss) the first lariat and caught the left front foot.

Step 2. Same procedure with the right rear foot. These lariats were jerked tight and allowed to trail in the dirt as the horse ran in a circle around the corral.

Step 3. The third lariat went over the head. By this time, the horse had gained speed, but Dad, with three tosses, had three lariats firmly attached.

Step 4. The head lariat was tied to the snubbin' post. The horse stopped and panted as Dad approached. He picked up the loose ends of the two, foot lariats. The horse stretched back from the snubbin' post and Dad. When the head lariat was tight, Dad jerked tight the ropes of the foot lariats, the horse fell and was hog-tied before he knew what had happened.

Step 5. Did you ever hear a wild stallion scream? Well, they do. It makes the hair raise up on the back of your neck! With rolling eyes, unable to move, the stallion laid there quivering. Dad then untied the snubbin' post rope and approached the weaving head of the stallion with caution. These horses can and do bite. With the loop, around the neck of the stallion, he flipped half-hitches around the muzzle, then up through itself to behind the ears, then doubled it for safety. The "War Whoop Hitch" was in place! Dad then pulled out the slack and tied the free-end of the "War Whoop Hitch" (which now resembled a hackamore or bridle) back to the snubbin' post. Got the picture? Wild horse, hog-tied, all four legs, neck stretched as far as man could pull it and tied to the snubbin' post, laying almost on his back, angry, excited, afraid, but unable to move anything except his eyes and his head a little.

Step 6. Two gunny sacks. One in each hand, approached slowly, talked smoothly, but softly, constant talk. This was the first rubdown. Every part of the horse's body. Twice around, then again, more slowly. By the third time, the horse had stopped quivering so violently, having found out the loathsome gunny sacks did not bite or hurt.

Step 7. Dad took off the piggin' string (the lariat which had tied the four feet together) and the horse jumped to his feet and flew back. This means that he backed, violently, away from the snubbin' post, but was brought up short by the "War Whoop Hitch." It hurt! The harder he pulled, the tighter the half-hitch around his nose got and then he stepped forward and flew back again. Eyes rolling! This half-ton of wild horse, stood pulling back as much as he could stand. Believe me, it hurt! Much more and the end of his nose would have dropped on the ground. But this horse was mean, ornery and tough. There he stood, all four feet spread out, pulling back, but standing, stock still.

Step 8. Two gunny sacks. One in each hand. Approached slowly, talked smoothly, but softly, constant talk. This was the second rub down. The same rolling eyes, mostly the whites. Slowly, Dad rubbed the sacks over every part of that stallion's body. Same result, the quivering subsided, the eyes did not roll as much, but the snubbin' lariat was still as tight as a steel rod. Then because Dad had an audience of one, he had to show off a little. He ducked under the belly of that stallion, going from one side to the other. He knew horses well, because that horse didn't move a muscle, just eyes. One more rub down to quiet the horse.

Step 9. Talked softly to the horse, one more rub behind the ears with his gloved hand, Dad stood in front of the horse saying firmly, "Here." Now remember, that horse was pulling back on the rope with all the force it could stand, as it was in pain. Lunging down on the center of the rope, which caused greater pain, Dad said again, "Here." Nothing happened. Again a lunge downward and the command, "Here," and the horse simply couldn't stand it and took one half step forward to lessen the pain on his nose. Dad had him!

Now at each command, with a pull on the rope, the horse took a small step forward. Dad led him in this fashion around the snubbin' post, then untied the lariat and held it in his hand. Backing up, commanding, "Here," with added pressure, Dad led the horse around the corral. Dad in reverse, the horse forward, both, of course, going in the same direction. Again around the ring.

Step 10. Now this is not breaking a horse in the strictest sense of the word, but the horse had been led. A big step from that wild-eyed, screaming, quivering piece of horseflesh. But, wait! This was not all.

Dad was a born showman and a natural show-off when it came to his favorite recreation--horses. He then indulged himself in:

Step 11. Removing the lariat from the horse's head, throwing it on the ground, there Dad stood, face to face with an animal, far superior in strength and weight.

In its own element, Dad would not have stood a chance, but here in his ring, with his psychology, and the "War Whoop Hitch," Dad had won!

Standing there, eye-to-eye, Dad took a backward step, his arms hanging loose at his side and he commanded, "Here." The horse followed him with a step. This process was repeated and Dad led the horse around the ring, freely, no rope, only a voice command, easily and proudly. Such was the power of my Dad and the "War Whoop Hitch! "

SOME KIND OF NEIGHBOR

By John A. Nelson, Jr.[2]

While we were living in the Chestnut Valley, two miles south of Cascade, across from the Missouri River, we had a variety of neighbors. Some were wonderful people. There was one man, however, who did not care to be neighborly. He had quite a reputation for his violent acts. One such act was when he hit one of his neighbors over the head with some muskrat traps.

Maude and Lawrence Squires were living next to this man, Emmett Swedblom. There was just a barb-wire fence between the two families. Lawrence had about 50 sheep that he had bought in the spring of the year and was getting them fattened up to sell. His son, Keith, was out in the field herding these sheep. There happened to be a low place in the fence that was big enough for the sheep to crawl under.

---

2   John A. Nelson dictaphone tape #23.

When one of the sheep saw this low place and crawled under the fence, all of the others followed the leader. Within a few minutes, all of the sheep were into Mr. Swedblom's field. There wasn't any feed there for them as the field was a dry lake. Mr. Swedblom noticed the sheep on his land. He got on his horse and found Keith had crossed the fence over onto Mr. Swedblom's land. Keith was trying to get the sheep around to the gate, in order to get them back to their own pasture.

Mr. Swedblom told Keith to get off of his property. Keith was afraid of Mr. Swedblom, because of his reputation and hurriedly ran home. Then Mr. Swedblom took the sheep over to his own corral and locked them up. Lawrence was greatly disturbed about this and went to get the sheep back. Mr. Swedblom threatened Lawrence and said, "Get off my land. I'll teach you to let your sheep get into my property."

Lawrence came to my home and told me the happenings of the day. About that time another friend, Marshall McComber, came to visit me. The three of us decided to go over and confront Mr. Swedblom with the problem. We felt quite brave because of our numbers. As we drove into Swedblom's yard and parked the car, I got out and went to the door. I knocked on the door. I could see that they were having their evening meal, when he came to the door. I said, "Mr. Swedblom, we have come to get Mr. Squires' sheep. Will you please come out and turn them out of your corral, so that we can drive them home?"

Calling his wife by name he shouted, "Go and get the 30.30 and shoot this son-of-a-bitch." He continued, "You get off of my land as fast as you can."

I knew he had the authority to run me off his place. I would have been whipped if I had struck the man or done anything forcible on his property and I knew the law was in his favor.

I told Lawrence and Marshall that we would have to leave the sheep there for the night and that the next day we would have to go into

Great Falls and see the county attorney. He would then give notice to the sheriff in Cascade to go and get the sheep so Lawrence could drive them home.

It was several days before we got to see the County Attorney. In the meantime, Swedblom had to feed the sheep as he knew that he would have been the worse offender of the two if he had let them die. He also had to draw water for them from his well. The county attorney wrote a letter for us to take to the sheriff with the instructions to go to the Swedblom ranch and have the sheep released.

We went with the Sheriff and Mr. Swedblom was forced to open his gate and let the sheep go. It had created a bad feeling in the neighborhood and no one was the winner.

A HOSTILE NEIGHBOR

By Bruce Nelson

When I was about eight to ten years old, my cousin, Keith Squires, and I were helping my father fix a hole in the fence, just north of the cemetery in Chestnut Valley. It was apparent that someone had cut the wires and opened the fence.

My father had a pair of beautiful black horses, who appeared to be identical twins. They had been captured from the unfenced, free area, where wild horses roamed. They were "fair game" for any rancher or group of riders who could bring them off the range. Father had brought this pair of horses off the open range some weeks prior; he set "great store" by them and planned to make them into a dandy driving team.

As we were there working, we heard a truck coming from the north. As it arrived, my father stepped out into the road and waved the driver to stop. As the car stopped, my father stepped around to the driver's side and addressed our neighbor, Mr. Swedblom, who was in the truck with his wife.

Father said, "Mr. Swedblom, we are fixing the fence that you cut and you have let my horses go back into the big Milligan Country. It is doubtful that we will ever see them again. I am sure that it was you, because the tire marks of this very truck are parked in the borrow pit, just behind you. Your tracks lead to the opening in the fence. Now, I am a patient man, but if your wife were not here with you today, I would pull you from your truck and thrash you soundly."

John continued, "Now you are my neighbor and I would prefer that we were good neighbors, but you seem not to want it that way. I warn you, that my patience is thin and I will not allow your hostility and vicious behavior to continue, or you will live to rue the day you were not a more Christian man."

Mr. Swedblom drove off and to my knowledge that was the last time he cut my father's fence. In those early years, Mr. Swedblom seemed to have the early-day, cattleman's impression that, since he was there first, the rest of humanity, who came along after, was not only unwanted, but was also infringing upon Swedblom's rights to even be in the same area as he was.

Another little run-in with this great neighbor occurred when Burt Paulson, who was working for my father, had just purchased a new 12-gauge shotgun. He invited Lovell and I to go with him to try it out. We made the mistake of going over into Mr. Swedblom's field, where there was a lake that was "alive" with Canadian honkers and fat, mallard ducks. Well, Lovell, Burt and I crept through the fence, went up to the lake, stood up and let go with our guns.

We had about 22 big geese and ducks lying in the lake and were quite happy about our good fortune, when we looked to towards the Swedblom ranch and noticed a cloud of dust approaching us.

Soon Mr. Swedblom descended upon us and confiscated Burt's new gun. He told Lovell and I that since we were under-age, he would not take our guns. (I wonder if my father's warning had anything to do with that?)

He then advised us that since there was ice out about 50 feet from the shore, which made it difficult to wade through, we had better go get a horse and come and get the birds we had killed. We went back home, about three-quarters of a mile and got a horse. When we got back, guess what? All of the birds were gone. Our good neighbor had confiscated all those fine birds and neither he, nor the birds were anywhere in sight. I believe, to this day, that Burt's new gun is with the heirs of our good friend, Mr. Swedblom.

THE BURIAL OF HARRY SMITHERS

By John A. Nelson, Jr.

One afternoon, while we were living in Cascade, Brother Jim Stoddard, who was in the Branch Presidency, came to visit me. His neighbors, the Smithers family, had an eighteen-year old son, Harry, who was in the Columbus Hospital in Great Falls, suffering from pneumonia. Brother Stoddard had phoned to see how the boy was getting along and Mr. Smithers told him that the boy was dying. He conveyed that they asked him to see if I would come with him to the hospital and offer a prayer for their son.

I, of course, could not refuse. Together with Brother Stoddard, we took a bottle of holy consecrated oil, consecrated for the healing of the sick, with us to the hospital. Mormons believe in the fifth chapter of James, wherein it says, beginning with the thirteenth verse, "Is any among you afflicted? Let him pray. Is any merry? Let him sing psalms. Is any sick among you? Let him call for the elders of the church; and let them pray over him, anointing him with oil in the name of the Lord. And the prayer of faith shall save the sick, and the Lord shall raise him up; and if he committed sins, they shall be forgiven him."

This scripture from the Bible was on my mind as I entered the hospital room. Harry was unconscious. Oxygen was being administered to him. I talked to his parents and told them that I felt honored that they would ask for me to come and pray for their son. I told them that we believed in the Bible. They were members of the Methodist Church.

I told them about the scripture in James and about the holy consecrated oil we had brought with us. I explained that it didn't matter if he was a member of our Church or not; this holy oil was for the healing of the sick. I told them that Harry was one of the sons of God and that he was loved by our Heavenly Father.

There were two nurses, Mr. and Mrs. Smithers, Brother Stoddard and myself surrounding Harry's bed. I asked Brother Stoddard to anoint Harry with the oil. When he was finished, we both laid our hands on Harry's head and I sealed the anointing. Harry remained unconscious all during the prayer.

Just the moment we removed our hands from Harry's head, he began to pray and he offered up one of the most beautiful prayers I have ever heard. It touched the hearts of all of us.

His parents said they had never heard him pray vocally before. He prayed for his mother and father. He prayed for his sister, Julia.

We were all in tears, even the nurses. There was such a sweet spirit in that hospital room. There seemed to be a heavenly feeling around his bed. We did not realize that death was so close, but within one hour after we left the hospital, Harry died and went on to his reward.

An article came out in the Cascade newspaper telling about Harry's death, and that the funeral services would be conducted by Reverend Little and Reverend Gridley, of the Methodist Church. Mr. and Mrs. Smithers came out to my farm and said, "Mr. Nelson, after what happened yesterday in the hospital and the beautiful prayer that Harry offered, we feel that if you hadn't been there in the hospital and given him that special blessing, he would have died without our ever hearing him pray. There was such a beautiful spirit in his hospital room. We would be very ungrateful if we did not ask you to conduct the funeral services for our son."

I told them that I would be happy to, of course, but I felt it was necessary to speak to their ministers before giving them my answer. I did not wish to usurp their authority. I felt it was important to know their feelings about my participating in the services. Mr. and Mrs. Smithers agreed. They wanted me to go with them, immediately, so we could discuss this with their ministers.

When we got to Cascade we found both of the ministers at their chapel. Mr. Smithers spoke and told them that he and his wife wanted to have Mr. Nelson conduct Harry's funeral service.

Reverend Little spoke up quickly, "We can not permit that. We cannot permit an outside minister to come into our chapel and conduct a funeral service for one of our members. That is unreasonable."

At this point, I spoke up, "Gentlemen, Mr. Smithers is asking this of me and I am a minister, the same as you are. I cannot refuse his request. However, if I do conduct this service, I would ask you gentlemen to assist me. I would ask you, Reverend Little, to speak and you, Reverend Gridley, to offer one of the prayers. I will also speak." The ministers both refused.

Mr. Smithers spoke up, "Well, then we will hold the funeral service over in your hall, Mr. Nelson." (At this time, the Mormons had purchased the old mercantile building, and were holding their services there.)

Reverend Little saw no other solution, so he said, "Well, in that case, we see that you are determined, Mr. Smithers; we will agree to Mr. Nelson's proposal." We left, with the agreement that I would be in charge of the service. I then asked Reverend Little to be the first speaker, and Reverend Gridley to give the closing prayer. I agreed to prepare the printed funeral program and have it ready for the service.

This was the third funeral service held in the little town of Cascade that week. In the early part of the week, a young man had been accidentally killed when his hunting companion had dropped his gun, discharging a bullet that went through the body of his friend. The other death had been caused when a young cowboy had been riding a bucking bronco. He had been badly shaken up from the ride and later that week, he dropped over dead on the streets of Helena, Montana. There was a gloom cast over the whole community because of these deaths.

It was a local custom that every one attend the funerals of their neighbors and friends, if possible. The Smithers were a prominent family in the community and it was one of the largest funerals ever held in that little town. There was not room for everyone to come into the chapel. Many people were standing outside on the sidewalk. Some were sitting in their cars because they could not find room in the chapel. Perhaps people were curious because it had been advertised, earlier in the week, that Mr. Nelson of the Mormon Church would be conducting the funeral service. Harry's funeral was held on a Sunday, so people were not working and many made arrangements to attend.

I had arranged to have a quartet from our church provide the music. They had sung before on numerous occasions and it was a treat to hear them sing. The quartet consisted of my wife Vera, Alverna Anderson, Lyle and Merrill Squires. They were to sing, "Oh, My Father, Thou Who Dwellest." The members of the Methodist choir were also to participate in the program. I had typed up the program and as we arrived at the chapel a few minutes early, I handed one of the programs to Reverend Little. He responded with the comment, "This is no funeral service! You have no scripture readings."

I said, "Reverend Little, you will hear plenty of scriptures read before the service is over. It doesn't matter to me, whether the scriptures are read at the beginning or at the end, it will be the Word of God."

Reverend Lyman, from the Congregational Church in Cascade, had also been invited to sit on the stand with the other participants. The

Methodist choir sang first. Then I gave the opening prayer. Then Reverend Little rose to speak.

His opening remarks were like this, "When I came here today, I thought that I was in charge of this service, but I found that the Mormons are." He did not say "Elder Nelson" or "Pastor Nelson," only drawling out the word "Mormons."

It threw a cold wave over the congregation and I could feel it clear down to my shoes. I did not know how I was going to counteract that remark when I arose to speak. He finished his talk and sat down. After another song, by one of the schoolteachers, a Miss Symes, then a song by the quartet, it was my turn to speak. I was nervous because of the Reverend's cold approach. I had brought my scriptures with me. I laid my hand on the Book of Mormon and the Bible. As I stood at the pulpit, I hesitated. Suddenly, a beautiful spirit came over me. It was a sweet and gentle spirit. I began by praising the words of Reverend Little. I said that I understood how difficult it was for Reverend Little to accept an outside minister to come in and conduct the funeral service for a member of his church. I said that, because I had been asked by the family, I could not refuse because, I, too, was a minister of the gospel of the Lord, Jesus Christ.

I had prepared a talk on the resurrection of the dead and the life of our Savior, Jesus Christ. I felt that I had the spirit of the Holy Ghost with me as I spoke and this beautiful spirit remained with me while I was delivering the funeral sermon. I told them that we believed in the Bible and quoted the eighth Article of Faith: "We believe the Bible to be the word of God, as far as it is translated correctly. We also believe the Book of Mormon to be the Word of God."

I informed them that the Bible is the history of the people on the eastern hemisphere; while the Book of Mormon is a complete and true record of the people who once lived and still live here, on this continent. I felt such a sweet, peaceful feeling and this feeling of love and peace also came to me from the audience.

Many people came up to me afterwards and expressed their gratitude for the services. They said they had felt of a special spirit and a message of simplicity and hope in the life hereafter from my message.

So, although it had been a difficult invitation to accept, the Spirit of the Lord was there to help me deliver the sermon. I acknowledge the help that I received and bear testimony of the truthfulness of the message that I delivered.[3]

WALTER SMITHER'S DEATH

By John A. Nelson, Jr.

We had moved to Great Falls by the time Harry's father, Mr. Walter Smithers, died. We had seen the obituary in the newspaper. The same day, there was a knock on my door. It was Mrs. Smithers and her daughter, Julia. Mrs. Smithers spoke, "Mr. Nelson, you will remember the difficulty we had at the funeral of our son. Harry? The Methodist minister rejected you being in charge of the service. Julia and I have decided to hold the funeral for my husband at the cemetery. We aren't going to have it in the chapel at all. We would be grateful to you, if you would conduct Walter's funeral service at the grave-side in Cascade."

I expressed my honor and gratitude at being asked, and replied that I would be very happy to do so. I asked Mrs. Smithers if a little platform could be erected so that I might be seen by those I knew would be attending. They agreed to take care of that detail.

The day of the funeral, Vera and Alverna Anderson sang one or two songs. I was the only speaker. The Lord helped me to deliver the words that I did that day. Mr. Smithers had lived his life in the Cascade area and was well known and well respected. There were many cars and a big crowd in attendance. I offered a prayer. I asked that those in attendance might hear and understand the principles of the gospel of Jesus Christ. I asked that the hearts of Mrs. Smithers and her daughter, Julia, might be consoled so that they could

3   John Nelson dictaphone tapes #17 and 47.

accept the passing of their father with a good heart and with real thanksgiving, knowing that they would meet him again.

I shared the experience that happened at the hospital just before their son Harry died. This was the day Harry had regained consciousness and had offered such a beautiful prayer. The Spirit of the Lord was with us that day. Many people thanked me for the words I had spoken. I thanked the Lord and gave praise to Him for His assistance and the inspiration of His mind and will that He had given me.

I bear my testimony to you, my children, that the gospel of Jesus Christ has been established upon the earth in this day and time, through the instrumentality of our prophet, Joseph Smith.

This gospel shall never be thrown down or given to another people, but it shall stand forever and when the Savior comes the second time, in all his glory, then perhaps there will be many other people who will yield obedience more readily to the wonderful plan of Salvation. This is the same plan that our Lord and Savior taught when he was here on the earth. This is my testimony and I leave it with you, my children, in the name of the Lord, Jesus Christ, amen.[4]

A METHODIST MINISTER

By John A. Nelson, Jr.

While we were living in Cascade, early one morning as I was shaving, the kitchen door banged open and a man appeared and angrily asked, "Did you see my car?" I replied that I had heard a car pass, but had thought nothing about it.

He responded, "Well, there were two of your large hogs standing in the middle of the road. As I drove up the road, I realized that I either had to hit the hogs, or take to the ditch, which is full of water. I knew if I hit the hogs, I might go into the water and maybe land upside down. I chose to run into the ditch and now my car is stalled and I can't get out. I am wet to my waist."

4   John Nelson dictaphone tapes #17 and 47.

I apologized as quickly as I could and said, "I am very sorry. I'll tell you what I'll do. I have a team right here. I'll go out to the barn and get one of them and since you are already wet, you can hook the chain on the back of your car and my horse will pull you out."

I went out and harnessed up Ole Rodg, who was a big 1600-pound gelding, who was ready to pull whenever I gave the word. The gentleman took the chain and hooked onto the back of his car. He got into his car and it started up. I just told Ole Rodg to pull, and of course, he just backed right up and pulled the car out backwards. I loosened the chain from the car and the man left.

Several days later, Marvin Turner, my nephew, and I were working on the fences. Marvin had come down to Cascade to spend the summer with us. Marvin's mother, Minnie, was Vera's sister. She and her husband, James, were living in Canada, but had made plans to move to Montana in the fall.

The same man I had helped out of the ditch the day before, came driving by and stopped. He said, "I guess you recognize me; I'm the man you pulled from the mud hole the other day." He continued, "I have a question to ask you. Would you please tell me if you are a Mormon?"

Yes," I replied. "I am a Mormon."

"Well," he said, "I have just one more question that is bothering me. Is it true that your missionaries go out into the world and pay their own expenses for two years or more and preach the gospel free of charge?"

I replied that it was true. I told him that I had gone to a foreign country for six and one-half years as a missionary. I told him that my dear father had sent me a check every month all that time. The Church had paid my traveling expenses after I became President of the Mission for over three years and they had also paid my expenses to return home. Other than that, my family had provided the funds to keep me on the mission. I continued, it's almost unbelievable, but that is really the way I feel the gospel of Jesus Christ should be preached. We shouldn't be paid for our service."

After this little conversation, my new friend left. A few days later, he came by again. This time I was out cleaning my corral. He said that he would like to talk to me and would I come and sit in his car for a few minutes. He told me that he was Reverend Davis, the new Methodist Minister assigned to the Cascade area. He said, "I have only been here a short time, but I have always wanted to meet a Mormon. I have read quite a bit about your religion; I'm sorry to say that it was not very complimentary, but have never had the opportunity to meet a Mormon."

I said that I would be happy to explain our beliefs to him. As he expressed an interest, I told him about the first principles of the Gospel of Jesus Christ. I told him that we believed in a God who has body, parts and passions. I told him that God, the Father, has a body of flesh and bones and that Jesus Christ, the Savior of the world, was His true and only begotten Son. I explained to him about the Godhead. I answered

Left to right: Gene and Cal Squires, Joyce and Verda Nelson

a lot of his questions and he seemed very interested in what I told him. He said that he didn't want to take me away from my work, but he wondered if it would be possible for him to come again and discuss religion with me.

I told him that would be fine. I invited him to come and meet my family and then we could have our discussion in my home. He brought his wife out and together with Vera, we went into the living room and talked about Mormonism. We told him about the

apostasy. He knew nothing about the restoration of the gospel. He was a man about 43-years old. He and his wife had three children. They both seemed very interested in our message.

About a week later, I went into Cascade with a team of horses to buy meal for my hogs and chickens. I stopped my team beyond the railroad tracks near the elevator where I bought my feed. I walked across the tracks over to the grocery store. Who should I see on the steps of the Great Northern Depot but my friend, Reverend Davis. He was walking up and down the platform. When he saw me, he came running over and shook my hand.

He said, "Mr. Nelson, I am quitting the ministry. After having discussed religion with you the past few weeks, I cannot preach from the Methodist pulpit anymore.

If I told them and preached the gospel that you've been telling me about, they would throw me out anyway. I cannot be deceptive and preach anything else, because I have received a knowledge that what you told me was true. I have been studying the chapters from the Bible that you suggested. I find that I have not been taught the correct principles of the gospel of Jesus Christ that He established here upon the earth when He was here. So I am quitting the ministry."

He went on to say that he was young and strong and that he could do manual work if he needed to. He said that he did not have any formal training for any other kind of work, but he felt that he would get along all right.

I didn't know whether to apologize to him or not. I knew that I was very happy to think that he had received the light of the Gospel. I said, "Well, I am very sorry if I have caused you to loose your salary and your position for financial gain, but I am excited to think that you have found the truth of the gospel."

In a few weeks we received a letter from Reverend Davis. He said, "We are living here in Great Falls. Will you please refer me to one of your Elders here in Great Falls, so that we may continue our

JOHN NELSON FAMILY--1931 Left to right: Lee, Bruce, Verda, John, Vera, Joyce, (sitting on Vera's lap) Lovell and Ruth. (Vera is pregnant with Robert.)

search for the truth of the restored gospel of Jesus Christ? I cannot think of anything but that I want to know more about what you have taught to me."

I answered immediately and referred him to an Elder Wood, who had just returned from the Southern States Mission. I knew Elder Wood was well informed of the gospel plan and could continue teaching this special family the gospel. In the spring of that year, I received a letter from Reverend Davis. He said,

"I suppose you will be happy to learn that my wife and family were baptized into the Church of Jesus Christ of Latter-day Saints yesterday. We have moved to Portland, Oregon and the missionaries here have continued teaching us the gospel. We are so thrilled to have found the truth and will always remember the day that I ran into your ditch. We will always remember your willingness to share the Gospel of our Master with us."

I bear you my testimony that this is a true story. I know that the Spirit of the Holy Ghost bore witness of the truth of the Gospel of Jesus Christ to this good man and his family.[5]

DOWN MEMORY LANE

By Bruce A. Nelson

My Dad was an organizer. In the area of Cascade, Montana in the years from 1924 to 1932, Dad was the moving force behind several of the 24th of July Celebrations. Dad always tried to involve the "outsiders." These celebrations were usually held near a grove of trees so that shade would invite attendance.

Dad and his committee planned activities that would be of interest to people of all ages. There were sack races, 3-legged races, backward running races, wheelbarrow races, ball throwing and other events designed to involve the entire crowd. Of all the events, I think the one that attracted the most adults and especially the cowboy class of that day, was the free-for-all horse racing events.

I had always thought that my horse, Flash, could outrun anything on four legs and I was always anxious to have this event come so I could prove his swiftness.

I always rode bareback, like an Indian, with only the reins and the squeeze in my knees to hold me on top of my swift beast. By this time, I had outrun all my competition of the boys in the Valley and was looking to wider fields to conquer.

The 24th of July was coming and my anticipation was high and my dreams of outrunning all those older cowboys and their swiftest mounts kept me training Flash, down the lane with fast starts and straight runs. The big day arrived and I remember about 25 horses all lined up between two points straining to hold their mounts behind the line.

---

5   Dictaphone tape #37.

The whistle blew and the horses surged forward to run about a quarter of a mile, straight to the east. Flash responded beautifully; the training had paid off. He knew what was expected of him and his desire to win equaled mine. No one was ahead of us. BUT WAIT!!

What was that roan horse, with four white legs, doing so far ahead? How did he get out there in front of all the rest?

Yes, the day belonged to Jimmy Moll and his horse. Second place was sweet to Flash and I, but the hero of the day was the Blacksmith's son from town. Jimmy and his horse had won, fair and square and to my knowledge were never beaten by any other horse and rider as long as they were together.[6]

MORE MEMORIES FROM CASCADE

By Ruth Nelson Miller

I remember the Christmas parties at Cascade. There was always a big dance at a large hall downtown for all of the youth of the Church. There was a big tree in the middle and we danced and had such a lot of fun. There was always a Santa Claus and he would come in singing, "Ho, Ho, Ho." He had a big pack with sacks of candy for each one of us. I especially loved the pyramid chocolates and would trade the boys for theirs with the nuts in them. Everyone in the Valley was poor, but the kids didn't realize it. We loved these parties, and thought that we had it as good as anyone else.[7]

---

6   Bruce Nelson's Writings.
7   Memories of Ruth Nelson Miller.

TENDER YEARS

The years spent in Cascade were memorable for the Nelson family in many ways. Their last four children were born while they were living in this community. There was a great bond of love and friendship formed with the other members of the Church. Many close family ties were formed as they all struggled to survive the hardships of an unsuccessful farm.

MEMORIES OF RUTH NELSON MILLER

John's employment of selling stock for the Merrill Mortuary Company necessitated his spending time away from home and family. He was trying to keep a growing family in shoes and the necessities of life. They were still living in the Chestnut Valley. He wrote this charming birthday letter to Vera from Great Falls:

Great Falls, Montana March 25, 1931

Dear Mama:

Today is your birthday and I will rush off a note of congratulation to you. I might be home before the day is over by the looks of the storm that is on. You know I would not be very contented away from home during a blizzard. I don't think that it will be a very bad one this time of the year, though. I hope the boys carried enough wood in to last you throughout the day. They are pretty good boys to help their mother and I have a lot of confidence in them. Bruce felt pretty big when I let him drive the car yesterday. He is going to be a good driver and I know he is a good milker, especially when he can find some big straws.

The Merrill Mortuary is busy today.

Well, Mama dear, who would have thought in fourteen years of married life we would have such a fine little family and you have been such a fine little mother to us all. We all love you and know your worth, even little Joyce shows her affection to a marked degree. I hope in the next 14 years that we will be blessed with wisdom to handle our children according to their age. No doubt the hardest struggle is still ahead, but as long as we can keep the Lord on our side, it will be made easy for us.

Well, if the storm gets too bad, I'll be home. Have the boys put the two cows they are milking in the barn; they have been leaving one out with her calf.

Tell Verda Cloe to eat an apple a day to keep the doctor away. Must hurry to catch the train.

With lots of love, Daddy

ROBERT DALE NELSON

By Verda Nelson Jensen

Robert Dale Nelson was born just a few months after the above letter was written. Robert was the last child of the Nelson children. He was born in the hospital in Great Falls, May 24, 1931. I can remember going with dad to the hospital. We stayed that first night at a hotel in Great Falls. I can remember sleeping on two chairs in the hotel. It was very uncomfortable. I remember visiting the hospital to see Mother. Joyce, who was only two, took off her shoes and climbed into bed with mother. She still wanted to be the baby. The next few weeks, Joyce and I spent at Aunt Maude Squire's home. By this time, the Squires family had moved out to Gibson Flats, three miles from Great Falls. I was five-years old, but I remember, very vividly, how much love I felt and how welcome they made us feel.

It was such fun having a baby brother. I hadn't remembered Joyce as a baby and this was my first recollection of a baby in the house. He was adored by all of his brothers and sisters. Maybe it was because there were more of us to love him, but I'm sure he was one of the most loved children ever born!

INSURMOUNTABLE DIFFICULTIES

From Peggy Squires Massey's journal: "The saints in the Chestnut Valley were worried, because after eight years work, they were still unable to get clear title to the land that they had been buying. There were difficult technicalities and some indebtedness on the land when they had moved into the valley to build their homes. Because of lawsuits throughout the entire valley and because the mortgages for the land were held by the Spokane Eastern Trust Company, the Saints found they were not able to get clear title to the land they had been buying. The people appealed to Church Headquarters in Salt Lake City for guidance. Apostle George Albert Smith was sent up to Cascade to investigate the conditions. After a thorough investigation, he realized that the indebtedness was so great that the people could never pay it off. It was his recommendation that the Saints leave the Valley and move elsewhere to find work and make a living for their families. This was a hard blow for the people who had come into the Valley with such high hopes and who had worked so hard to build their homes in the beautiful valley.[8]

GOOD-BYE TO CHESTNUT VALLEY

John and Vera were active in the Branch during the time they spent in Cascade. A Cascade Branch minute book chronicled the date John was released as the Branch President. It stated: "President Wm. R. Sloan, President of the North Western States Mission gave John A. Nelson an honorable release as Branch President of the Cascade Branch, Church of Jesus Christ of Latter-day Saints, May 2, 1932."

The minutes continued: "Retiring J. A. Nelson felt sorrow on being compelled to leave us. [John and Vera had made the decision to move into Great Falls.] Our new President, J. L. Stoddard felt to go and do his best. First Counselor Marshall McOmber felt to thank our retiring President for his laboring with him. Marvin Turner, second

---

8   Life and Times of Peggy Squires Massey, used by permission.

counselor, felt good having been called to labor as counselor. Brother Bartino favored us with a solo. Brother Barlow, our former old President, told of our early organization, eight years ago. Brother Hardy, from Great Falls, enjoyed the spirit here. Brother Reed Molen, from Vaughn, spoke on authority. Brother Lyle Squires favored us with a solo. Brother Ball was glad to be with us. President Sloan spoke on the favored people of the world and the blessings they receive. Closed by singing page 102. Benediction by Brother Simpkins."

John and Vera, along with many of the other Mormon families who had settled the Chestnut Valley, moved into Great Falls. It was in the middle of the Great Depression in 1932. What a hard time to make a transition. With their big family of seven children, the question and worry on their mind was, "How are we going to provide food and clothing and the necessities of life for our family?"

15

NELSON FAMILY IN GREAT FALLS

HARD TIMES FOR THE NELSON FAMILY

By Verda Nelson Jensen

The move from Cascade to Great Falls in 1932 was a very difficult time for our family. The whole country was in a devastating depression. My mother and father, John and Vera, gained very little materially from the eight years they lived in Cascade; however, special friendships and family relationships they made there endured the rest of their lives. They hated to go, but they had no other alternative than to leave the land in Cascade, when they learned that they could never get clear title to their land until everyone had paid their mortgages in full. Too many problems surrounded obtaining clear title to the land, so under recommendations from the Church Headquarters in Salt Lake City, many of the Mormon families left the beautiful Chestnut Valley.

This was a very discouraging time for my parents, John and Vera. Several years before they left Cascade, my father John, had begun selling stock for the Merrill Mortuary Company in Great Falls. The company wanted to build a new mortuary in Great Falls, Montana. Due to some type of financial problems, the company did not pay the stockholders anything for the money they had invested. Many of these people had sacrificed to buy the stock and lost everything they had invested. Consequently, John's employment with this company terminated.

John began selling automobiles for the Ford Motor Company. It was a hard time financially, because few people had enough for the necessities of life, let along enough for the luxury of a new car.[1]

Our first home in Great Falls was at 312 -28th Street South. We brought Old May, our cow who was a big producer, with us when we came from Cascade. My brother Bruce, remembered once slicing his thumb while he was cutting beets for Old May.[2]

Then we moved to 1223 -4th Avenue South. This was across the alley from the Emerson School. It was here that the younger children of the family came down with the Red Measles. There was a sign put on our house, "Quarantine--Measles." As I recall, Ruth didn't get the disease. We all were terribly sick. Mother kept us in a dark room, because the doctor said that light was hard on our eyes. It was a bad memory.

The home just a few houses west of ours was for sale. A deal was made for us to purchase this home at 1209-4th Avenue South. A big vacant lot went with the home. It was a wonderful place for a big garden for our growing family. Every spring our whole family, Mother, Dad, and all the children, would work together to get the garden planted. Vegetables of all kinds were grown. We all thought the corn was a great treat when it finally became ripe. There was an abundance of all good vegetables and enough to share with neighbors and friends in the church.

---

1   Verda Nelson Jensen's Memories.
2   Letter from Bruce Nelson, dated April 3, 1989.

This garden also provided a little spending money for Joyce, Bob, and I. We would load our little red wagon with the fresh vegetables and "peddle" them around the block. It was all profit for us as Mother and Dad let us have whatever money we could earn from the garden. Tomatoes and fresh peas out of our garden were easy to sell. And when the corn came on, selling it was another easy way for us to make a few dimes.

Let me digress for a moment to tell you a few little events about my brother, Robert, commonly called "Bob." Bob had such fair skin and he freckled easily, like his father. Bob really didn't care too much for these freckles and some times he was teased about them. One person who always made him feel that freckles were special, was Peggy Squires Massey.

She loved Bob and it seemed that he had one special freckle on his nose that was Peggy's favorite. Every time she came, she would always ask, "Bobby, how is my freckle? Are you taking good care of it? It is my favorite and I love little boys who have freckles, because that is a sign that the sun has kissed you."

One day after one of the special women from the ward had been to our house, Bob noticed that she had a lot of freckles. His observation was that maybe freckles weren't too bad after all, as he said, "Sister Henderson has freckles and she is purdee!"

During those years, we had a family pet that we all loved dearly. Bob seemed to take over the main ownership of her. She was a baby Boston Bulldog. She had never been spayed and so every year there was a batch of puppies. As I look back now, it seems too bad that we didn't have her bred, because she was such a beautiful, little thoroughbred. She had been given to the family by a dear lady, Sister Clara Dupler. Mother and Daddy had converted her to the Church and we all loved her and called her, "Auntie Dupler."

It seemed that Mitzi was always expecting a batch of puppies. When they were born, she usually would have four puppies and most of them looked like the neighborhood scamp. Bob and Mitzi were inseparable pals. Mitzi was with Bob day and night and would even sleep at the foot of his bed. It seemed that she was dog.

One day Bob had gone over to the fairgrounds with some friends for an outing and as usual, had taken Mitzi with him. She became excited when she saw some other dogs and jumped out of the car window before Bob could stop her. She was attacked by a big German Shepherd dog. She was mortally wounded and although tender-loving care was given to her, there was no way she could be saved. The only alternative was to have her put to sleep.

Lee was the big brother who took the responsibility of doing this unpleasant task. He and Heber Nelson found an old gun and fixed it up to use. It was a shame they had to shoot the little dog who was like a member of the family, but there was no alternative for Mitzi had been too badly chewed up to save.

I am sure that was one of the hardest things Lee ever did. It was especially tragic for Bob, also, to loose his little pal. We all cried for days. It was our first experience with death of any kind and we all took it so hard and felt such a keen loss in the death of our family pet.

CHURCH SERVICES

Our church services were held in a rented hall. I think it was the ELKS CLUB or such as that. I can remember going to church on Sunday morning with Dad and have him and some of the other priesthood members there, cleaning out the beer bottles and the whiskey bottles left from the Saturday night dance. The memory of the odor of some of the rooms where we held class in, still lingers in my nostrils.

Although we didn't have a lovely chapel to meet in, the Spirit of the Lord was there, and happy memories are recorded of giving the Two and One-half Minute Talks, and the Sacrament Gems. There was a closeness with the other members of the Branch and it seemed that we all were concerned about each other and took care of one another. There were lots of young children in our Branch and birthday parties and Church parties were such fun.

I loved to celebrate the 24th of July. It was called "Pioneer Day" and what a big occasion. Parades, games, carnivals, good food and lots of friends made it a special day.

One of the special Sunday School teachers was Marcella Van Orman. She and her husband, Melvin, had moved to Great Falls from Utah to take over one of the department store management. We all adored her and she was such a good teacher, always having special stories and experiences for us to use to become better citizens.

Dad and Mother were some of the stalwarts of the Branch. It was fun to have lots of family members, aunts and uncles and cousins, attend the same Church as we did. I felt sure that I had more special cousins than anyone else in the world.

A MEMORABLE CHRISTMAS

By Verda Nelson Jensen

I think I shall always remember the Christmas when I was eight years old, not because of any special present, or the amount of money that was spent on any of the seven children in our family, but because of the love we shared and the feeling of happiness we experienced being together. Sharing this happiness and love with my dad's brother, Cleve, and his family made this occasion even more special.

Our family was living at 1209 -4th Avenue South, Great Falls, Montana at this time of my life.

Montana winters are times that you can never forget. The snow had been falling all day on the day before Christmas until it was piled in deep mounds, glistening like new diamonds on the fingers of newly- engaged girls.

Finally, as the snow stopped falling, the temperature began a steady descent until it reached a low of 35 degrees below zero.

Dad was afraid the water pipes in the house might freeze so he took gunny sacks and wrapped the pipes coming into the house. I knew why he was worried, as I had seen him have to light torches soaked in gasoline and thaw out the pipes that had frozen before on the occasions when it had been so cold. The windows of the house were all painted in a beautiful scene by our old friend, "Jack Frost."

Testing the coldness, I remember putting my tongue on the metal doorknob outside. If my tongue stuck on the metal, I knew it was "pretty darn cold." I can still almost feel my skin being pulled off as I struggled to gain my freedom on such occasions.

Whenever the temperatures was this cold, we could plan on having frozen milk, if we left the milk delivery out overnight. The caps of the bottles would rise and the cream would peek out of the bottles like a ground hog might peek out of his burrow on a cold morning.

Preparations for the grand day had been taking place for several weeks. The Christmas tree stood majestically in the little-used parlor, with gifts surrounding it. Each gift had been carefully wrapped, tenderly fondled, and lovingly placed beneath the tree where it longingly awaited the magic hour when it could be opened. Popcorn and cranberries had been strung laboriously into long chains and draped artistically among the branches of the tree. Tinsel had been strung painstakingly and the bows were heavy with treasured ornaments.

Special treats had been prepared. Mince pies and pumpkin pies lined the shelves on the unheated porch. We had spent hours mixing, rolling and baking cookies and gingerbread men. Then the fun task of decorating all these goodies began. The frosting had been placed in a paper folded into a cone. It was necessary to get just the right "squeeze" on the paper or else the frosting would come oozing out the top of the paper instead of out the hole cut in the bottom of the cone. In either case, the taste was delightful. Mother had made cans of plum and carrot pudding and had cooked them in empty Crisco cans on the top of the giant, black, coal stove.

Uncle Cleve, Aunt Luella and their family arrived in time for Christmas Eve supper. Having their family come to spend the holiday with us was now a family tradition. I don't remember the menu that mother and Aunt Luella served, but I will always remember the creamed, oyster stew and the bite-sized, round crackers that were served along with the hot, spiced cranberry juice.

After the dishes were cleared away, the Christmas program commenced with each of the children taking a part. Mother played the piano and led the singing, leading out with her mellow contralto voice. We all gathered around the piano and raised our voices in praise to the Christ Child. After singing the new Christmas songs we had learned in school and hearing the Christmas story read from the Bible by my father, we were ready for one of the most important parts of the evening-hanging up our Christmas stockings. Each of us used the longest stocking we could find and pinned our name on the top so Santa would be sure to know. We hung them on the rack in the hall. Then it was time to go to bed.

The children's bedrooms were on the second floor of the house. There had been no provision made to keep these rooms heated. Long, flannel nightgowns were donned, flatirons were heated and hot-water bottles were filled and wrapped in towels.

Mother took the flatirons and ironed the flannel sheets for us, warming them before we hopped into bed. My younger sister, Joyce, and my cousin, May, and I slept together. We always insisted that May sleep in the middle so we could "share" her better that way. Sleep came tardily as we listened to the bells from the magnificent cathedral ringing in the distance. Even though we firmly believed we must hurry to sleep before Santa Claus could make his appearance, we listened cautiously for the sound of his sleigh bells and the sound of the reindeer's hooves beating on the roof.

Clockwise from top left: John, Lovell, Lee, Robert, Bruce.

The next sounds I remember were familiar every morning. Dad was shaking the stove and shoveling out the ashes into the coal bucket. Realizing how cold the house would be until the fire was made, we remained quietly in bed for a few minutes longer until our curiosity could be contained no longer. Bounding down the stairs, we rushed to find our stockings to see what Santa had placed in them.

Bruce ready for the fair, about 1935.

We always found the stockings lumpy with the most interesting bumps. Always in the top was a big candy cane. A little further down in mine, I found a little house, encased in glass, with a real snow storm occurring when the house was shook. There was hard-tack candy with its ribbons of color shaped in curly-que designs, sugary chocolates with big cherries in the center, and crystal-clear animals in a variety of shapes, sizes and colors. After we played with these little animals for a few hours, it was fun to break them a little at a time and nibble at their legs or heads. Always at the very toe of the stocking was a big orange and a red apple.

After a breakfast of blueberry pancakes and thick-sliced oranges, covered with snowy-white, powdered sugar, we spent the day sharing our treasures with one another, playing "Old Maid," Pit," or "Monopoly."

Looking back on this Christmas, I can't remember the new bicycle, or the skis or stereos that our children might be expecting for their Christmas, but I do remember the exciting times and the love and fun we had planning for this glorious day. We had shared an experience with loved ones always to be remembered and talked about for many years, as a "memorable Christmas.[3]

---

3   Written as a University English assignment by Verda Nelson Jensen, January, 1968.

SELF-SUFFICIENT, ALWAYS

By Verda Nelson Jensen

My mother, Vera, tried to talk John into getting some assistance from the county during those days of the Big Depression when it was so difficult to make a living. But, John was too proud and always felt that it was a disgrace to seek assistance regardless of how little they had. Vera would can fruits and vegetables and make her own bread. This was a special treat to all her family and their friends, as we would come in after school and the fresh bread would be hot out of the oven. Vera would tell us to go get a bottle of our favorite jam, which was usually huckleberry, and with hot rolls or a loaf of hot bread, it was a delicacy that remains fresh in my memory. Mother baked about seven loaves of bread twice a week, plus a big pan or two of biscuits.

John began making collections for the Metropolitan Life Insurance Company and later he was given the territory of Northern Montana to sell for the Mutual of Omaha, Life and Health and Accident Insurance.

John and Vera were stalwarts in the Great Falls Branch and District. John served as Branch President for many years. He also served as President of the Great Falls District for fourteen years. There were 23 branches in towns and cities throughout Northern Montana under his leadership. This covered an area

Verda and her pal, Jean Jahr, dressed for the Helldorado Parade, about 1936.

of over 100 miles each way from Great Falls. Consequently, John and Vera did a great deal of traveling, at their own expense, to attend meetings throughout this District. As District President, John gave inspiration and guidance to those branches. He met with them on a regular basis to hold District Conferences. Under the inspiration of the Lord and with the guidance of the men on the High Council, it was their responsibility to select the Branch Presidents and direct the affairs of the branches within his district. There were many special conferences held and speeches to be given; he counseled and encouraged the members whenever he could.[4]

Vera served along with John as the Relief Society President. Later she was a counselor to the first District Relief Society President, [Sister Charlotte Barlow], for four and one-half years. Then Vera accepted the call to be President of the District Relief Society. She serve a total of fourteen and one- half years in the Relief Society organization.[5]

VERDA, OUR MIRACLE CHILD

From Vera's diary:

"January, 1937, the year Verda Cloe was ten years old, she was stricken with appendicitis. She had attended her fourth grade class in the morning. She came home that afternoon with a violent pain in her stomach. Because John was out of town, I called my brother-in-law, Lawrence Squires, to come and administer to her. He brought the Elders. They gave her a blessing and she had a good night. The next morning she was worse. I called our family doctor, Dr. Allred. He came and examined Verda and could find no reason for the high temperature she was having. "

"He asked me to take Verda to the hospital so she could have some further examinations and x-rays to find the cause of her problem. It was apparent from the tests that she was suffering from appendicitis. It was soon obvious that her appendix had burst and surgery

4   33 Vera Nelson's journal.
5   34 Ibid.

was necessary immediately. John arrived home by this time and together with Uncle Lawrence Squires, they again administered to this darling child."

"After the operation, it was necessary for the doctor to place drain tubes in the incision, to drain off the poison that surrounded the tissue.

On the third day after the operation, the infection stopped draining. Gangrene and peritonitis had set in. The doctor informed us to expect the worst.

He suggested that the family be called to bid Verda 'Good-bye' as he did not think she would live until morning. All of the children came and we all knelt around her bed and offered a prayer in her behalf. They all kissed her 'good-bye' thinking that there was little chance they would see her again.[6]

From a letter written by Ruth Nelson Miller, another viewpoint is expressed:

> *"I shall never forget how frightened I felt as I got the little ones, Joyce and Bobby, ready to go to the hospital to say 'goodbye' to our dear sister, Verda. Val, Bruce, and Lee helped. When we got to the hospital, we waited for daddy to come. When he arrived, he took us into Verda's room and told us that only our Father in Heaven could save her life now. He wanted all of us to kneel around her bed and he would administer to her. We should each use our faith in her behalf. Everyone was crying but we knew that our daddy could use his Priesthood power to save our little sister's life.[7]*

Continuing from Vera's diary:

> *John had gone to bring another Priesthood bearer to help with the administration. When they arrived, John told all of the children, as they knelt by Verda's bedside, that she could be healed through*

6   35 Vera wrote a letter to Verda concerning this operation.
7   36 Letter dated April 6, 1989 from Ruth Miller while on a mission in Brighton, England.

the power of the priesthood and the faith of those who loved her. The children all had a great faith. Verda, too, had great faith and seemed to know that she could be healed through the power of the Priesthood that her Father bore. In the blessing, John said, 'Heavenly Father, if it be thy will, as the sun comes up in the morning, may this child awaken to a new life, free from pain and suffering.' After the blessing, she fell asleep.[8]

Lee was twelve years old at this time. He recently recalled some of the events that took place in Verda's hospital room:

"At the request of Doctor Allred, all the family came to say good-bye' to Verda. With the gangrene and peritonitis so far advanced, the doctor had given up hope of Verda's recovery. Mother was sobbing softly, Ruth was crying silently, Joyce and Bob were round-eyed and silent and we older boys stood there with sad, uncomprehending faces."

"We were waiting for Dad to come. It seemed an eternity. We believed the Doctor. It was scary and to look at Verda's still, white face, it was easy to believe that she would never leave her bed of affliction alive. When Dad came, Brother Russell Crandall was with him. Brother Crandall anointed Verda's head with the holy, consecrated oil, that had been consecrated for the healing of the sick. Dad sealed the anointing and blessed his baby girl. By now we were all in tears." [9]

Ruth has added this to the story: "Lovell, Bruce and I took the other children home and put them to bed. That night was the Gold and Green Ball in our Ward and Sister Vera Croxford had lent me a long formal to wear for the first time. When we got home, none of us felt like going."[10]

Vera's diary continues:

8   37 Vera Nelson's journal.
9   Letter from Lee Nelson dated March 24, 1989 to Verda Jensen.
10   Letter from Ruth Miller dated April 6, 1989 from Brighton, England.

"The infection had stopped flowing from the drain tubes placed in Verda's incision. While John was giving Verda a beautiful blessing, I had the inspiration of the Holy Ghost come upon me that I should ask the nurses to place hot epsom salt packs on Verda's side. I felt that this would start the infection to begin draining again. The nurses said that they would have to ask the doctor. When he was told of my request, he said, 'If it will make Mrs. Nelson feel better, then by all means, do it.' Within a short time after they placed the hot packs on her incision, the infection began flowing again."

[Remember, this occurred before the modern miracle drugs, the sulfa, penicillin, or other life-saving drugs had been discovered.]

"As I sat holding Verda's hand and wiping her forehead, she awoke and asked me a strange request. She loved music and always loved to hear me sing. She said, 'Mamma, will you sing to me? I want to hear the song, I Had Such a Pretty Dream Mamma. As hard as it was for me, concerned that this little child was dying, I sang all of the verses of this beautiful song. She went to sleep while I finished the last verse."

"She slept all night through. Just as the sun was coming up, she awoke and said, 'Mamma, what are you doing here? Have you been here all night?'" I replied, 'Yes, my darling, both your daddy and I have been with you all night. Verda replied, 'Well, doesn't this hospital have any funny papers?' Her temperature was down from the 106 degrees the night before to nearly normal. The poison in her body was flowing from the drain tubes in her side. We had witnessed a miracle."

"When Doctor Allred, who was of the Catholic faith, came into her room, he made a classic remark to John and I when he said, 'A power higher than I has saved this little child. We have witnessed a miracle in this hospital room today.'"

"The Branch was holding their annual Gold and Green Ball the night Verda was so sick. Many people left the dance and came and waited in the hall corridors to offer their faith and prayers in Verda's behalf. The next day, members of the Branch brought dozens of balloons that had been used as decorations from the dance the night before, to fill Verda's room. They filled the corridors and all of the children's rooms on Verda's floor."

How grateful we were for the Priesthood of God and for the opportunity of having Verda anointed and administered to with the holy consecrated oil that had been blessed for the healing of the sick.

How grateful we were for the faith and prayers extended by our dear children, our family and our friends in her behalf. How grateful we were to a kind Heavenly Father who saw fit to answer our prayers and save the life of our dear daughter."[11]

A STAKE OF ZION IN THE MAKING

In July of 1937, John was set apart by President Melvin J. Ballard and the Mission President, Preston Nibley, to prepare Northern Montana to become a Stake of Zion. A letter written by John to his parents in Cardston, Canada, October 26, 1937, concerning this calling, contained the following excerpt:

"I find it a big calling, but have plenty of able men in the priesthood to help out. We have held three district priesthood meetings. The peo-

John A. Nelson and President Preston Nibley of the Northwestern States Mission. John was District President, Great Falls, Montana.

---

11   Verda Nelson's journal.

ple come for nearly a hundred miles around and our hall is filled. The support of the Latter-Day Saints is wonderful ... On the 14th of November we are holding our regular District Conference and Priesthood convention. President Nibley will also be in attendance. We have invited President E. J. Wood, from the Canadian Temple, to also come and speak to us. The Church in this part of the world is growing by 'leaps and bounds.'"

"Our children are, at present, all in school, but Lovell who has a job and works at a grocery store. Bruce was the main actor last night in the high school play. He will finish high school this coming spring. Ruth is quite a young lady and a very good student. Lee, Verda, Joyce and Robert are also wrapped up in their school work. Bob thinks that he is quite a man now that he goes to school. Vera is home alone most of the time now. Of course she keeps busy with her work in the Church and serves as P.T.A. President." [12]

A LETTER TO GRANDMA & GRANDPA NELSON

The following letter is one that Ruth Nelson Miller wrote to her grandparents John Sr. and Ella Nelson who were living in Cardston, Canada. Ruth was about seventeen years old at this time:

Great Falls, Mont. February 23rd 1939

Dearest Grandmother and Grandfather,

I've been thinking of you both for a long time and really have been neglecting to write. Aunt Mary wrote that Grandpa wasn't feeling so well a week or so ago, and I hope this letter finds you both in the best of health.

Have you been having a cold winter this year? We really can't complain much, as the very coldest spell didn't last longer than two weeks at a time. The temperature has dropped below zero since Tuesday, and we have received a foot or more of snow. This will cheer the farmers up I'm sure as we really need the moisture.

---

12   41 Letter from John A. Nelson, Jr. to his parents dated October 26, 1937.

Great Falls is having their annual Gold and Green Ball tomorrow evening. We all hope it turns out to be the grand occasion it is planned for. The proceeds from the ball are to go on the fund for our new church house here in the Falls. We hope to have our own church house some day soon and know it won't be so long now. At least we all have hopes that it won't.

Well Grandma, it's your turn to come and see us soon. We'd love very much to have you and Grand Dad both come down and spend a couple of months with us. Why don't you see what can be done about it? Bobby still talks of when Grandpa was down and says he'd sure like to see him and Grandma again. Maybe we'll be able to get up that way this summer. Let's hope so.

Well, take the best of care of yourselves and don't go out without your hats and coats on, so that you won't catch cold. Remember, we all think of you every day and love you both very dearly. Write often, as we always enjoy receiving your letters and read them through many times. Give my love to all the good relations in Cardston and keep a lot for yourselves.

Love and Kisses, Your Granddaughter,

Ruthie

A LIFE OF SERVICE

John was asked to speak at numerous funerals. It didn't matter how far away the service was to be held, he willingly went, always at his own expense.

John and Vera's home was headquarters for numerous missionaries who were called to the North Western States Mission. The missionaries knew that they would always be welcome and usually were invited to dinner once during the week, plus always on Sundays. They were provided with fresh bread and garden produce and occasionally Vera would help out with ironing a shirt or two.

RUTH BECOMES "MRS. IVAN MILLER"

Ruth married Ivan V. Miller from Hyrum, Utah on January 29, 1941 in the Logan Temple. A lovely wedding breakfast was held at the Bluebird Restaurant in Logan. They will be living in Hyrum where Ivan is in business with his father, Lester Miller and his brother, Max Miller. Lester Miller had been a missionary in the California mission and had been friends with Vera when she lived there in California. Ruth had gone to Utah to see her friend Norma Stoddard. While she was there, they paid a call on the Miller family and met Ivan. The romance and subsequent marriage followed.

ELLA ELIZABETH NELSON'S FUNERAL

John's mother, Ella Elizabeth Nelson, died in Cardston, Alberta Canada October 30, 1941. At her funeral, the tabernacle was filled to overflowing. John recorded:

"I was touched as my wife Vera and I went from Great Falls to Cardston to Mother's funeral. We always had an idea that Father would go first but mother died at the age of eighty-six after having filled a long and useful life. She taught her children many wonderful lessons, how to live and be good neighbors and to be kind and loving to each other."

"During the funeral service of Mother, Sister Lilly Pitcher spoke. This good woman had assisted my mother on many occasions in delivering children and healing the sick. She was a very fluent speaker. She was a woman who had the touch of the gospel and the spirit of it and she did extol the beauties and character of my mother to the satisfaction of all we children who were there. So I give thanks to my Heavenly Father that my parentage were people who were willing to serve."

"Both Father and Mother were willing to give their lives for the Gospel of the Master and for their neighbors and for their friends. Mother rode all over the neighborhood, sometimes on horseback

Ruth and Ivan's Wedding Day-(Ivan is taking the picture.)
Notice Aunt Lileth and Aunt Rae are among the guests.

and sometimes in an old buckboard with no springs on them. It just had four wheels and a box on the axles with a railing around the back of it to make the buggy. There was no such thing as a fine carriage or automobiles or anything of that sort in those days. My mother lived to be a good old age and she has a posterity that runs into the hundreds. I am grateful for her life. I am grateful for the example that she set and the things she taught. I love and extol her name because of the virtues she had and her willingness to serve mankind."[13]

LETTERS TO DEAR OLD PA

Vera was thoughtful of her father-in-law after his wife Ella died. Vera would faithfully write letters to him and keep him informed about the happenings of their family. A few excerpts from these letters follow:

13   John Nelson dictaphone tapes #31.

November 12, 1941

Dear Grandpa and all,

We think of you every day and wish we were near you. Do hope you are feeling all right. The children all want to see you. Bobby said he didn't see why he couldn't have gone to grandma's funeral too. But we left in such a hurry and all. Next time we go we will try and take him.

Tomorrow night is Frank's farewell party. [Cleve and Luella Nelson's son.] He is such a grand boy and will make a fine missionary, I know. I hope I can send some of my children on a mission.

The weather is still very nice, no storm here since the first of the month before we left for Canada. I wrote to Lileth and Rae. Now I must write to Ella. [These are John's sisters.]

Lovell and Lee went hunting yesterday. It was Armistice Day so the stores were all closed. They each got two chickens. Wish you could come and have dinner with us. Little Janell is here for the day. Her mama is going to a party this afternoon so Lovell brought her over. She loves to come to our place, just like her dad used to love to go see you. Remember when you used to set him on the table and give him a glass of water and the sugar bowl? He sure loved his grandpa!

Cleve and Luella were here to see us Sunday night. They are all well. Lee and Heber Dean went hunting deer in the mountains last week. Heber got one, but Lee lost his. It got dark as they tracked it by the blood. They had a grand time anyway.

The ward here is putting on a big carnival and fair. Turkey dinner and all the trimmings on the 21st and 22nd this month.

Well, dear old pa, we all love you and pray God to bless you and keep you. Love to Lola and Doran and all the rest.

Yours always, Auntie

[John, Sr. always called Vera, "Auntie" from the time John and Vera first announced their engagement. It was a term of endearment and an expression of love.]

16

WAR YEARS

UNITED STATES AT WAR!!

Verda remembered, "We were on our way home from Sacrament meting December 7, 1941. Dada always stopped to pic up an early edition of the newspaper, "The Leader". There across the top of the newspaper in bold red headlines were the words, "JAPS ATTACK PEARL HARBOR!" As a young girl of 15, I didn't completely realize the full importance of these words, but it wasn't long before the full force of it hit all of us."

WAR-TIME LETTERS

Many letters were exchanged during the war. John and Vera were faithful in writing letters to John's father and to their children away from home. The following are excerpts from these letters:

March 3, 1942

Dear Father,

I will try and write you a few lines this morning as it is snowing quite hard and difficult for me to get out on the road to take care of my business.

Lovell is in the hospital having slipped on the ice and put his right ankle out of place. The doctor told him that he would have to be down for two or three weeks, as a dislocation is almost as bad as a break. He has had a rupture that has bothered him for a number of years, so he had that attended to while he is in the hospital. He was operated on Saturday morning and is now feeling fine again, but will stay in the hospital for about two weeks longer.

Margaret, Lovell's wife, is staying with us, with their two little children, while Lovell is in the hospital. Janell is sixteen months old and the baby is two months. They named this little guy John Lovell, and they call him "JOHN".

Bruce is still in California, but we expect him home the first of April. Then, no doubt, the Army will want him to help run down the Japs and the Germans.

Lee and Lovell were thinking about going to Alaska in defense work, but now that Lovell has had this set-back, they may not go for awhile at least.

We only have three of our children in school now, as Lee graduated the last of January from high school. Verda is in high school and Joyce is in junior high school and Robert is in the grades.

We have sure had a lot of snow this winter and the side roads are drifted full of snow, but the oiled roads can always be traveled.

Vera is feeling pretty good now, since her operation last June. The girls are getting pretty well grown up now, so they can do a lot of the work, which helps their mother a great deal.

I hope that you are strong and able to get around some at least. You always said that you would live to be a hundred years old, and I trust you will if you want to. I only wished that we lived closer to you so we could take you for a ride once in awhile. I have been trying to build up an insurance agency the last two years, and it has been quite a struggle. I did not want to work for the other fellow, but rather work for myself, which is a lot better in the long run.

Where is Hazel's son, Cleve? Is he in the war yet? I suppose that you will have a number of grandsons, etc. in the war. The Japs are not so easy to lick all at once, but just wait a little while and we will sure make them back up, when Canada, England and the United States all get going together.

I have signed up to go back to the Islands, where I was on my mission. The U.S. Government wants some interpreters for a number of those islands in the Pacific. A man that I am well acquainted with left Great Falls last week for Samoa to work for a construction company, building air bases, etc. [Editor's note: John never got this assignment, so never had the opportunity to go back to his beloved Samoa.]

Do you ever write any more letters? Vera and I would love to have you write us a short letter, if you can. Tell everybody "Hello" and that we hope to meet again this summer.

Love and best wishes,

Your son, John

On March 16, 1942, John wrote a letter to his father. Part of it follows:

"The war is getting real serious now and more boys are leaving every day or two. We do not know just when some of our boys will have to go. Bruce is coming home from California the first of next month. Lee will have to register now that he is 18 years old."

The following is a letter from Vera to her father-in-law, Grandpa Nelson:

Spring, 1942

Dear Ole Pa:

We all think of you every day and pray God to take care of you. How are you getting along anyway? Hope Lola and Doran are getting along alright. It is nice and warm here today. The snow is almost gone and what there is left will soon go, for the temperature is 48 degrees.

I had a nice letter from Lileth. She is feeling some better, but is still not well.

Bruce and his wife are sure having a nice time in California this winter. They are both working at the big dude ranch at Palm Springs. The movie stars all go there to spend their holidays and it is such a grand place, so they say. Wish we were all there for a nice sun bath.

Well, Lee will soon be out of school. Do you remember the day he was born in Cascade? Those years have gone by so very fast. Then I just had four babies. Now I just have four at home and three married. My four at home are all so grown up. Some day Dad and I will be the old folks and Lovell and Bruce and the rest will step into our role. Such is life, but it is rather nice to have been entrusted with seven fine spirits from Heaven. I have tried to do my part, the best I knew how and I have loved the job.

Dear old grandpa, you have ever been an inspiration to me and I think you from the bottom of my heart for your many kind words and deeds of kindness to me and my family. I hope we can see you before too long. We all love you.

Sincerely your kids,

John, Vera and Family

Top left:
Growing up years for ROBERT
and JOYCE NELSON, about 1942.

Top right:
JOHN and his first grandson,
JOHN NELSON. JOHN was employed
in the security department at
East Air Base, Great Falls, Mont.

Bottom left:
Grandson, Johnny, age one year-
1942.

In John A. Nelson, Sr.'s eighty-second year, the driest year in the history of Cardston, he produced a wonderful garden from which he distributed to those who were in need or unable to grow their own. He was not anxious to give an ear of corn to those who had been lazy, but he would not see anyone suffer.[1]

Lovell wrote a letter to his grandfather, John A. Nelson, Sr. We will include it here:

Great Falls, Montana

August 25, 1942

Dear Grandpa,

I suppose you thought that I had forgotten all about you, but I haven't. We had figured on coming up to see you this summer but I was in the hospital in February and had to lay off work for two months, so I didn't get any vacation.

Is the world treating you okay? I sure hope so. Things are going okay for us. Bruce is going to a special school and when he gets out he will be a Second Lieutenant in the Air Force.

Dad is a guard at one of the Air Bases. Lee is working in Utah on a hospital. He is a carpenter and has saved enough money this summer to put himself through a year of college.

I am going to run a store for the Army, starting the first of September, then when I do get in the Army for sure, I will get a rating of Sergeant.

Say "Hello" to every one and tell them to keep their chins up, we'll soon win the war. Hope to see you soon.

Your grandson, Lovell

---

1   History of John A. Nelson, Sr., written by his son, Seth.

John, Sr. was eighty-eight when he died in Cardston, Alberta, Canada, on September 29, 1942.

MORE WAR-TIME LETTERS

Many of our loved ones were enlisting and being drafted into the war efforts. It was a difficult time as each family bid good-bye to their sons. Boys from all of the various family groups were called to service in the American and Canadian Armed Forces. These boys, young men in their prime, served with honor and dignity. We can be proud of them as they defended our country's honor and protected each of us from the aggressive nations. Many were wounded in battle.

In John and Vera's family, their son, Bruce, joined the United States Air Force Officer's Training School. He and Betty Ruth (Ruth Molen) were married before this time. Bruce was sent to India with the Air Force. Their son, Lee, joined the Merchant Marine as soon as he was old enough. He was able to come back home occasionally during the war between his voyages. There were black, lonesome, worry-filled days. Vera changed from a carefree sort of a person, to a woman whose heart was heavy over the safety of her sons. Her hair went from its beautiful coal-black shade, to nearly grey within the next few years.

Merchant Marines: Lee (left) and his buddy.

John was a good one to write letters and always put a carbon copy in the typewriter so that he could keep a copy of his correspondence. It is from these carbon copies written to his sons while they served in the Armed Forces during World War II. John also sent a copy of many of his letters to his daughters living away from Great Falls. The following are excerpts from these letters:

Great Falls, Montana April 18, 1943

To Bruce and Lee, Our Dear Sons,

This is Sunday and we all went to Sunday School, including Johnny and Janell and Ruth and little Marsha Ann. [Ruth was married and living in Hyrum, Utah] Lovell and Margaret, with Vivian and Gladys went fishing out to George and Ada's place. It was funny to watch that boy, John, in Sunday School. He does about as he pleases when it comes to make people laugh, etc. His grandma finally had to take him outside as he got started to sing and wanted to keep it up after the rest of the crowd had stopped. Janell, of course, is still the little lady and is a good girl in her class.

Everybody wanted to see the new "Miss Marsha Ann," and she received many fine compliments from Ruth's admiring friends.

The weather is sure fine and the grass is growing very fast. To mention grass might sound strange to you fellows in such green beautiful country as California, but the sight of green grass is appreciated in Montana.

Last Wednesday I went out to the Lloyd Croxford ranch and broke four head of wild horses to lead and I harnessed them up and drove them around the corral for a while. This was real fun for me as I love horses and take a lot of pleasure in making them gentle and submissive.

Two of them were the real bronco of Montana type and being large and well-fed, we had to reset the snubbing post and put it deeper into the ground.

Jene McKay is home for a while and army life seems to agree well with him, as he is much heavier than he was before he left.

Mr. Lyons, one of the guards I work with, was run over while walking on 1st Avenue North and Fifth Street and killed. He has a son in Australia and a daughter who works at the sub-depot.

Another accident happened Friday when LeRoy Savalsted was killed when he was thrown from his motorcycle as he hit a truck. He will be buried tomorrow. I think this lad was about the age of Joyce, as he was in some of her classes in school.

I will have to let mother finish this letter if it gets posted today, as I have to go and put Johnny and Janell to bed in their own beds.

Bob is getting his right arm wound up for baseball, I am not sure if it is for the world series or not, but he seems to think it is just as important.

The gospel is true. Remember your Heavenly Father is just as close to you as you let him be through your prayers.

We love you both, Dad

April 20, 1943

Dear Son Bruce,

Your letter from Fresno came a few minutes ago and I will add a line or two to the letter I wrote you and Lee on the 18th and send them both to you this morning.

No doubt Ruth is with you before this. She can tell you all the latest news of Great Falls and surrounding country. We just closed a deal for a place on the West-side near the brewery. A five-room modern house with one acre of land for Bob to work, a $700 up-to-the-minute chicken coop, garage under the house, where it will always be warm in the winter, as it is in the same room with the furnace. It looks like a good deal for us, as there is plenty of space for garden, etc. etc. A nice lawn around the house. It looks like a deal as we have made a down-payment.

Glad you have a nice uniform to wear home. Hope Ruthie can stay with you, as it will then not be lonesome for you. I am sure you are making the best of Army life and by trying to find the best, it will be of vast importance to you later in life. You always can learn, no matter where you are and what your surrounding conditions might be, if you look for the best.

I will close as mother has called me to dinner. If we locate on the West-side, I think I will get a cow for Bob to milk. It will do him good to have a little responsibility. Always keep us posted as to your address.

Love from All, Dad

Great Falls, Montana
May 16th, 1943

Dear Bruce and Lee:

This is Sunday and about time that I should write you fellows
another letter.

We all attended church this morning, even Lovell and Janell went,
but Margaret and Johnny stayed home as Johnny has not been
too well the past week. He is better now.

Joyce is preparing a formal for the Green & Gold Ball which will
be held this coming Thursday night. This will be her first formal
affair and she seems to be very much enthused about it. I suppose Verda will also be there in her formal. They are both young
ladies now and Bob is really the only little one we have, outside
of the grand children.

The people are moving today out of the house we bought and
they hope to turn it over to us about Tuesday morning. We will
move immediately as we are anxious to get our garden planted.
It has been so cold and stormy that there are only a few gardens
put in around here. It snowed a little as late as yesterday and
the ground has been very wet and cold. I have had a man hired
to plough the garden plot for the last ten days but every time that
he planned on doing it, it rained.

Bob is sure anxious to get moved as he is going to do great things,
like raise chickens and rabbits and he talks about buying himself
a pony and even a cow to milk. The house sits on a whole acre of
ground with plenty of Great Northern vacant land joining. This
land will do to picket a cow or pony on it.

I took an annual leave from work, for five days, planning to move,
etc. but we could not get possession as the folks living in the place
had no where to move to. I have to go back to work Monday

night and then I am off again Tuesday and Wednesday so this will give me ample time to move.

You may address your letters from now on to 224 14th Street South West. We hope to be out of here by Wednesday night completely.

I have some pretty good life insurance business lined up in the country as soon as the roads get passable. I will, however, write most of my insurance in the city.

We have two men from Salt Lake City who will speak to us to-night in church. You boys should attend church whenever it is possible, even though it may not be your own church you go to. All churches give a man some good thoughts on how to live, etc. etc. There are quite a few Latter-Day Saint soldiers that attend church here every Sunday.

We are always anxious to hear from both of you boys, so please write as often as you can.

Love from us all,

Dad

Reunion of Nelson Family During War Years - 1944
Back row: Robert, Lovell, Ruth, Bruce, Lee,
Front row: Verda, Vera, John and Joyce

January 21, 1945

Dear Bruce:

We have received your letter telling us that India is quite the place. It is a relief to know just where you are. You saw plenty of water on the way over and no doubt, it became tiresome. The old sailors get tired of the land, so there you are.

You may remember me telling you that I saw thousands of Indians from India in the Fiji Islands many years ago. I saw the sacred cow and other things they worshipped. Of course, the real India where you are is much different, I am sure. It is a great experience for you to visit foreign countries and learn the customs of the people. Learn as much about the country as you can and it will be a great value to you in your later life.

WAR-TIME FAMILY: BRUCE AND LEE in Armed Forces:
Left to right: Lovell, Robert, John, Vera
Ruth, Verda and Joyce.
About   1945

Left: John with
Johnny, Janell,
Margaret, Ruthie,
Lee, Joyce and
baby Bruce.

Right: Joyce,
Margaret, and
Vera

Ruthie and Alice just came in after church. They are not staying long. [Ruth was living in Great Falls, while Bruce was serving in the Air Force.] We all went to church tonight. Lovell and his family came over and Joyce and Bob tended the babies.

That Bruce Allen Baby Boy, well it would now take pages to tell all about him. Needless to say, he likes his old grand-dad. He is very willing to stay with me as long as I will tend him. He can just about sit alone, I practiced him on the table for quite awhile today. He is the most wiling little guy I have ever seen. He will try anything you start him out on. Ruth is a very capable little mother, but I will say that she has got to work fast to keep ahead of that lad.

Yes, Lee is home and has been for two weeks. I think he intends to leave about Tuesday the 23rd for Utah. He is going back to San Francisco to sail the Pacific again. Last trip he took, he left from New York and came through the Panama Canal and left the ship in Portland, Oregon. Quite a trip for a small lad.

A man by the name of Brown was at the Church meeting tonight. He is from Salt Lake City to look over the Chestnut Valley. He says the Church is going to buy the land and bring in about 32 families as settlers. This will be a good move for our people.

Well, Brucie Boy, keep up the good fight till the war is won. Remember there is comfort and safety in prayers. We will all be waiting for you when you come home. We all send our love.

Dad

CASUALTIES OF WAR

Keith Squires [Maude and Lawrence's son] was badly injured when his plane crashed in Southern England in 1944 or 1945. Nothing was left of his plane. He came down amid fire and wreckage. He landed with only the seat and a big log across his legs. He was severely wounded about the face and head; his right leg was broken in five places and the left leg was cut and badly bruised as well as sprained.

Jack and Boyd Squires also joined the services and the Nelson family was concerned over these dear cousins. Heber Nelson was in the Navy, serving on the aircraft carrier, the Enterprise.

John and Vera's special friends, Marshal and LaVerne McOmber, lost their son, Calvin, was he was shot down over Sicily. He was buried there but a memorial service was held for him in Vaughn, Montana. John had always been someone very special to Cal and the McOmber family, so he was asked to preach the funeral sermon. He spoke eloquently about the first principles of the gospel and the meaning and purpose of this life. He offered comfort and consolation to the family. He told the family, "It matters not where we die, but how we die. Go to the Lord in humble prayer that your hearts might be touched with comfort and with faith that will mean peace, that will mean contentment, that will mean joy and pride in the fact that your son has given his life for his country and that he served his country and his Church with honor and dignity."[2]

What joy we all felt when that terrible war ended. It had taken a toll in every family we knew and we all gave thanks to a kind Heavenly Father when our loved ones returned to their homes and families.

17

POST-WAR YEARS

FOR THE NELSON FAMILY

WEDDINGs, AND MORE WEDDINGS With the war at an end, there were thoughts of college, careers, and marriage for the Nelson children. By no means a complete account, but the following information concerning the wedding dates of the four younger Nelson children is available: Verda married Leon James Jensen, of Hyrum, Utah on July 31, 1946 in the Cardston Temple, Alberta, Canada. Lee married Linda Anna Hall on March 8, 1947. Joyce married Earl Thomas McMaster on June 5, 1948. Robert married Geraldine Linnell on February 9, 1951.

DOING COMMON THINGS IN AN UNCOMMON WAY

By John A. Nelson, Jr.

In 1945, President Samuel A. Bringhurst, President of the North-western States Mission came to Great Falls, to hold the regularly scheduled Conference with our District. He wanted to advance the missionary program in our area, but because there was not enough full time missionaries to do the needed work, he decided to call a number of local missionaries. Vera and I were chosen to, along with about three other couples, to serve as missionaries.

After about a month, because of my business, we found that we did not have sufficient time to spend on the missionary activities. It was necessary to write to President Bringhurst and tell him that we had not experienced the success that we had hoped for. In time, we received a letter back from him, encouraging us and saying, "I commend you and your wife for the fine work that you are doing. Do not get discouraged, but proceed ahead with your work and the Lord will bless you in your endeavors."

As we took this counsel, I remembered a Mutual lesson that I had taught when we were living in Canada. The message was "Doing Common Things in an Uncommon Way."

The thought came to me, "Why can't Vera and I do missionary work in an uncommon way?" The common way for missionaries to teach is to go from door to door to visit the people in their various homes.

The thought came to me, "Why can't Vera and I call a group of investigators together once a week and hold a meeting with them all together? Perhaps we could arrange to meet in the Church and this way we could teach more than one at a time and satisfy the limited time we had to spend on missionary work."

After discussing the idea with our Branch President, and receiving his blessing and his permission to use the Church, I went home and called about 12 people. Some were acquaintances of ours, some were strangers. I explained, what I was doing by saying, "Hello, John Nelson is my name. I am an Elder in the Church of Jesus Christ of Latter-Day Saints, commonly called the Mormons. I am holding a class every Thursday evening at eight, in the Mormon Chapel. I will be teaching the Gospel as taught by Jesus Christ when He was here on earth. It would be a pleasure to have you and your companion attend this class."

Sometimes, the response was, "Yes, you can count on us."

Sometimes, the response was, "No, we are not interested."

At the appointed hour, eight people showed up at the chapel. We were there to escort them in. They did not know each other, except for those with their companions. I explained that while we were in our class, I would like them to call us Brother and Sister Nelson and I would call them Brother and Sister, also. They all looked at each other and smiled as this was something new for them. They were being taught the gospel of Jesus Christ by two concerned missionaries. It was a marvelous experience and one that neither Vera nor I shall long forget. We met each week as planned and at the conclusion of the lessons, six of these people asked for baptism.

We have always been proud of the special award certificate .presented to us with a picture of Prophet David O. McKay and signed by the presidency of the newly organized West Central States Mission.[1]

---

1   John Nelson's Dictaphone tape #30

Only Vera's certificate has been located concerning their mission call,
but both John and Vera were awarded the same type of certificate.

HAPPIER DAYS

JOHN AND VERA WITH THEIR THREE OLDEST GRANDCHILDREN:
Vera holding Marsha Ann Miller,
John holding Johnny Nelson
with big sister, Janell Nelson, in front.
About 1946.

Tough jobs for the Nelson Boys
Bruce and Robert
operate the concessions
at the swimming pool.
1946

Not much family history was written during these post-war years, but plenty of living was going on. Jobs were being taken care of. New homes were being built. New grandchildren were being born, blessed, baptized, and confirmed members of the Mormon Church. With all of these new families being formed, John and Vera find themselves in the "empty-nest syndrome." However, their lives continue to be full and rich by their dedication to their Church and the callings that they respond to.

As the grandchildren come along, family get-to-gathers become a natural occurrence with family pictures resulting and good times being shared.

John with Grandson,
Richard Alexander Nelson
1948

GRAND KIDS!

Left to right front: Richard, Janell, holding Carol. Susan and Marsha, with John and Bruce, Jr. in back. 1948

Vera holding Beverly McMaster. About 1951.

Pam, Rick, and Vicky Nelson Bob and Gerry's kids, about 1960.

Patty Bev Debbie Lori
B. H Mary

McMaster family, 1966

ENTIRE NELSON FAMILY GROUP - SUMMER, 1953

Front row children: Carol and Lana Jensen, Patti and
Beverly McMaster, Gregory Nelson, Randy Nelson, Judy Nelson,
Richard Nelson, Susan Miller, Johnny Nelson,
Bruce Nelson, Jr. and Marsha Ann Miller.
Back row: Leon Jensen, holding Julie, Verda Jensen,
Lee holding Sheila, Ruthie Nelson, Vera, Bruce behind,
holding Michelle. John, holding Sheryl. Linda. Joyce,
holding Debra. Janell, Robert and Gerry behind.
Margaret, Lovell, Ruth, Ivan, holding Jeff.

JOHN AND VERA NELSON,
THEIR CHILDREN AND SPOUSES, 1953

Front row left: Gerry Nelson, Linda Nelson,(Baby Sheila)
Joyce McMaster, Verda Jensen, Margaret Nelson, Vera Nelson.
Ruthie Nelson, and Ruth Miller.

Back row left: Earl McMaster, Lee Nelson, Lovell Nelson,
Leon Jensen, Robert Nelson, John, Bruce Nelson, Ivan Miller.

JOHN WITH HIS FOUR SONS,

Left to right: Robert, Lee, Bruce,

Lovell, and John

VERA AND HER THREE DAUGHTERS,

Left to right: Joyce, Verda, Vera, and Ruth.

DEDICATED TEACHERS

By Verda N. Jensen

Both John and Vera were dedicated students of the scriptures. John had his little Ready-Reference that enabled him to look up the scriptures he needed in a hurry. He was in great demand to speak at Sacrament meetings, at funerals, or other special occasions. He was one who could keep the interest of his audience. He taught the first principles of the gospel in a simple manner, telling stories that fit the ideas he was teaching to make his talks interesting.

Vera never went to a Sunday School class or a Relief Society meeting without first having studied the lesson that was to be presented. She loved to teach the gospel lessons and would often take over the difficult classes to teach. One particular time, when Lee was about 14 or 15 years old, his class was made up of a group of "rowdy" boys. Several of them were Vera's nephews and included, Lee, her own son. The Sunday School Superintendent had a difficult time keeping a teacher for this class. Vera took over the assignment and she literally had them "eating out of her hands" as she invited the class over on numerous occasions to fry donuts or have parties. Vera had a fun personality and a real sense of humor. She and John were always organizing parties, picnics, family reunions and camping trips with their friends and families.

Vera and John's home was "home-away-from-home" for many missionaries who were called to the Northwestern States Mission. The missionaries were always invited to dinner at least twice a week. They were provided with fresh bread and garden produce. John and Vera provided many contacts for the missionaries.

DANGERS ALONG THE HUCKLEBERRY TRAIL

By Verda N. Jensen

John and Vera loved the great outdoors. They loved to camp and each summer would go to Glacier Park, where they would meet with Grandma and Grandpa Nelson, as well as Uncle Seth and his family, as well as some of John's other brothers and their families from Canada. Trips were planned to go gathering huckleberries to can for our winter supply. Nothing was a nicer treat than a couple quarts of ice cream from the Central Avenue Ice Cream Shop and a bottle of huckleberries to top it off.

Sometimes we would 'go for huckleberries with Aunt Maude and Uncle Lawrence and their family, or Cleve and Luella and their children. On one particular trip to Glacier Park to gather huckleberries, Uncle Lawrence and Aunt Maude had joined us. It had been a stormy week, but because there was some blue in the sky, it was decided that we would take the chance on going up the trail for huckleberries.

Maude and Lawrence were walking along the trail and visiting with Vera when they discovered some beautiful big huckleberries.

They began filling their buckets with the treasured berries When suddenly Vera screamed as she came face to face with a big grizzly bear.

The bear took one look at Vera and ran the opposite direction. Vera threw her bucket in the air and grabbed Uncle Lawrence on the way down the hill. They both grabbed Maude and ran as fast as they could to safety. They could laugh about it when it was all over, but we all wondered if they could have "trained" the grizzly to pick huckleberries. We also wondered who was the most frightened, the pickers or the bear?

SQUIRES FAMILY

Maude and Lawrence Wedding Picture - December 21, 1900

Squires Family Left to right front: Maude, Peggy, Lawrence. Left to right back: Vivian, Merrill, Boyd, Lyle, Keith and Jack. About 1945.

TEMPLE WORKERS

John and Vera were dedicated temple workers. The fact that the closest temple was in Cardston, Canada, over 150 miles distance didn't keep them from attending every month. Often groups of people from the various towns and cities from the Branches of their District would attend the temple in 'caravan.'

In one of John's dictaphone tapes, he records:

"We had been to Canada to attend the temple. We had invited Brother Chadwick to ride home with us. It was a stormy winter day as we left Cardston, heading back to Great Falls. As we came along the highway on the eastern side of Glacier Park, a terrible blizzard was in progress. It was so bad that we could not even see the road. There were no homes that we could turn in to and wait out the storm. We were very concerned and did not want to become stranded in the blizzard, as we could likely have frozen to death before the storm subsided and someone could rescue us.

Vera said, "John, the only way we will get through this storm is if the Lord opens up the road for us. We could perish here on this highway. Will you offer a prayer that the road will clear up enough for us to drive on through this storm, so that we may travel on in safety?" We all bowed our heads in humble prayer, knowing that our Heavenly Father could control the elements and help us travel through this terrible snow storm.

As we finished our prayer, we looked ahead. It was as if the snow had been plowed from the middle of the road and although the blizzard was still raging, a path was cleared right down the highway and we drove right on through the storm, without another minutes trouble.

As we neared the town of Shelby, the storm had subsided to a certain extent and the road was clearly visible. Vera said to me, "John, let's stop on the side of the road and thank the Lord for our deliverance for truly a miracle has occurred in our behalf." So we did.

I asked Vera to offer the prayer and it was, indeed, a touching prayer that she offered. She gave thanks to our Eternal Father for his blessings to us and for delivering us out of that terrible storm.[2]

YOU MUST HEED THE WARNINGS

By John A. Nelson, Jr.

In the summer of 1957, I was working in Choteau and vicinity, with my insurance business. I had decided to return home that day and after eating a late lunch, I started on the trip back home. Sometimes I get sleepy while I am driving, especially Just after eating. When this happens, I often just pull off the road and take a few minutes nap,

After reaching the top of a hill, I noticed a side road ahead just off the highway and determined that this would be a good place for me to stop and rest before continuing my journey.

Just as I was prepared to turn off the main road, to the side road, a voice came to me and said, "Don't stop! I had the impression that I could see a car with two men in it behind me.

I looked through my rear-view mirror, but saw nothing. But this impression did not leave me. I could see no reason for any feeling of anxiety or fear and I am sorry to say, that I disregarded the still, small voice that had warned me not to stop. I pulled off the road, turned my car facing out toward the highway, and was just ready to turn the motor off on the car. Suddenly, a big, black car appeared, and as was my impression, there were two men in the car.

They circled in around behind my car and hit the back of my car a good jolt with their car. I felt, immediately, that these men had a plan to rob me. They both jumped out of their car and each ran to one of the front doors of my car. I always made it a practice to keep

2   John Nelson dictaphone tape #50.

my car doors locked and at this time, three of my doors were locked. All I had to do was push the button down on my left door on the driver's side. As I did, the men grabbed the door on each side. The motor of my car was still running and as I stepped on the accelerator, my car gave a lunge. Through my rear-view mirror, I noticed one of the men as he fell and rolled in the dust. I have no idea whether either of them was hurt.

As I sped on down the highway towards Great Falls, I noticed in the rear-view mirror, that my "would be attackers" had turned back towards Choteau. I am writing this story to remind my dear children and grandchildren that if we live worthily, we have the blessing of the Holy Ghost as our constant companion. However, it is up to us whether we heed the warnings that are given us by the Holy Ghost.

If we choose not to pay attention to these impressions and warnings, then we may possibly be the losers.

I know that I had been warned not to stop. I failed to heed that warning and, in so doing, I put myself in a very dangerous position.[3]

VERA'S LETTER TO THE WILCOX BULLETIN

Great Falls, Montana February 8, 1960

Dear Relatives:

My, oh my, how the years go by. When I was a child, it seemed endless from one birthday to the next. Now, well it is just no time at all. We had a very nice year, 1959-60. Two more little spirits have been added to our family. A boy, Reece Allan, to our Lee and his wife, Linda. A baby girl, Joyce Ann, to Verda and Leon Jensen, who, by the way, left Salt Lake City on January 10th for Washington, D.C. Leon is on a special assignment with the

---

3   John A. Nelson, Jr. dictaphone tape #10.

United States Geological Survey, his employer. They will live in Washington for the next five months. Their address is 4212 - 4th Street South, Arlington, Virginia. They have five children now, and the three oldest girls are in school there. They will always remember this experience.

Our son, Bruce, and his wife, Ruth, are at this time in the Hawaiian Islands. This will be a nice experience for them. They flew to Frisco and then took the regular steamship from there. They will be gone about two weeks. You see, we have some gypsy blood in us, somewhere.

Now that a Stake of Zion has been organized from the mission and is called the Great Falls Stake, we are all very busy working in the Church. My husband is a High Councilman and we both work in the Stake Mutual. John is to also in charge of the Stake genealogical work. We go to the Cardston Temple the third of each month, a distance of a little more than 200 miles. I also work in the Ward Genealogical Society and travel with John to all of the other wards. Our towns are so far apart, 20 miles to 160, so I go to keep him awake on the way. I still sing with the Singing Mothers, so you see I have not time to get old. I also teach a class in Relief Society and love it. I am also Stake Era Director.

We were in Salt Lake City for conference October 1st. I thought may be I would see some of my people, but not a soul I knew.

We had our Nelson reunion last July in the beautiful Glacier Park, 225 miles from Great Falls. It was so nice to see all of the family again. We are really scattered over a lot of territory, from Edmonton, Canada on the North, to California and Salt Lake City, etc.

My only sister, Minnie Turner, spent most of the summer here last year. I do enjoy her so much and hope that she can come again this summer. Her baby daughter, Ada McKamey, lives here, I'm sure you all know.

Our oldest grand-daughter, Janell, attended the BYU last year and until Christmas this year. Now she is attending the University in Salt Lake City.

We have long outgrown our chapel and there are three congregations in our group. So everyone is wearing old clothes and giving until it hurts to help build our new tabernacle. We have lots of missionaries here. Then, too, we have the stake missionaries here. It is not uncommon to baptize fifteen or twenty a month. It is wonderful how fast the Church is growing all over the world. Sunday will be our Stake Conference and our main speaker will be Apostle Hugh B. Brown of the General Authorities.

We did a lot of sealings for our Wilcox people last month in the Cardston Temple and it seemed so wonderful to attend to this work. I only wish we could find more names on the Wilcox line. We seem to be up against a stone wall on my mother's line. Grandpa Laughlin was one of the Mormon Battalion that left when the pioneers were at Winter Quarters. We have found his father and grandfather and that is as far as we have any record of him or his people.

Well, I trust everyone is well. I should love to be with you all this year. We will plan on that. We were sorry not to have been there last year, when my niece, Olive May Wilcox Parker, was there. She was disappointed, too.

Vera Nelson.[4]

AUNT MINNIE TURNER

By Verda Jensen

Aunt Minnie Turner and her husband, James, were some of our other special relations. Minnie was Vera's older sister and for many years lived out on a ranch south of Cascade, Montana. It was always such fun to visit their ranch, because Uncle James would always saddle up "Old Smiler" and we could ride as long as we wanted. We could

---

4   Wilcox Family Bulletin, 1960-61.

sleep in their upstairs and when it rained the sound of the rain on the metal roof was so exciting.

Every summer we would make an annual trip out to Aunt Minnie and Uncle James' home to pick chokecherries. It was always fun because something unusual always happened. For instance, the year we got to ride in the back of the new Ford truck all the way to Cascade. Then how Dad drove the truck way up onto the foothills where Uncle James had spotted rattlesnakes. James and Dad had their shovels, and when they turned over some big rocks, there was dozens of baby rattlers. They killed them with their shovels. It was a sight a child never forgot. The rattlesnakes had been coming down to their home and Aunt Minnie had nearly stepped on one that was coiled up by her front steps. Consequently, the pilgrimage and war on the rattlers!

Aunt Minnie Turner, age about 87.

Aunt Minnie and Uncle James had the nicest little root cellar that I had ever seen. It was so cool in there during the summer and it was always so well stocked with all kinds of good things to eat. I remember her churn and watching her churn the butter and then giving us the cold buttermilk that was left. Every time I have a glass of buttermilk, I think of those happy days, visiting at the home of dear Aunt Minnie and Uncle James.

During the later years, they moved to North Hollywood to be by their daughter, Jean. Their family all adored them, and they made frequent visits back and forth from California to Montana and Canada. I'm sure that Aunt Minnie must have been close to 65 or 70 years old when she drove her little Ford car all the way to California. On their return trips, she and James would always stop in Salt Lake to stay a few days with us.

After Uncle James died, Minnie was a frequent visitor, only then she traveled by way of airplanes. She would call from the airport and we would have the privilege of having her come and spend a few days with us. Our children thought of her as a "Grand-ma" and we all loved and respected her so much. The following picture was taken on her last trip to Utah and Montana, about 1962. She was about 88 when she died:

A LETTER FROM GRANDMA VERA

The following letter was written by Vera Nelson in Great Falls, Montana to her granddaughter, Carol Jensen, (Verda and Leon's daughter) in Salt Lake City, Utah in 1960:

Great Falls, Montana November, 1960

Dear Carol,

Your letter was so nice and Grandpa and I are both so very proud of you. Some day maybe you can play the big organ in the Tabernacle. Would you like that?

I hope you can keep on practicing so you can be as good or better than any one. I am so homesick for you all. I loved little Joyce so much. Wasn't she cute the day we went to the Big Falls?

We have had no snow to speak of since in the first part of November. Today it was 52 degrees plus. I hope it stays nice now over the weekend till we get home from Canada.

We had a nice movie at the church after our literary lesson of all the ladies who have graced the White House from George Washington's wife down the line to Mamie Eisenhower. It was really nice. I'd love to go to see Washington during Cherry Blossom Days. These pictures were taken when the blossoms were just the loveliest. You are lucky you got to go on that wonderful trip. You will never forget that.

We are going to have the big missile base near us. We do hope peace will come to this old world before long.

I must write to Pattie. She sent me a nice letter last week. Aren't I the lucky one to have so many nice girls in my family. Twenty-one isn't it? Seems to me one could be with me most of the time. I sure thought Aunt Ruth's four girls looked nice. Sue is so like her Mama. Study hard. Practice the piano well and be good. I love you all. Kiss baby Joyce and Jim for me. God bless you all ever and ever.

Grandma N.[5]

DON'T FORGET THE 26TH

The following entry was written in Carol Verlee Jensen's baby book by her mother, Verda:

"I can't begin to tell you how thrilled we were to have an adorable little girl to love. You were called a 'miracle baby' by your two grandmas. Grandma Jensen often said you were a miracle baby because she had worried for over 3 1/2 years while daddy Leon had been in the Air Corps and had been so far away from home on a foreign shore. And she didn't know when he would ever get home and settle down and have a family. Grandma Nelson thought it was a miracle that you were born because I had been so sick when I was a child, and she didn't know if I would ever be able to carry a child."

"Grandma Nelson came Out to Vernal to be with us when you were born. I had written to her and told her not to come until the first part of February, but on the 24th of January, she told

---

5   A Letter from Vera Nelson in Carol Jensen Lasson's "Treasures of Truth Book."

Grandpa Nelson she had to go to be there when the baby was born and she knew that it would be the 26th of January, 1948. She lived 800 miles away from us, but she got there Sunday night of the 25th and my how happy we were to see her."[6]

Fourteen years later, the following letter about this event was written by Vera Nelson to her granddaughter Carol Jensen:

January 30, 1962 Dear Carol,

I surely did not mean to let your "big" day pass with out a note from your Grandma. I have been down with the flu and thus the delay.

I am sure you are a very special person and some one loved your Mama very much, My sister Chloe Robinson, was with me when your mother, Verda Cloe, was born. Chloe was my older sister and I had always loved her so much. Because of this, I named your Mama for her. [I added the " Verda" to the Chloe and changed the spelling of Chloe, to "Cloe".].

Aunt Chloe had died a number of years earlier, but I felt that she was with me on numerous occasions as my guardian angel. Just before you were born, she appeared to me and woke me in the night to say, "Don't forget the 26th." I kept thinking, "What does she mean?"

The next morning as I was doing the dishes, Aunt Chloe passed between me and the sink in the kitchen and said, "Don't forget the 26th." I realized what she was trying to tell me and took the hint and told Grandpa I must take the noon train to Verda because her baby was coming the 26th of January and I felt it was important to be with her When her first child was born.

I am sure no one could have been happier than I was to be with your mother and father in Vernal, Utah the day of the 26th of January, because, just as Aunt Chloe had told me, you arrived on schedule.

---

6   Carol J. Lasson's Baby Book written by Verda Nelson Jensen.

That is my strength in my testimony of the Gospel, that God lives and hears and answers prayers. I do feel Grandpa and I are very fortunate because we have been blessed with such wonderful children and that means all of our grand-children, too.

Your Mama was so greatly blessed when she was a little girl. The doctor said she couldn't live until morning and so all the family came to see her, to bid her "good-bye". Through administration of the holy Melchizedek priesthood by her father, with the help of another priesthood holder, she was blessed that she might recover. She had strength and faith, too, as did all of her family. How precious she is to me, too, darling. She loves you like as we all do.

Please accept my good wishes for your 14th birthday, even if I did procrastinate terribly. HAPPY BIRTHDAY and GOD BLESS AND KEEP YOU!

Ever,

Grandma Nelson[7]

MY VISIT TO THE RANCH OF STONE PAULSON

By John A. Nelson, Jr.

(John always said that if he couldn't sell a customer insurance, he would try to teach them the gospel, or he would talk about horses. On one of John's dictaphone tapes, he recorded an experience with one of his insurance customers.)

One evening without an appointment, I felt impressed to go to Belt, Montana which was a distance of about thirty miles. I had no idea of where I was headed. I almost automatically pulled into an open gate at a large farm house. The people were very warm and friendly to me. They introduced themselves to me as Mr. and Mrs. Stone Paulson. Mr. Paulson told his wife that they were going to buy some insurance from me. Then he told me that I had been sent to their home. He said that several times.

---

7   Letter from Carol J. Lasson's "Treasures of Truth Book."

He told me that his daughter, Emily, had been sick and had recently returned from the Mayo Clinic in Rochester, Minnesota. I told him that I was not sure whether the insurance company would be able to cover her because of her illness, even though at that time I didn't know that it was cancer.

Just as I prepared to leave, though we had never mentioned religion, Mr. Paulson asked me a strange favor, "Mr. Nelson, would you offer a prayer for our little Emily before you leave?"

I told him that I would be happy to. I asked Emily to sit over on a chair and we would all lay our hands on her head and ask a kind and eternal Heavenly Father to bless her.

I do not remember what I said in the prayer, but the prayer had touched the hearts of these good people, for as I finished and looked up, tears were streaming down their faces. This was a very touching time for all of us.

Several weeks later when the insurance policy came to my home, I, as usual, took the policy out to the Paulson's ranch and explained to them that the company would not cover Emily and had returned her premium. Mr. Paulson said, "Mr. Nelson, we understand. However, Mrs. Paulson and I have been thinking how nice it would be if you and Mrs. Nelson would come out here and have dinner with us some day. I responded that I thought it would be a lovely idea and I was sure that Mrs. Nelson would enjoy meeting them.

Mr. Paulson told me that he and his wife had wondered, after I had given Emily that beautiful prayer, if maybe I was a Mormon. He said that he had seen my name in the paper several times, that I had conducted funerals for some of the Mormons in Great Falls. I asked him what church they belonged to and he said that they were Lutherans. He expressed an interest in the Mormons. He said that he had never been in a Mormon chapel, but that he knew some other Mormons.

I asked if he would like to have two Mormon missionaries come out to dinner with us when we came and we could hold a little cottage meeting with them and let them know some of the beliefs of the Mormons. He agreed that this would be a nice idea. I mentioned that I thought it would be special if all of us were to fast for and in behalf of their daughter, Emily, on the day of our dinner appointment. Neither Mr. Paulson nor his wife knew what I meant by "fast," so I explained it to them. I told them that a "fast" meant to abstain from food for twenty-four hours and while under that spiritual influence, to pray to the Lord, in behalf of the person who needed a special blessing.

Mr. Paulson suggested that we might bring as many as we wished with us when we came to dinner. I told him that I would let them know several days ahead of time so they would know how many to plan for. Vera had been in Utah, visiting with Ruth and Verda and when she got home, I told her about our invitation. She thought it was a lovely idea and agreed wholeheartedly. We wrote the Paulsons a letter and told them about the day we could arrange to come.

In the meantime, I had met our District President, Brother Lyman Tracy, on the street and told him about this little experience. He thought it would be a nice occasion for he and his wife to go along with us. He had just bought a new car and suggested that this would be a good way for him to "break it in." He said that there would be room in the car for six; two missionaries, Vera and I, and he and his wife.

As we had planned, the six of us arrived for this special dinner party at 6:00 p.m. The table was set and decorated so beautifully. Everything was just lovely. We had all been "fasting" for the benefit of little Emily. There was a feeling of thanksgiving in this home. I suggested that before we had our dinner, we hold a short, twenty minute meeting. Mrs. Paulson invited us all into their parlor where there was an organ. I had asked the mission-

aries to be in charge and they had invited me to say a few words to begin the meeting.

I explained our practice of addressing each other as Brother and Sister and asked if this would be alright with them. They thought that was very nice. As I was speaking, I turned to Brother Paulson and said that I had been wondering, since the first night I was out to their home, why it was he mentioned three times, "Mr. Nelson, you were sent here tonight." I said that it must have some significance and I would be happy to have him tell us what he meant.

The tears began to stream down the face of Brother Paulson as he said, "Brothers and Sisters, I have always been a praying man, and just recently I had asked the Lord to send someone to our home who could give us consolation, because of the sickness of our daughter.

The moment that you drove up, Brother Nelson, it came over me that you were the man sent here to give us this consolation. That is the reason that I took the insurance policy with you, without any hesitation. I truly felt that you had been an answer to my prayers."

Brother Paulson's story touched each of us. We explained the administering of the oil for the restoration of health of whomever might be sick and we administered to little Emily before we broke our "fast." I explained to the Paulsons that Emily was in the hands of the Lord. I told them the scripture where the Lord says, "If they die, they die unto Me, if they live, they live unto Me." I explained this to the Paulsons so that they would not expect too much from this administration. But they felt a peace and a love of a kind Heavenly Father, comforting them and helping them to accept His wishes. After the dinner was over, we spent an hour or so, explaining the various phases of the Gospel of Jesus Christ to this special family. Brother Paulson got up and took the two missionaries to his son's bedroom. The son was away to college. He told the missionaries that the bus from Great Falls traveled right by their home once a day. He said, "Any time you wish to come out here and visit us, the bus makes a round trip in one day. If our visit is not over, you may stay here in this room for as long as you wish to stay, without any cost to you." What a "Golden" opportunity for missionary work. We all thanked the Paulsons for their kindness and returned to our homes.

The story does not end there. The missionaries didn't go back and were soon transferred out of the area. Busy with the daily chores of earning a living, I was unable to follow through with teaching this family further truths of the gospel myself. A short time later, I read in the paper that Emily had passed away. We sent a wreath of flowers and signed it from the six of us who had enjoyed the lovely meal at the Paulson home. I asked the next pair of missionaries to contact this golden couple. When they made the contact, the Paulsons were not willing to let them come in. They told the missionaries the Lutheran minister had wholeheartedly accepted their return to his congregation.

Because of the pressures of time and distance, these people were neglected, They had been ready to receive the truth when I first met them, but without the opportunity at the right moment to continue in the gospel lessons, they lost interest. I learned from being in the insurance business, that the only way to succeed is to follow up all good leads and prospects. Follow up carefully and consistently and finally, you will reap the harvest. It is the same with teaching the gospel; you must do the same thing, follow up carefully and consistently and finally you will reap the harvest, or those interested in the gospel will be able to reap the harvest and gain a testimony of its truth.[8]

---

8   John Nelson dictaphone tape #62.

A BLOW OUT

By John A. Nelson, Jr.

I had been asked to speak at the funeral of Brother Stott of Bynum, Montana. This is a distance of about 65 miles from Great Falls. I thought I had given myself plenty of time to make the trip comfortably. Vera was travelling with me. Our car was in good condition. As we got past Fairfield, going towards Choteau, there is an area called "Freeze Out Lake." It is a straight, good highway and I was travelling at a high rate of speed. All of a sudden, the car began twisting out of control. Vera and I both realized immediately, that we had experienced a tire blow out.

I stopped the car as quickly as I could, grateful that I had not lost control of the car and pulled over on the right side of the highway. As I got out, I could see that the left rear tire was flat. It had been a comparatively new tire. As I walked around the car to see how the other tires were, I uttered a little prayer. "Dear Father in Heaven, please help me to change this tire quickly, as I have only a few minutes left in which to travel to Bynum where I am to speak at the funeral of Brother Stott."

As I came around the car again to the tire that needed fixing, I discovered, to my great astonishment, that the tire was up and in place just as it should be! I looked at it again and then went and got in the car.

Vera noticed my astonishment and said, "Daddy, you're as white as death! What is the matter?" I told her that the tire was all right. I got back into the car and continued my journey. We arrived just as the funeral was beginning.

Vera also bore witness of this event. I know that the Lord can help you, regardless of the trouble you might be in, if you are faithful and humble and prayerful. This was a very sacred experience to me and one I have not felt I could share before.[9]

9   John Nelson, Jr. dictaphone tape #4.

A STAKE CENTER UNDER CONSTRUCTION

By John A. Nelson, Jr.

The following letter was sent by John to his daughters and their families living away from Great Falls, Montana:

Great Falls, Montana March 28, 1963

Dear Daughters, Husbands and Children,

As I am on guard duty at the construction sight of the new Stake Center again tonight from 2 a.m. until 7:30 in the morning when the men start coming to work, I will write you another family letter. It is now just 2:30 a.m. and after sweeping the place out, so I can sit down and feel a little better about it, I am ready to write.

The new Stake Center is going up quite rapidly now that the Labor Union has stopped bothering us. The Union stopped us from driving a nail or laying a brick for three weeks. We had an agreement with them when we first began building, that we could use non-union men. However, as the building progressed, they claimed we were using too many of this type of workmen. You see the Church pays 70% and we pay 30% of the cost of construction, etc. Of course many of the members like to work out their assessments as much as possible.

When the Union saw that some evenings we would have as many as twenty-five or thirty non-union men working under the big flood lights, they claimed we were using too many such men.

The Church had allowed the members to pay off their assessment using their own labor throughout the Church, wherever buildings were constructed, so it was a firm policy within the Church. The Union placed pickets around the building and every-body driving up and down could see them. People began to inquire of us, "Why do they picket your church when other churches build pretty much the same way?"

Then the ministers took it up with the Union, realizing this same thing could happen to any building projects they might begin. Letters and phone calls began coming into the Union office until they were swamped with questions. They even refused to answer the phones. Still, the Union would not change their minds and they held out. The Church leaders could not change the policy of the Church as to how the labor should be done, so the work on the Stake Center was at a "stand-still."

Non-Mormons all over the country were calling and asking if they could do anything to help the Church to be completed. This union trouble was the best advertising boost our church has ever had in this country. We really didn't know we had so many friends before. Everybody seemed to be on our side. Catholics and Protestants were alike in their willingness to help us. Finally, we Just had to do something about it, as the building was scheduled to be ready for the Dedication Services in November, 1963.

The Stake Presidency called the High Council in and we had a special prayer one evening.

Early the next morning the Union called and informed us that they were ready to settle any way we wished and that they would not interfere again with us. In fact, they congratulated us for holding out.

We only had one plan and we stayed with it and all other churches helped us out. As I said before, we received more favorable publicity than the Church had ever received in Montana.

We almost believe now, at the rate we are going, that the building will be completed by September instead of November. Mother and I will sure be happy when it is completed because we will only have a short distance to go to church. We are grateful to the Lord for His help and realize that through efforts and through prayer we were able to continue in the construction of our new Stake Center.

Mother and I are going to spend Easter with Joyce and family in Columbia Falls. The Branch President has already made an appointment with Joyce that I speak during the Sacrament Meeting on the 14th in her ward. It is always a pleasure for me to speak at the different wards.

Mother and I have just finished a three months assignment out to the Malmstrom Air Base from the ~ Church. We have 208 members out there and they a~' very wonderful people coming from all over the country and staying for a few months or a few years at the most. We have a number of officers and a very intelligent group of members. Since we were there a month ago, a Major and his wife and family have been baptized.

We were assigned to speak at this branch last Sunday.

When I first arose to speak I noticed two little boys sitting on the front row so I asked the question, "I am wondering how many boys and girls present this evening intend to go on missions when they grow up?"

The two little fellows raised their hands so I invited them to sit on the stand and when I looked around again I noticed many more hands had gone up. Consequently I had to invite them all to sit at the front. As the subject for the meeting was prayer, I then asked each one to explain the meaning of prayer. One little fellow, age ten, said "Prayer means to talk with God." A little girl said, "Prayer means to ask God for what you want and He'll give it to you." So all eight of my speakers gave like answers to the meaning of prayer.

Last night Mother and I were invited to attend the 50th wedding anniversary of Brother and Sister Eugene of Simms. It was held in the new chapel and we enjoyed meeting so many old friends from all over the stake again. Brother Eugene is 83 and she 75.

I got a kick watching Mother and Brother Gray dance. Mother still enjoys putting on a little act.

Lee is in a play which will hold forth at Fairfield Friday night. Mother and I did not get to see it here last week so we are going out there. Lee works hard in the church as well as in his construction building program. He hires a lot of men and pays them $29.50 a day. This makes a big payroll for forty men or more. Bruce is doing about the same and he is building another row of homes back of us. He has bought all the land to the top of big hill 57. There are a lot of members from the other wards buying over here near the new Stake Center. This will, no doubt, be known as the "Mormon Settlement." Bruce has played his cards well.

I think we will have to wait and go to Utah later in the summer, even though we are home-sick to see you all. We go to Canada quite often. We were there just two weeks ago. We stayed all night and had a good visit with some of our friends and relatives.

Mother is tying another quilt. She can almost make one in a day after she gets all the material together. We enjoy our new home and have quite a few visitors. Some come because they like us and really want to visit. Others come just to see where we live. One lady came this evening because she claims she likes us and wished us to explain the gospel to her. I conducted the funeral for her husband last September. He was a member; she is not, but I am sure she will soon join.

Verda, dear, your nice letter about forming a family organization has not been entirely forgotten. We must get busy and organize. Thank you. Love and kind wishes to each one of you. I could write much more but will stop for now. We enjoy all your letters please keep them coming.

God bless you all, Mother and Dad[10]

---

10   Letter in Verda N. Jensen's possession.

[Editor's note: The Stake Center was completed and dedicated on schedule.]

GATHERING OF THE PRIESTHOOD

By John A. Nelson, Jr.

Sometimes a cowboy must run a great number of wild horses into a corral in order to capture the one gentle horse that had become lost or gone astray. I found this to be true with men of the priesthood well. A number of men living within our Branch as boundaries had become inactive in the church. They were not attending any of the meetings at all. Many had been married in the temples. Many had held jobs of responsibility in previous wards and branches. Some were from part-member families where the wife was not a member of the Church.

I had been asked by the President of the Branch, Brother LaMar Killpack, to teach the adult priesthood class. I told him that before I took over the class, I would like to try a program to reactivate the priesthood members. I recruited the aid of Brother Ernest Blackburn. When I contacted him, he agreed to help and to attend the meetings if I promised not to call on him to speak. He became the secretary of the group and searched the church records to bring up-to-date, all possible members.

I also recruited two more men and gave them responsibility to contact three more men each to help on our team. We made phone calls, personal visits, wrote letters and gave encouragement. Each week our class grew in size. We felt that if there was a well prepared lesson and the men knew that we needed them to be a part of our Branch Priesthood Quorums, they would attend. Our class started out with 22 men attending. Within a few weeks, we had an average of 70 attending.

With this success, we set a goal to have 100 priesthood holders to attend a special priesthood meeting in two weeks. We planned a special program and asked some of the inactive brothers to speak and help out. I have a slogan, "I dare not doubt that the faithful will work, if given something to do."

I appealed to some of the men, saying, "Brother, So and So, you hold the office of Elder or High Priest, or Seventy, in the Church. I will be disappointed if you do not come out next Sunday and our goal of 100 priesthood bearers is not met, because you do not attend." Usually, the Brethren would say, "You can count on me, Brother Nelson, I'll be there."

On the appointed day, 103 men holding the Holy Melchizedek Priesthood, attended our special meeting. It was a grand occasion. Many of these men remained active to the church. Some of them, of course, fell back into their old pattern. But we had been successful in activating many who became faithful once again. They needed to know that we needed them in our Quorums.

So my old saying, "Sometimes a cowboy must run a great number of wild horses into a corral in order to capture the one gentle horse that had become lost or gone astray," applied once again to human nature. [11]

FAMILY REUNIONS

By Verda N. Jensen

We all looked forward to summers for that meant "Reunion time for the Nelsons." About every two years, all of the John A. Nelson, Sr. clan would gather in Glacier Park or vicinity for a few days. It was always held around some lake and many of the family members brought their boats, fishing gear, and swimming suits. This was part of the fun activities, with maybe a tug- of-war held in the water and water skiing lessons for all the kids. There were always lots of good food and hugs and kisses from relations you loved and from some that you had to introduce yourself to every year.

---

11   John A. Nelson, Jr. dictaphone tape #9.

HUSBAND   John Alexander NELSON

Birth   12 October 1859
Place   Farmington, Davis, Utah
Chr
Married   9 Jan 1879
Place   Salt Lake City, Salt Lake, Utah
Death   29 September 1942 Cardston, Alberta
Burial   1 October 1942 Cardston, Alberta
Father   Robert NELSON
Mother   Elizabeth JOSEPH
Other Wives   (2) Frances FURSER div

WIFE   Ella Elizabeth THOMAS

Birth   9 October 1859
Place   Lehi, Utah, Utah
Chr
Death   30 October 1941 Cardston, Alberta
Burial   Cardston, Alberta
Father   Preston THOMAS
Mother   Maria HADLUND

John Preston born & died 3 August 1886

Irene, twin to Hazel, died 21 January 1900

1st Child Maria Elizabeth NELSON
Birth   7 March 1880
Place   Smithfield, Cache, Utah
Married to   Alonzo Bray LAMB
Married   11 September 1901
Place   Cardston, Alberta, Canada

2nd Child Ella NELSON
Birth   5 June 1882
Place   Smithfield, Cache, Utah
Married to   Joseph Franklin ALLEN
Married   23 March 1899
Place   Cardston, Alberta, Canada

3rd Child Lileth NELSON
Birth   9 February 1884
Place   Smithfield, Cache, Utah
Married to   Heber Chase SMITH
Married   2 September 1902
Place   Magrath, Alberta, Canada

4th Child Rachel NELSON
Birth   28 September 1887
Place   Smithfield, Cache, Utah
Married to   William Adamson WOOLFORD
Married   4 September 1911
Place   Salt Lake, Salt Lake, Utah

5th Child John Alexander NELSON
Birth   13 September 1889
Place   Smithfield, Cache, Utah
Married to   Martha Vera WILCOX
Married   1 Jan 1917
Place   Raymond, Alberta, Canada

6th Child Seth Henry NELSON
Birth   15 October 1891
Place   Cardston, Alberta, Canada
Married to   Mable Caroline HANSEN
Married   15 December 1917
Place   Cardston, Alberta, Canada
Married M D (2) Freda Ethel Broadhead
Cleveland NELSON

7th Child NELSON
Birth   20 March 1893
Place   Cardston, Alberta, Canada
Married to   Hattie Luella BROWN
Married   1 December 1920
Place   Salt Lake City, Salt Lake, Utah

8th Child Lorenzo Snow NELSON
Birth   2 July 1896
Place   Cardston, Alberta, Canada
Married to   Mary Ireta TURNER
Married   1 November 1920
Place   Raymond, Alberta, Canada

9th Child Hazel NELSON (twin)
Birth   15 December 1899
Place   Cardston, Alberta, Canada
Married to   Milton Leo BURGESS
Married   13 April 1919
Place   Cardston, Alberta, Canada

10th Child Darrel Thomas NELSON
Birth   20 December 1901
Place   Cardston, Alberta, Canada
Married to   Mary Critchfield
Married   7 December 1922
Place   Napa, Canyon, Idaho

Left to right: Seth Nelson, Darrell and Mary Nelson, Luella Nelson, Hazel Burgess, Rae Woolford, Lileth Smith, Freda Nelson, in front of Wren Nelson, Cleve Nelson, Milton Burgess, with Vera and John Nelson front right.

On the off-year, John and Vera would organize a reunion, just for their immediate family. One time it was at White Fish Lake, where the hornets almost ate us up, but that didn't stop us from having a marvelous time. One time it was at Lake Gregory, in Montana, where we just about had the entire lake to ourselves. For several years we have met on beautiful Lake McDonald in Glacier Park. Can you imagine how cold the water was for the swimmers and the water skiers? No matter where the reunion was held, everyone arrived with tents, campers, boats, fishing tackle, mosquito repellent, stories and good food, all geared for another super reunion.

Occasionally, the reunions were mini-reunions, with just those we could gather on the spur of the moment. Sometimes it would be a trip to Uncle Lee's lovely cabin, not far from Great Falls. One time, in particular, John and Vera engineered the trip with 17 of their little grandchildren and a few mamas to help out.

One memory the kids still talk about was when Grandma Vera and Uncle Lawrence Squires decided to dress up as hobos and surprise the grandchildren. They got moss from the trees to make beards and extra hair. They found old clothes from the trunks and really had a good disguise. They sent John ahead down one road, with the little ones. Vera and Uncle Lawrence circled around to meet the group head-on, coming down the road. The funny thing was, the disguise was so authentic, that no one recognized that it was really "Grandma and Uncle Lawrence." All of the kids were in tears, afraid of the strangers.

Lileth and Chase Smith

The crowning moment of disappointment came, when, much to their amazement, the moss was securely stuck on with the pine gum from the trees and scrub as they would, it would not come off. What a disaster! It is one we can laugh at now, but it wasn't so funny for the two hobos, at the moment. But these are memories!

Dear Uncle Cleve Nelson, with Julie, Verda, David, and Joyce Ann Jensen

No matter if the reunion was a regular scheduled reunion, or a mini-reunion, we would always have our own Sacrament Service on Sunday with the sacrament and the speakers. It was always

Nelson Family Reunion at Lake Gregory, Montana in 1961.

well- planned and included a time for sharing our testimonies and love with each other. John would usually conduct and would always tell one or two of his special missionary stories. He could always keep the audience spell-bound with his good stories.

One nice thing about family reunions was they did not stop when John and Vera died. The family all treasured times like these and many other occasions were enjoyed at various parts of the world: Flathead Lake in Montana, Colter Bay at Jackson Hole, and one was held in 1983 at Garden City, Utah on the Bear Lake. Each one were so special and well attended. What happy times we remember getting reacquainted with cousins and aunts and uncles!

18

JOHN'S LATER YEARS

JOHN'S HEART ATTACK

On July 9, 1960 at two-thirty in the morning, John suffered a severe heart-attack. The ambulance was called and then the doctor. John was admitted to the hospital, where he was immediately placed in an oxygen tent to help him breathe. He said that he was treated very kindly by the nurses and Dr. Allred, the family physician.

A sign, "NO VISITORS ALLOWED, FAMILY ONLY," was placed outside his door. He recalled that there were still a lot of people who came and stood in the hall and, unobserved by the hospital attendants, talked to him when his hospital door was open. The missionaries came in several times and offered prayers for his recovery.

John's children all rallied to his support. He wrote how kind his sons were to him and how concerned for his complete recovery. Ruth and Verda came from Utah and Joyce came from over in Columbia Falls. He said, "I had all the attention that was necessary. I was administered to by the Elders and by my sons. Dear Vera was by my side every possible moment and she was a marvelous nurse when I was released to go home."[1]

John was in the hospital for 26 days before the doctor told him that he could go home. He was extremely weak, although he was not in any more pain. The doctor gave him orders not to go back to work. This was hard for John.

His son, Bob, brought him a dictaphone and he decided to use the recovery time, recalling some of his life's experiences and putting them on tape for the use of his posterity.

John said, "I have a lot of wonderful experiences that I wish to relate for the benefit of my children and my children's children; that they may profit thereby. That their faith might be strengthened, because my faith is of such a nature that even though the doctors were well-informed and highly educated, there was still a higher power over them, to guide their actions in my behalf, I have always been a firm believer in the fifth chapter of James, beginning with the thirteen verse, 'If there is any sick among you, let them call for the Elders of the Church and let them pray over him, anointing him with oil in the name of the Lord: And the prayer of faith shall save the sick and the Lord shall raise him up; and if he has committed sins, they shall be forgiven him.'

I know, as I live, that the Gospel of Jesus Christ is here upon the earth and if we would adhere to the teaching of the scriptures, the Book of Mormon and the Bible, we would not go far astray."

John recovered and enjoyed three more years on this earth. He was well enough to continue on with the work that he loved: his insurance business and his missionary service.

---

1   John A. Nelson Jr. Dictaphone tape #41.

VERDA'S FATHERS' DAY LETTER

In June, 1963, about six months before John died, the following letter was written:

Dearest Dad:

Just because it is "Father's Day" doesn't mean that our love for you is any greater today, but only that it perhaps makes us a little more thoughtful and realize how very blessed we have been to have such a wonderful Daddy as you.

When I think back over the years, I have such fond memories of you and I am so grateful to you, for the love and security you gave to me.

Whether it was going on a trip to Glacier Park, or only to Sunday School, I always felt that with you at the wheel, we would be safe. I had, and still do have, such faith in your power as a holder of the Priesthood and what comfort and peace it always gave me to have you anoint my head and give me a blessing when I was ill.

You have been such a wonderful example to all of us with your missionary activities. We could never have had better teachers than you and Mother have been. My humble prayer for my family is that we might follow in your footsteps, loving and serving our family and serving our Heavenly Father.

Leon and I are so proud of our darling little family. Carol is quite the grown-up young lady this summer. She is trying to get me better organized and I am working on her, too. She is going to start driver's training this month, and she is pretty excited about it. Lana is a bundle of energy and into so many activities. She enjoys her music and has so many friends around all of the time.

Julie is thoughtful and sweet and enjoys her music, also. She is working hard to try to catch up with Lana. She loves to baby tend now, and if any of the neighbors need a tender, she is the first to say, "I'll go."

Jim is mostly interested in baseball and his Dad is the assistant coach. Jim has a uniform with his name on the back and a hat for the team. He loves to swim and he is looking forward to being baptized this summer.

Everyone needs a little girl just half-past three and our Joycie fills the bill so well. She is such a lot of fun, and all of the family adore her and her cute ways. And life wouldn't be complete without our David John. His sweet little personality has made our family complete. He is so smart, saying lots of words. He gets up and down the stairs and into the lady's chamber before you can hardly bat an eye. He is just past one. He calls, "Jim-mee," and adores his big brother. Well, let's face it, he is pretty much the apple" in the eyes of the Jensen family.

I feel so blessed to have such a special husband, Leon, honoring his Priesthood and guiding the affairs of our family. He is providing the same kind of love and leadership to our dear children as you did to your family.

We all love you and Mother so very much. We send our love and hope you are well and enjoying your life. We are really looking forward to getting together with all of the family for another big "Nelson Reunion."

Thanks for being our Dad and Grandpa. Thanks to Mom, too, for all the love we have always felt. We love you both.

Verda, Leon and Family

ANOTHER HEART ATTACK HITS JOHN

In a letter from Vera to her daughters, news of another heart attack is given:

Great Falls, Montana November 3, 1963

Dear Daughters,

Once again I must tell you your dearest Daddy is in the hospital. He suffered another severe heart attack. Friday morning at 2:00 o'clock they took him to the hospital. Dr. Allred was called. Dr. Allred seems to think it was not quite as severe as the other one, but it is bad enough. I am up to Lovell's and he says I am to stay here until Daddy is able to go home. I am so thankful for my good boys. They have all been so concerned.

I should have written you before, but it seems that I have been in a daze. Today is our Conference, but I don't feel I could sit that long, so will stay here. Janell has a car and will take me any place I need to go. Lee and Linda are close to Maggie's. Little Reese loves me so much and he was with me when Daddy took sick. Lee says about every other day, Reese thinks he should come to see me.

Johnny is in Provo, I guess. Val says he thinks he has a girl friend. Lee and Bruce are up to their eyes in building. Lovell has lots of things he is doing, too. Bob is such a dear and hates to see his Daddy suffer. I can't think of much to say, so will close with love to all. We will keep you posted. Keep praying. We all love you so much.

As ever,

Mother[2]

It was while John was in the hospital that President John F. Kennedy was assassinated. What a terrible shock to the people of America

---

2   Letter in the possession of Verda N. Jensen.

and in fact, people all over the world. We all grieved at the loss of our President. It is hard to believe that something like this could occur.

JOHN'S DEATH

John died December 9, 1963 after suffering several heart attacks. He was in the hospital in Great Falls at the time. He said on several occasions, "If I can't get well enough to do the things that I love doing, being a missionary, enjoying my family, doing my Church assignment, I don't want to live. I want to wear out, not rust out." His family all thought that he had accomplished his goals in life and that he did indeed "wear out, not rust out." All of his children had come to see him prior to his death.

JOHN'S FUNERAL SERVICES

John's funeral was held on a terribly cold day in Great Falls, Montana on December 12, 1963. John's nephew, Vivian Squires, who gave a beautiful talk, was not listed on the original printed program. He shared happy memories of his "Uncle John." Vivian recited the following poem (author unknown) at the funeral and dedicated it to the memory of "Uncle John:"

> *He has gained success who has lived long,*
> *Laughed often, and loved much.*
> *Who has filled his niche and accomplished his task.*
> *Who has gained the respect of intelligent folks,*
> *And the love of little children.*
> *Who has always looked for the best in others,*
> *And never failed to express the good.*
> *Who has left the world a better place in which to live,*
> *Than he found it, whether by an improved poppy,*
> *A perfect poem, or a rescued soul.*
> *Whose life has been an inspiration,*
> *Whose memory a benediction!* [3]

---

3   Letter from Vivian Squires, dated December, 1963.

In Memory of

JOHN A. NELSON

Born September 13, 1880
Smithfield, Utah

Passed away December 9, 1963
Great Falls, Montana

Funeral Services
December 12, 1963
Latter Day Saints Church
Great Falls, Montana
2 P.M.

Bishop James J. Johnson, Conducting

PALLBEARERS
And
HONORARY PALLBEARERS
Members of Great Falls Stake
High Council

Earl Stanard   Ariel Hulse
Clarence Bingham   Lloyd Peterson
Dr. Robert Phillips Ray Geilmann
Reid L. Molen   Alvin Ecker
Robert Hansen   Donald L. Briggs
Clyde Allen   Gerald Stott
        Edward E. Midgley

Interment Sunset Memorial Gardens
Great Falls, Montana
CHAPEL OF CHIMES FUNERAL HOME

Family Prayer..........William Jones

Prelude Music..........Betty Wilson

Remarks........Bishop James J. Johnson

Opening Prayer..Bishop Thomas Williams

Song.............Pauline Sanderson
                  Maureen Madsen
        "Oh, My Father"
Accompanied by...........Betty Wilson

Speaker........President Victor Bowen

Song..............Lyle Squires
"God Be With You Til We Meet Again"

Closing Prayer...Bishop Harold Porter

Postlude Music...........Betty Wilson

****

Dedication of Grave....Arden S. Payne

THE GIFTS OF MEMORY

By Peggy Squires Massey (John's niece)

U-*ntil I die, his name will be one I'll recall most gratefully.*
N-*or can I hope to ever repay all the kindness he showed to me.*
C-*ountless lessons of faith and courage,*
L-*ove for the Gospel and sharing its message,*
E-*ver a missionary, devoted and true,*
      And what a legacy, he passes to you!
J-*ust the sound of his name brings memories,*
O-*f a dear, kind, wonderful friend.*
H-*ow grateful I am he gave to me the*
N-*ame of "Peggy," which set me free from a hateful set of*
      circumstances which saddled me with the name, "Hortense."
N-*o kinder service could ever be, than what this dear Uncle did for me!*
E-*venings too, I oft recall, we gathered at his side,*
L-*istening to stories of South Sea Lores*
S-*ince he spent seven years on Samoa's shores;*
O-*ften he told how as a Elder so young,*
      he was given the gift of the Tongan tongue.
N-*umerous stories of faith stir our souls even now,*
      As when we were young.
I am sure that up in Heaven
      He is teaching those people still;
For that has been his mission
      And I'm sure it always will.
And there with Aunt Vera beside him
      they will go on serving together,
And the mansion they've built with service on earth,
      They'll eternally share forever!
They, too, will live on within our hearts,
      And through their posterity
Their hopes, their love and their influence,
      Will extend through out Eternity![4]

---

4   The Gifts of Memory, by Peggy Squires Massey.

A TRIBUTE TO UNCLE JOHN AND AUNT VERA

By Boyd Squires

One of my early recollections of Uncle John, was at a picnic when I thought he was the smartest man in the world. A couple and their daughter had just returned from Samoa and were telling their experiences. Uncle John was talking to them in the Samoan language. I can still sing today some of the songs he taught us in the Samoan language.

Uncle John had some Indians stay at his place to work on his farm. I remember going into their tepee and they sang and danced for us. Uncle John was able to communicate with them and they seemed to hold him in high esteem. The Indians had some really beautiful costumes, but their tepee was pretty smokey. Most adults would have left the kids out when they went to a program with the Indians, but not Uncle John. He made us feel as important as anyone and he always had time for us.

He would let us do things that would bother most men. I remember one time when the Branch went on a picnic up in the mountains. Uncle John had a real nice team of black horses and on the way up the mountains, he let us kids ride on them. This was a great thrill and only Uncle John would think of letting us do a thing like that.

When we got to the camping place in the mountains, it began to rain and we all got under the wagons to try and stay dry.

Uncle John had some beautiful black work horses. I always liked to watch him "break" wild horses. He seemed to be able to get them doing the things he wanted in a very short time. He seemed to understand their feelings, and they responded to him. He could have a wild horse following him around the corral in no time at all.

One day we went swimming in the canal and I remember what a good swimmer Uncle John was. I always thought he must have learned to be a good swimmer from swimming island to island in Samoa.

One Halloween, a bunch of us, including his own sons, took his wagon apart and put it together on top of his barn. We also took a few other things that he used to work with every day. When he was ready to go to work, he seemed to know who to call to help him find his equipment. We were all invited to come down to his place and gather things up, so he

John and Vera, several years before his death about 1960.

could go to work. The thing that really impressed me was his calm firmness. He didn't get angry, so it took all the incentive away to ever do it again.

Uncle John was blessed with one of the nicest ladies I ever knew to be his wife. We always felt just as much at home at Aunt Vera's as we did our own home. We had many a good meal at Aunt Vera's. It was a special treat when she would recite some of her readings for us. One of the last times I saw Aunt Vera, she told me how much she thought of me. This was her life, giving of her love to others.

I remember the talks and the prayers Uncle John would give in church. Some of the older folks used to talk too long and about things that kids weren't interested in, but Uncle John always had stories to keep us listening. I especially remember a prayer he gave at a prayer circle for someone who was sick; I remember the prayer and even some of the words he used in the prayer. When he spoke, it was worth listening.

Thinking over the people I have known in my life, outside of my own family, no two people had a greater influence on me during my growing up years than Uncle John and Aunt Vera.

I appreciate Ruth for asking me to write a few of my recollections of Uncle John. I also want to express my appreciation to his children for the opportunity of growing up with them and of sharing part of their lives with them. The good lives you have lived and are now living are testimonies to the influence your parents had in teaching you the real values of life. From what I know of the grandchildren, this influence is being passed on from generation to generation; may it so be until the end of not only time, but of eternity. [5]

IN MEMORIAM: A EULOGY OF MY FATHER

By Bruce A. Nelson

I have sometimes wondered if Father (John), who spent nearly seven years as a missionary, was not somewhat out of place in the world of realism that we all face. I feel he truly belonged to a more spiritual and idealistic world. I often remember feeling that his spirituality was so sincere and so intense that his influence should have been shared more widely than in the limited area in which he lived. But this may be the fate of unsung heros and of unsung geniuses of many periods of human history.

Even after leaving Cascade and the ranch life behind, John always carried a hard-twist lariat in his car and he often got calls to take the "rough" off of a horse that others had given up on. His famous "Mormon Hitch" is still used after all these years in the Cascade

---

5   Letter to Ruth Miller, from L. Boyd Squires.

area. Dad had the respect of the cowboys of his time, which respect was not easily earned.

As I look back over Dad's life, I think his greatest accomplishments were in the area of being able to stimulate men to become involved

J. Nelson Dies; LDS Leader

John A. Nelson, 74, 921 Ave. B, Valley View Addition, a Latter-day Saints leader and an insurance man, died late Monday morning in a local hospital after a short illness.

Funeral services will be from the Church of Jesus Christ of Latter-day Saints, 16 14th St. S., Thursday afternoon at 2, with Bishop James J. Johnson officiating. Burial will be in Sunset Memorial Gardens.

The body is at the Chapel of Chimes Funeral Home, where it will lie in state until 1 p.m. Thursday afternoon.

Nelson was born Sept. 13, 1889, in Smithfield, Utah. When he was two, his family moved by wagon train from Smithfield to a ranch near Cardston, Alta., where he spent his early youth and received his schooling.

When Nelson was 20, he was called as an LDS missionary to go to the Samoan Islands, where he served three years. He was asked to remain as president of the Samoan Tongan mission for the church for an additional

four years and returned to Canada when he was 27.

He was married to Martha

JOHN A. NELSON

Vera Wilcox, Jan. 1, 1917, at Raymond, Alta. Nelson and his wife came to Montana in 1923.

Continued on page 2

Continued from page 1

when they settled on a farm in the Chestnut Valley near Cascade. He farmed and broke horses for fellow ranchers in this area until 1931, when he moved with his family to Great Falls.

Throughout his life he had been known as a lover of horses and as a fine horseman who could break a wild range horse to lead in less than an hour. Throughout his life, he always carried a hard-twist lariat in his car to break an occasional colt to lead for friends as he traveled in his insurance work.

Nelson also had been active in his church. At Cascade he served as branch president, a position he held later in Great Falls. In 1937, upon formation of the Great Falls District, comprising Great Falls, Augusta, Sun River, Browning, Fort Benton, Conrad, Choteau, Cut Bank and Fairfield, he served as the first district president.

At the time of his death he was a member of the High Council of the Church for the Great Falls Stake, of which he had been a member since its formation.

Surviving, besides his wife, are four sons; J. Lovell (Val), Bruce A., Leo C., and Robert D., all of Great Falls; three daughters; Mrs. Ivan (Ruth) Miller, Hyrum, Utah; Mrs. Leon (Verda) Jensen, Salt Lake City, and Mrs. Earl (Joyce) McMaster, Columbia Falls; four brothers; Seth H., Cardston, Alta.; Cleveland, Salt Lake City; Lorenzo, Woolford, Alta., and Darrel, McGrath, Alta.; three sisters; Mrs. Chase (Lileth) Smith, Salt Lake City; Mrs. Will (Rae) Woolford, Smithfield, Utah, and Mrs. Milton (Hazel) Burgess, Raymond, Alta.; 36 great grandchildren and one great grandchild.

in causes deemed important and to change the lives for good of the people he came in contact with. Dad touched the lives of hundreds of people and was a missionary all of his life. The great crowd who came to pay their respects to him at his funeral, attested to the love his neighbors and his fellow men had for him, as we all said "good-bye" to him that cold day in December, 1963. Long may his memory live!

Beverly, Patti, and Debra McMaster with Grandpa John Nelson

A TRIBUTE TO MY DAD AND MOTHER

By Joyce Ione Nelson McMaster

March 2, 1989

In Great Falls, when Beverly was a baby and Mother and Dad would baby-sit for me, I would go to their home to pick Beverly up and there would be Dad and Beverly asleep in a rocking chair.

On other occasions, Dad would take two or three of the grandchildren and set them all on his lap and sing very loudly in Tongan or Samoan. Soon the children and Dad would be sound asleep. We used to tease him that the children would go to sleep to get out of the misery of hearing him sing. He wasn't the best singer in the world, but he did keep a strong beat and he knew the songs. Whether they were love songs or war-chants, we never could tell.

Dad loved all children so much, almost like the Savior. And all of his grandchildren adored their Grandpa Nelson and talked about him every day. I remember when we lived at 610-3rd Avenue South. Dad would come over and pick up any of the children who were there and take them for an ice cream cone. He would always say, "Put a wet washcloth in some wax paper so I can keep them clean!"

Mother loved all of the grandchildren with the same love and she especially enjoyed baby-sitting Beverly while I worked. She called her "my baby" and I think Beverly began to think that was true! The love and kindness Mom and Dad always showed to their children and their grandchildren was just wonderful.

I remember one time we all went up to Uncle Lee's [John's son's] cabin and had so much fun! Verda and Leon were also there with their children. Ruth Miller was there with her children, too. Mom and Uncle Lawrence Squires got all dressed up and stuck moss on their faces and old hats and coveralls. When the children saw them, they cried, as they didn't recognize Mom and Uncle Lawrence.

I remember Dad had bought a big box of plums and on the way home, he had everyone stop at the creek and then he brought the plums out and gave some to everyone. He wanted to be by the creek, so all of the kids could get washed up after eating the juicy, yummy plums!

I remember that Mother would come to Columbia Falls to take care of me when each of the babies was born. Earl would always laugh as she would rearrange each cupboard and he never knew where anything was! But, I just told him, we could rearrange them when she left. She always worked so hard and especially loved rocking and singing to each baby. It was always such fun to have her come and lots of times, Dad would stay for several days, too. Everyone who came to see me just fell in love with Mother and Dad. They were always so friendly and loving to all people.

Mom would say her poems to all of us and when she got where her memory was failing her, Earl thought it a good idea to write them down. So that is what we did. It was always such fun to sit and listen to her quote all of the poems she had memorized so long ago. What a fantastic memory she had!

I recall whenever Mother and Dad would come over to Columbia Falls for a visit, Dad would call from East Glacier and say, "Get my little doodles cleaned up and we'll be there in an hour and a half, so we can take them to Kalispell and go to our restaurant, MARVIN'S.' I want them to be on their best behavior!" Once Mom and Dad arrived in Columbia Falls, the children were so exited they could hardly stand it. We would go to 'MARVIN'S' and usually we were the only ones there. We would get a huge table and place our orders. Then Dad would proceed to tell the children stories of his horse breaking days and his love for the horses. It got to be a joke, because the waitresses would ask if they could listen, too! Dad truly had a gift of story-telling.

One time when Mother and Dad were visiting with us in Columbia Falls, Dad had parked his car in the back driveway, facing South. (We didn't have a fence up then.) Bill was five years old and unbeknownst to us, Bill got into the car and somehow shifted it. It started to roll down the hill. We happened to see it out the window and ran out. It went into the next door neighbor's yard and, very luckily, stopped by a big pipe! Bill was one scared little boy, I can tell you! But, Dad didn't even get upset, but just took Bill out of the car and loved and hugged him and told him, "Well, Bill, now you know how to drive a car." Dad was so dear to all of us!

I remember all the love Mom and Dad both showed to us when we were growing up. I remember how much they loved the Lord. We are very lucky to have had them for our parents!"[6]

FROM VERA'S MEMORY PAGES

Vera wrote in her genealogy book on March 24, 1965 concerning John's death:

> "On December 9, 1963, my dear companion left us. He had been ill one month, one week and one day. He had been in the Columbus Hospital in Great Falls. I had known that he was failing, but had faith he would be better soon. I had gone to the hospital every day to be with him. On December 9, 1963, I went as usual. Before I entered the hospital, I could see Bruce in the foyer. He came to meet me. I knew when I saw Bruce, that my dear husband was gone."

> "John was truly a kind and loving companion. We lived together over 46 years in happiness and joy. Our family consists of four sons and three daughters: John Lorin Lovell, Bruce Allen, Ruth Maurine, Lee Carl, Verda Cloe, Joyce Ione and Robert Dale. We were always so proud of all of our children and if I do say so myself, and I mean it, they are all outstanding citizens. They

---

6   Letter from Joyce McMaster, April, 1989.

all have their own homes and our grandchildren are so good and kind to me. "

Today I spent with Margaret. She hasn't been very well. I stayed with her today and we visited some. I am very fond of all of the special daughters-in-law and also my sons-in-law, too. They have always treated me with such respect and kindness."

Another entry on July 14, 1965:

"I hope that we can go to the Canadian Temple soon. I haven't been to Canada since my husband left me. I went to Oakland with Ruth and Ivan Miller. We went through the Oakland Temple. It was rather different from our temple in Canada."

"While I had the privilege of attending the temple in Oakland, I was reminded of the day when John and I were privileged to take our children to the Canadian Temple to be sealed. When we got married, the Temple on Cardston was under construction. The advice given to us was to save our money rather than travel to Utah to the temple. We were asked to wait until the Canadian Temple was completed. Well, we waited and it was almost seven years before it was finished."

"Our oldest son, Lovell, was six years old. Then came our Bruce Allen and two years later, our sweet Ruth Maurine. What a wonderful event, when we finally went to be sealed to our family. It seemed to me that was one of our finest days; when our three children were brought in to us, all dressed in white, to be sealed for 'Time and all eternity.' I am sure we have never regretted that day! Later, it was a wonderful feeling of security when our other children were born, Lee Carl, Verda Cloe, Joyce Ione, and Robert Dale, to know they had all been born 'In the Covenant' and we would be an 'Eternal Family' if we all lived worthily."[7]

Vera had a strong testimony of the Gospel of Jesus Christ. She felt it was a privilege to share this testimony with others. On April 9, 1960 she wrote: My testimony is that Jesus is the Christ, the Son

---

7   Entry in Vera W. Nelson genealogy book, July 14, 1965.

of the Living God. I would love to bear this testimony to the world. The more I study, the more I feel that I need to study. Our Church gives us good experiences to build testimonies on."[8]

MORE THAN A CHANCE MEETING?

By Verda Nelson Jensen

In July, 1969, as we were getting ready for our daughter, Carol's wedding, Carol and I had spent all day shopping for material for the bridesmaids' dresses. Carol and I had looked in several stores in the Sugarhouse area and had not found what Carol wanted for these dresses. Then we drove to downtown Salt Lake and spent several hours more in all the fabric stores there and still did not find what we were looking for.

Disappointed, we decided to give up for the day, when I suggested that we go back into one of the stores in Sugarhouse where we had been that morning.

I said, "Maybe we have overlooked something and we should go back." I had a feeling of urgency, a feeling that it was important to make one more stop.

As we retraced our steps into the same store we had been in that morning, a pleasant man, about 40 years old, came and asked if he could help us. He introduced himself as Wayne Turley, the store manager. He was so kind and when we explained what it was we were looking for, he said, "Some new fabric has recently arrived. It isn't even unpacked, but it may be just what you are looking for."

He went to the back room and brought out exactly what Carol had in mind for her bridesmaids' dresses. We had an opportunity to visit with Mr. Turley. He had just come in for his shift of work. In our conversation, we found that he had lived in Great Falls for a number of years. He had moved back to Salt Lake and was managing the fabric store and teaching in the Church Seminary program.

8   Ibid.

Then he made the comment that I felt Heavenly Father had sent us back into his store again to hear. He said he had met an older gentlemen while he was living in Great Falls and had become close friends with him.

He remarked, "If I had a copy of some of his life stories, I could keep my seminary class interested for a year."

I inquired as to the name of his friend and he said, "His name was John Alexander Nelson. He had served a mission to the Samoan Islands, had been a Mission President, had been a Bishop and a Stake President and had lived the life of a dedicated Latter-Day Saint missionary."

I was extremely touched by his comments. I told him the man he mentioned was my father. I cried as I told him how we had spent all day shopping and had not found the fabric we wanted. I told him the urgency I had felt to return to his store and search one last time for just the right material. I know that the reason we had not made our purchases before was because it was important that I meet Mr. Turley and hear his experiences with my father, John.

Several years later, while I was teaching in second grade, I had a student, the kind of bright child that a teacher never forgets, named Sue Ann Turley. Her mother was my room-mother. Mrs. Turley came to my class once a week to teach music to my students. She was such a delightful person and the children as well as I, looked forward to her coming each week. I told her about my experience with the man named Mr. Turley and she said he was her husband. Unfortunately, he had died with a sudden heart attack a year or two before.

Brother and Sister Turley had lived in Great Falls for several years. She told me they had been close friends with Lee and his family and had been invited to have breakfast at their home the morning they moved to Utah. I have had a special relationship with this dear family and I know that Heavenly Father wanted me to meet Brother

Wayne Turley so I could hear of his love and high regards for my dad and for me to develop a friendship with him.

Since that time, I have enjoyed my friendship with Sister Turley and Sue Ann and I feel that Heavenly Father was aware of our circumstances. We have had a special bond of love.

19

VERA'S LIFE WITHOUT JOHN

VERA'S LIFE GOES ON

Vera had suffered several slight strokes before John was hospital-ized. While he was in the hospital with his last heart attack, Vera suffered a stroke and was found in her back yard, unconscious. The strokes seemed to affect her memory. She was still the same sweet, gentle, loveable person, but she became quite forgetful. After John died, Vera had a hard time adjusting.

Vera stayed in her lovely new home for several years. Then her sons felt she would be happier in a place where she could just walk to church. They found a nice apartment almost next door to the chapel in her old ward where she was known and loved. She felt comfort-able in the apartment and didn't seem to mind being alone.

She was proud of her children and loved them all very much. Her children in Great Falls were all kind to her. Her fine daughters-in-law, Margaret, Ruth, Linda and Gerry, were close by and they shared the responsibilities of looking after her needs. They would see that her apartment was cleaned up and her refrigerator and cupboards were well stocked with food. They would wash her hair and take her for rides. Her sweet Nelson grand-daughters, Janelle, Judy, Michele, Noelle, Sheila, Sheryl, Shauna, Sharla, Pam and Vicky who lived near-by, would often come, two at a time, to spend the night with her and to keep her company.

VERA GIVES UP HER HOME

By Verda N. Jensen

Eventually it was not safe for Mother to live alone. She needed constant care and supervision. At this time, it was necessary for her to give up her apartment and from then on, Mother spent her time living in the homes of her children. For awhile, she lived with Margaret and Lovell and then with Bruce and Ruth and also Lee and his family.

Vera, surrounded by grandchildren, daughters, sons-in-law, 1969.

As long as she was able to travel, she shared some of her time with her daughters, Ruth, Joyce and I, who lived away from Great Falls. She didn't seem to mind flying and the air line personnel were good to help her out and keep track of her until one of the girls could pick her up at the airport. Sometimes Mother would stay with one of us for a month or so, but she was never very content after being moved from her own home.

Mother very often became disoriented and likely suffered from what is now known as Alzheimer's disease or hardening of the arteries. She still knew that we loved her, however, and she responded with her love. It was interesting that her grand- daughter, Carol, was still able to communicate with her so well. Carol would take time to talk to her and hold her hand and pat her. It sometimes seemed like "the old" Vera was back. There was a special bond between the two of them.

One time I invited a group of my neighbors to come to celebrate Mother's birthday. These ladies always made a "fuss" over Mother and had all brought her a nice gift. When I brought in the birthday cake,

Admirers of Vera. From left: Marsha, Beverly, Joyce, Vera, Carol, Ruth, Julie, Lana and Verda in Hyrum, Utah, 1972.

I told Mother to blow out the candles and make a wish. Without batting an eye, Mother said, "I wish I was home!" Bless her heart. As much as she loved all of her children, it was hard for her to understand why she wasn't able to stay in her own home.

THE MOVE TO HYRUM

By Verda Nelson Jensen

As a family, we found that it was hard on Mother not to have a permanent residence. Eventually Mother could no longer take care of herself at all, so Ruth and Ivan moved her into their home in Hyrum, Utah. They treated her kindly and each of their children were good to her. Steven often cheered her up by swinging her off her feet and saying, "May I have the next dance, Grandma?" Then he would waltz around the room with her.

Rosie often had the responsibility of taking complete charge of Mother's care. One time while Ruth was ill and in the hospital for a week, Rosie, who was still in high school, stayed out of school the whole week to care for her grandmother. Ruth and Ivan's other children, Jeannette, Marsha, Sue and Jeff, showed similar love and care for Mother during her last years.

Because of her increasing inability to care for her own physical heeds, constant vigilance was required by the Miller family. Other members of Mother's family were concerned about the hardship it was on Ruth and Ivan to be responsible for Vera's constant care. Ruth replied, "It is a pleasure to have her here. She brings out gentleness and love in my children that I didn't think possible and her sweet spirit radiates love to each of us. She is so appreciative of whatever we do for her and she is always so uncomplaining about her problems."

Each of Mother's other children and their families gave financial support for her care, showed their love and concern for her welfare, and helped whenever they could. However, the responsibility for Mother's continuous needs were assumed willingly by Ruth and Ivan.

They and their children are indeed fine examples of unselfish, compassionate service. As a family, we are truly indebted to them.

DEATH AND FUNERAL OF VERA

Vera fell and broke her hip some time in October, 1972. She was in the hospital in Ogden, Utah for several weeks. Her doctor recommended that she go to a convalescent home for an additional recovery period. She was only in the convalescent home in Ogden for a short time when she died on November 29, 1972. A copy of her obituary follows:

Her funeral was held in the Hyrum 3rd Ward. A copy of her funeral program is reprinted on the next page.

Vivian Squires had been invited to come and preach the funeral service, however, because of a storm which grounded all of the airplanes and stopped all ground travel, he was unable to come from his home in Fort Benton, Montana.

Vivian sent a lovely letter of apology and a tribute to Vera. It was read at her funeral. Part of it is included here:

I wanted to tell the folks about the Aunt Vera I loved and remembered. Not the 'last leaf on the tree in the spring', but the woman in her prime, 'ere the pruning knife of time cut her down', who could play the leading lady in a drama, who played the organ and who used to sing so beautifully with Lyle (Squires) and others. How she could make chills run up and down our spine, when she recited, "It Takes a Heap of Living in a House to Make it Home," "The Cattle Thief," and many other poems. I wanted to tell of the woman who helped raise a family of seven children during years that included the depression years and who could always make room for others at her table at mealtime."

Now she is gone, we'd not recall her from her paradise of bliss
Where no evil can befall her to a changing world like this.
But her name shall never perish nor her memory sleep in dust.
For the many friends will cherish the remembrance of the just.
Faith's sweet voice of consolation, soothes our grief--the spirit's flown,
Upward to a holier station, nearer the celestial throne.
Tho' her earthly form is sleeping, lowly 'neath the prairie sod,
Soon the grave shall yield its keeping,
yield to life this CHILD OF GOD-
When the heaven and earth shall tremble,
when all things shall be restored,
When the trump of God shall awaken,
those who sleep in CHRIST THE LORD![1]

Because Vivian was not able to attend, Ivan Miller, Vera's son-in-law, capably consented to speak in Vivian's place; he gave a lovely tribute.

Leon Jensen, another son-in-law of Vera's, also gave a beautiful tribute to Vera and told of some of her special talents and early life experiences. Her grand-daughters, Michele Nelson, Sheila Zolman, Sheryl Boyer, Patricia Rowles, Lana Jensen, Julie Jensen, Carol Lasson, Debra Parry and Lori McMaster sang a lovely rendition of "Oh My Father," accompanied by two other granddaughters, Marsha Thompson and Susan Stockwell.

---

1   Letter from Vivian Squires, Dec. 4, 1972, in possession of Verda Nelson Jensen.

An original poem written by Vera, THE PIONEER TRAIL, was read by her niece, Peggy Squires Massey:

THE PIONEER TRAIL By Vera Wilcox Nelson

This was the trail the wagons made, And the teams of horses and open stayed. And the feet of women and children small-- And the men who had listened to the call.
What was the cause and what the quest Of this vast concourse marching west? Over the miles of endless plains Fording the streams through sun and rains
To find a place where all might be Safe and protected, happy and free. To build their homes and till the sod Freedom to serve and to worship God.
Year after year, others followed the trail, Some pushing hand carts, o're hill and dale, With stout hearts and brave they strove fearlessly With unfaltering faith in their destiny.
Can you not see them? The fair, the bride, Trudging along by her husband's side. And children, heedless of trouble and care, Playing a game on the old trail there. And the mother soothing a little child. When into the camp rode the Indians wild.
And then when the long days trek was done And down in the west sank the blazing sun, They gave thanks to the Giver of all good, For kind protection and simple food.
Oft' round the campfires burning bright They sang their songs in the starry night And often to a merry tune They danced to the light of a golden moon.
And along the way in the earth's broad breast Are the graves of many who sank to rest Whose strength had failed e're they won the race And heard the welcome, "THIS IS THE PLACE."

HYRUM CEMETERY

Vera was buried in the beautiful Cemetery in Hyrum, Utah. Several years before Vera died, there had been a devastating flood in Great Falls, Montana. The new cemetery in Great Falls, where John had been buried, was seriously damaged by the flood. Because of the flood, the cemetery was no longer functional and the caskets all had to be removed from there and taken to other cemeteries.

Since it became necessary to move John's casket from this cemetery, Ruth and Ivan generously arranged for a burial plot for it in the Hyrum Cemetery where it is now.

4—The Herald Journal Logan, Utah, Thursday, November 30, 1972

Obituaries

Vera Nelson

Vera Nelson

Vera Wilcox Nelson, 83, formerly of Great Falls, Mont., died Wednesday in an Ogden convalescence home following a short illness.

She was born March 25, 1889 in Sunnydell, Idaho; a daughter of Samuel Allen Wilcox and Julia Ann Laughlin. The family moved from Idaho to Alberta, Canada and later to Sacramento, Calif., where she lived until the time of her marriage. She was the eighth of 10 children. One brother survives her; Lorin Elmo Wilcox of Columbia Falls, Mont.

She was an active member of the Great Falls PTA, serving as president a number of times. A member of the LDS Church, she had an active career in church auxiliary organizations. For nine years she served as the District Relief Society president in Great Falls.

For the past several years she made her home with her daughter of Hyrum, Mrs. Ruth Miller.

She married John A. Nelson Jan. 1, 1917, in Cardston, Alberta. The marriage was later solemnized in the Cardston Temple on Nov. 23, 1923. Mr. Nelson died Dec. 9, 1963.

Seven children survive Mrs. Nelson. They are John Lovell, Bruce Allen, Lee Carland, Robert Dale, all of Great Falls; and Mrs. Ivan (Ruth) Miller of Hyrum, Mrs. Leon (Verda) Jensen of Salt Lake City and Mrs. Earl (Joyce) McMaster of Columbia Falls, Mont. Also surviving are 37 grandchildren and 15 great-grandchildren.

Funeral services will be conducted Saturday at 1 p.m. at the Hyrum 3rd Ward Chapel with Bishop Seymour Nielsen officiating. Friends may call at the Thompson Funeral Home in Hyrum Friday from 7 to 9 p.m. and Saturday one hour prior to the servvice.

Burial will be in the Hyrum City Cemetery.

Services

Family Prayer .... Lovell J. Nelson

Organ Prelude and Postlude .... Rosemarie Miller (granddaughter)

Invocation .... Pres. Glen Baird

Introduction and Obituary .... Bp. Seymour Nielsen

Tribute .... Leon J. Jensen

Musical Selection by granddaughters .... Michele Nelson, Shiela Zolman, Sheryl Boyer, Patricia Rowles, Lana Jensen, Julie Jensen, Carol Lasson, Debra Parry, Lori McMaster

Acc. by Susan M. Stockwell, Marsha Thompson

"O My Father"

Original Reading .... Peggy S. Massey

Speaker .... Vivian Squires

Vocal Solo .... Lyle Squires

Benediction .... Bp. Ivan Miller

FUNERAL SERVICES FOR

Vera Wilcox Nelson

Born March 25, 1889 – Died Nov. 29, 1972

Saturday, December 2, 1972

HYRUM 3RD WARD CHAPEL

Bishop Seymour J. Nielsen, Conducting

Dedication of Grave .... Lee C. Nelson
   Hyrum Cemetery

PALL BEARERS – GRANDSONS

John Nelson	Jim Jensen
Bruce Nelson, Jr.	Bill McMaster
Steven Miller	Greg Nelson

HONORARY PALLBEARERS

Brad Nelson	David Jensen
Reece Nelson	Robby McMasters
Rick Nelson	

(Pallbearers are all grandsons)

Flowers cared for by
Hyrum Third Ward Relief Society

Upon Vera's death, her remains were buried in a grave next to John's. It is a peaceful spot and comfort and happy memories come to those who take the time to visit their gravesides.

Photograph taken the day of Vera's funeral in Ruth Miller's yard, Hyrum, Utah, December 2, 1972.
From left: Lovell Nelson, Bruce Nelson, Ruth Nelson Miller, Lee Nelson, Verda Nelson Jensen, Joyce Nelson McMaster, Robert Nelson

CONCLUSION

To the ancestors of John and Vera Nelson and to anyone who reads this history, may we live worthily to know and love these great people in the eternities. As we read the following words from the Book of Mormon, Helaman 5:6, may we also remember the lives of John and Vera Nelson and know that they were good.

Behold, I have given unto you the names of our first parents, who came out of the land of Jerusalem; and this I have done that when you remember your names, ye may remember them; and when ye remember them, ye may remember their works; and when ye remember their works ye may know how that it is said, and also written, that they were good."

PHOTOS

Bruce Nelson, Jr., as he prepares to leave on his mission to Michigan in 1963, with mom Ruth Nelson and Dad, Bruce Sr.

Sisters Minnie Turner and Vera Nelson in 1965

Left to right: Julie Jensen, Verda Jensen, Vera Nelson, Lana Jensen, Joyce Jensen, 1967

1982 - Michele Nelson and Jean Nelson

Cousins - 1979 - left to right: Julie Mendenhall, Lana Jardine, Debra Parry, Beverly Brink, MaryKay Phelps, Lori Seely, and babies. Front: Joyce Jensen.

1982-left to right: Steve Miller, Rick Nelson, Reece Nelson, Greg Nelson, Aunt Ruth Miller in front left.. At Family Reunion in Bear Lake, Utah.

Jeanette Miller and Noelle Nelson - 1982.

1982 Bear Lake Reunion - Ruth and Ivan Miller's Family - Prize for best attendance.

1970-left to right: Michele Nelson, Lana Jensen, Patti McMaster,
Judy Nelson, Sheila Nelson, Sheryl Nelson, Julie Jensen.

Left to right, back row: Verda Jensen, Leon Jensen, La Verda Stuehser, Betty Ruth Nelson, Margaret Nelson, Lovell Nelson, Robert Nelson. Front row: Ivan Miller, Minerva Molen, Ruth Miller, Bruce Nelson, Vickie Nelson, Lee Nelson, Ginny Nelson. Bear Lake, 1982.

McMaster Family: Joyce, Beverly, Patti, Debra, Lori, Mary, Bill, Rob, Earl - 1983.

1984 - from right: Sheryl Boyer, Shauna Rohbock,
Lee Nelson, Sharla Nelson

1985-left to right back row: Verda Jensen, Carol Lasson, Sheila Zolman, Debra Parry.
Front row: Lana Jardine, Sheryl Boyer, Shauna Rohbock, Beverly Brink.

Leon and Verda Jensen Family - 1988

Lovell and Margaret Nelson - 1986 Cardston Temple

416

Dorene - The girlfriend who waited!
Rick Nelson - The Missionary!

Rose Marie and Brad
Johnson and children
- 1986

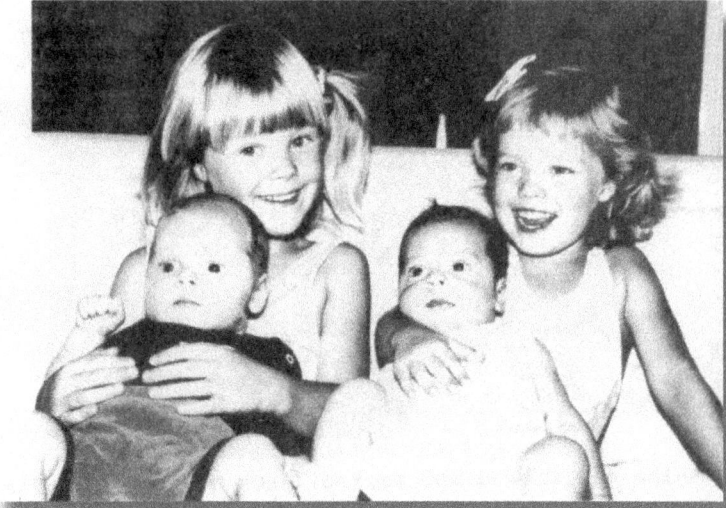

Drew, Natalie, Rhett and Kristi Nelson -
Children of Bradley and Jean Nelson - July 1989

Dr. Bradley Nelson

David John Jensen and
Brooke Jensen

Bruce A. Nelson, Sr., Bruce A. Nelson, Jr., Lee Nelson

John, photo taken when he was working
as a security guard, WWII

John A. Nelson, Jr.,
dressed more casually

Clockwise from top left: Bruce A. Nelson, Jr.,
John Nelson, Greg Nelson, Dick Nelson

Grandpa John , Jeff Miller (on John's lap), Julie Jensen,
Michele Nelson, Greg Nelson, Lana Jensen

Clockwise from top left: Lovell Nelson, Bruce Nelson, Lee Nelson, Robert Nelson, Ruth Nelson Miller, Joyce Nelson McMaster, Verda Nelson Jensen

Woolford, Alberta, 3/87. Home built by J. A. Nelson and Sons
for John, Jr. in about 1917, now abandoned

*From Left: Sheila Nelson, Patty McMaster, Minerva Molen,
Debra McMaster, Sheryl Nelson, Judy Nelson, Beverly McMaster*

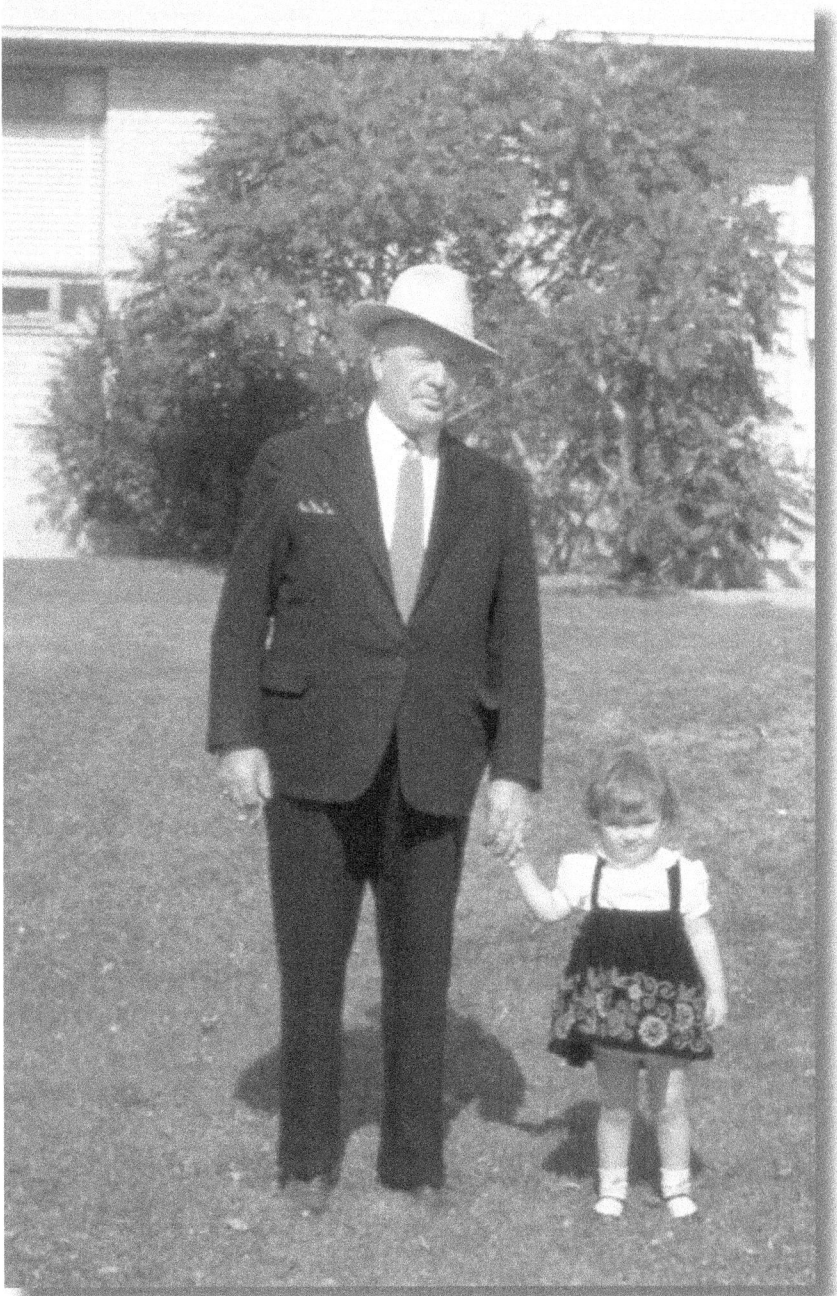

Grandpa John Nelson and Michele Nelson in front of
14th St Chapel, Great Falls, Montana

The Miller family, taken at a family reunion long ago

From left: Sheila, Randy, Sheryl and Shauna Nelson, a Christmas long ago

Another generation of Nelsons

From left: Aunt Gerrie, Pamela, Uncle Bob Nelson

Beautiful Aunt Linda Nelson, Lee's wife

More cousins!

Lee on hunting trip

Lee and pet dachshund

From left: Bruce Nelson, Bradley Nelson, Betty Ruth Nelson, Linda Nelson, Sheryl Nelson, Sheila, Shauna

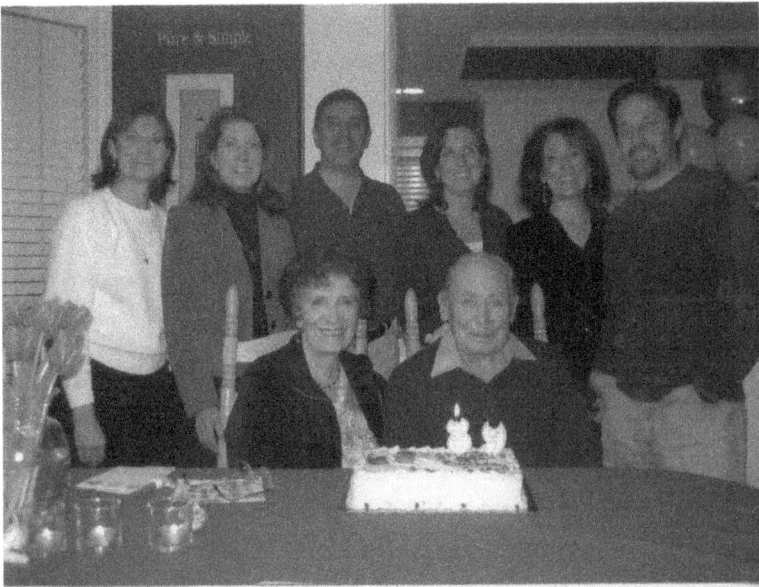

Clockwise from left: Julie Larson, Carol Lasson, Jim Jensen, Joyce Morgan, Lana Jardine, David Jensen, Leon, Verda at Leon's 89th birthday party!

Grandpa John and grandchildren, taken at a family reunion, possibly 1960 or late 1950's

Grandpa John, Janell, and Robert, taken when Janell was about 17 months old

From left: Bruce Nelson, Sr., Ruth Nelson Miller, Lovell Nelson,
Joyce Nelson McMaster, Lee Nelson, Verda Nelson Jensen, Robert Nelson

Bruce A. Nelson, Sergeant in the Army Air Corps,
China/Burma/India Theater, WWII

Clockwise from top center: Bruce Nelson, Jr., Noelle Nelson Lundahl, Gregory Nelson, Betty Ruth Nelson, Bruce A. Nelson, Sr., Bradley Nelson

From left: Grandpa John Nelson, Verda, Joyce, Wren, Ireta, Bob, Bruce, Vera-WWII

Dear Aunt Maggie (Margaret)
Nelson and Uncle Lovell

More cousins!

From left: Ivan Miller, Ruth Miller, Joyce McMaster, Verda Jensen, Leon Jensen, Robbie McMaster, Lee (wearing lampshade), Vicky Nelson, Lovell Nelson, Bruce Nelson

In Samoa to get Greg Nelson from his mission, from left: unidentified, Noelle, Greg Nelson, Betty Ruth, Michele, unidentified, Bradley, Bruce A. Nelson, Sr.

Lee, Bruce, Lovell. Three of the best men who ever lived

Bruce and Lovell had barbecue aprons made for each other, printed with their favorite old sayings for the other brother. Bruce used to tease Lovell, saying "Lovell loves Mary Lake!", and Lovell used to say "Bons By Boobie, he does stink on a Summer's Day!"

Bradley Nelson, Grandpa John, Noelle

On the back of this old photo is written in John's handwriting,
"This is the Mormon Mission House at Pesega, Samoa"

*In the town of Pesega on the island of Upolu there now stands this
beautiful L.D.S. Temple, (shown on the cover of this book as well)*

INDEX

www.ingramcontent.com/pod-product-compliance
Lightning Source LLC
Chambersburg PA
CBHW031228090426
42742CB00007B/120